HOOVER INSTITUTION PUBLICATIONS

THE STEEL INDUSTRY IN COMMUNIST CHINA

Research and publication sponsored by
The Hoover Institution and the Stanford Research Institute
in cooperation with the University of San Francisco

中共鋼鐵工業

張弓權題

THE STEEL INDUSTRY IN COMMUNIST CHINA

by

YUAN-LI WU

with a contribution by

RONALD HSIA

Published for
THE HOOVER INSTITUTION
ON WAR, REVOLUTION, AND PEACE
by
FREDERICK A. PRAEGER, *Publishers*
New York · Washington · London

THE HOOVER INSTITUTION on War, Revolution, and Peace, founded at Stanford University in 1919 by Herbert Hoover, is a center for advanced study and research on public and international affairs in the twentieth century. The views expressed in its publications are entirely those of the authors and do not necessarily reflect the views of The Hoover Institution.

FREDERICK A. PRAEGER, *Publishers*
111 Fourth Avenue, New York, New York 10003, U.S.A.
77–79 Charlotte Street, London W.1, England

Published in the United States of America in 1965
by Frederick A. Praeger, Inc., Publishers

Library of Congress Catalog Card Number: 64-8250

Printed in the United States of America

FOREWORD

The Hoover Institution is pleased to sponsor publication of this second volume of a projected four-volume series of studies of the contemporary Chinese economy by Dr. Yuan-li Wu. It follows <u>Economic Development and the Use of Energy Resources in Communist China</u>, which appeared as an Institution publication in 1963. A third volume, <u>The Spatial Economy of Communist China</u>, is also scheduled for 1965.

Dr. Wu's studies, as well as many of the others which stem from the research programs conducted by the Hoover Institution, are designed to serve both as guides and reference sources for the advanced student and as interpretative analyses of current problems of world significance. The control of the Chinese mainland by doctrinaire Communists, implacably opposed to the United States and other free nations, is unquestionably one of the most serious problems we face.

Steel and its components are basic to any nation's ability to wage effective war. The author's careful appraisal of Communist China's resources in coal, iron ore, and other raw materials necessary to the development of a steel industry does not include any attempt to confirm or deny China's intentions to continue its self-elected role as a primary agency in creating international tensions. It does, however, provide disturbing evidence that, with a relatively narrow but adequate base for a major steel industry, Communist China is making substantial progress towards building an industrial economy which ultimately could support large-scale international aggression.

In addition to background and training in China, the author is a 1942 honors graduate from the London School of Economics. He has been Professor of International Business at the University of San Francisco since 1960, a consultant to the Hoover Institution since 1962, and is the author of a number of books and major articles on various phases of Communist China's economy.

The Hoover Institution
April 15, 1965

W. Glenn Campbell
Director

PREFACE

This volume follows <u>Economic Development and the Use of Energy Resources in Communist China</u>, published in 1963, as another sectoral study undertaken both because of the crucial role of the sector in over-all economic development in Communist China and because of the light its examination is expected to throw on the performance of Chinese economic planning. It is also a companion volume to another broader inquiry, currently under preparation, into the general course of development of the economy of mainland China, and consequently, it does not contain a full discussion of Communist China's economic development in general, nor of that peculiar phenomenon euphemistically described as the "Great Leap Forward" and its aftermath. As a sectoral study on a strategic industry, the pages that follow should nevertheless be of interest to the earnest student of Chinese affairs, the economist interested in problems of development and planning--especially planning in practice--and the businessman who wishes to know about Chinese steel. If the book succeeds partially in meeting the anticipations of any of these readers, it will not have been written in vain.

As an intellectual exercise, this book owes a great deal to many scholars who have previously written on the subject. In particular, the works of Ta-chung Liu and Kung-chia Yeh on Communist China's national income, of Gardner Clark on Soviet steel, and of Kung-pin Wang on Chinese mining and metallurgical development have proved immensely helpful at every turn, and their intellectual aid to the author should be publicly acknowledged. The important contribution of Ronald Hsia included in the volume must also be mentioned at the outset. Both Professor C.M. Li and Professor T.C. Liu have read the study at its manuscript stage, and the author is most grateful for their many helpful comments. Needless to say, there are many others who have helped in the unfolding of our work by furnishing information and references. Among them are Anton Wei at the Bureau of Mines and the research staffs of the Cabinet Research Office and the Iron and Steel Federation, both of Japan. Other scholars and friends,

vii

scattered in many places, cannot all be named. To all of them we extend our sincere thanks.

As a research undertaking this book owes its existence to the unwavering and staunch support of the Hoover Institution under its enterprising and understanding director, Dr. W. Glenn Campbell, and of the Stanford Research Institute. The author is also most grateful to his own institution, the University of San Francisco, for having made it possible for him to find the time necessary for long-term and continued research. Discussions with Francis P. Hoeber of SRI, especially during a joint study trip in 1962 in the Far East, have often provided valuable insight.

The study which has led to this volume has benefited at every step, as did the previous volume, from the generous and considerate assistance of Eugene Wu and his staff at the East Asian Collection of the Hoover Institution. Their logistical support has most assuredly gone beyond what any researcher can possibly demand. In the search for Japanese language sources the invaluable help of Tamotsu Takase should be especially mentioned.

Preparation of this book began in late 1960. During these years, the assistance of Kuan Y. Lee and H. K. Kao preceded that of many others. May Liu and K. C. Ng did most of the computations. In the finishing stages, Grace Hsiao and Janet Wang did a great deal of checking. Without their patient and painstaking effort, such an analysis as we have been able to make based on extensive, albeit still limited, data would not have been possible. Nor should the maps drawn by K. S. Yao, the constant counsel of H. C. Ling, and the comments and assistance in many ways of Dennis Doolin escape mention. The careful and meticulous typing of the preliminary draft by Madere Olivar and its final composition by Mark Grant have proved a tremendous boon. In a very real sense, therefore, this book is as much a product of their efforts as it is the author's. The errors and deficiencies that remain in spite of all the effort to avoid them are, however, unquestionably the author's alone.

This is but another small landmark in the researcher's continuing journey. The toll of research is found in preoccupation and neglect of many other no less important, and sometimes even more important, obligations. To have been excused for all these failings, the author must thank his wife and

have been excused for all these failings, the author must thank his wife and daughter for their long indulgence and their understanding hearts.

Yuan-li Wu

Menlo Park, California
July, 1963

Note: All proper names used in this volume are spelled according to the Wade-Giles system with the exception of those place names which are more widely known in their traditional spellings. Throughout the tabular material in this book, ... indicates "no information"; --- means "nil."

CONTENTS

TABLES

FIGURES

MAPS

APPENDICES

To Connie Ann

INDUSTRIALIZATION AND
THE DRIVE FOR STEEL

Introduction

The First Five-Year Plan of Communist China (1953-1957) devoted its attention primarily to the development of industry. Within the industrial sector emphasis was placed on producers' goods, and among the latter the ferrous metals occupied a most prominent place. In 1958, when Communist Chinese planners made their fateful decision to accelerate the process of industrialization by developing many small-scale industrial enterprises simultaneously in a "Great Leap Forward," their battle cry was again "Steel!" It can be argued that the severe economic crisis which beset the Chinese mainland in 1960 and continues up to this writing (spring, 1963) was triggered by overexpansion during 1958-1959, in which the movement to produce iron and steel on a massive scale played as intimate and responsible a part as the establishment of agricultural communes. In this sense, therefore, steel has played a dual role. It has provided a central focus for the frenzied drive to industrialize. It has also become the nemesis of this drive. Somewhere, somehow, the planning and, most likely also, the execution of the plan appear to have been in error.

Whether or not the above surmise can be proven will be seen later in this volume. What is needed is a detailed examination of the steel industry of Communist China or, more appropriately, the iron and steel industry, inasmuch as iron smelting still predominates in some mills and localities. To the increasing number of students of Communist Chinese affairs, such a study should cast some useful light on a vital sector of the Chinese economy and on Chinese performance in economic planning as a whole. This function alone would perhaps be sufficient to justify the effort we have devoted to the present inquiry.

Actually, our horizon can be broadened a great deal more, for Communist China has not been alone in stressing the importance of steel production to industrial development. The Soviet Union, mentor and major contributor to

Communist China's First Five-Year Plan, has herself followed the same route before. Many other underdeveloped countries share the same aspirations--to possess steel mills of their own.

Has Communist China really been wrong in placing too much emphasis on developing the steel industry? Has the Soviet Union in her turn been wrong as well? Can both countries have been mistaken? An interesting comment on the Soviet steel industry has been attributed to a recent statement by Khrushchev to the Communist Party Central Committee of the Soviet Union[1] to the effect that Soviet officials had put on "steel blinkers" and that in spite of the appearance of better and cheaper materials their cry continued to be: "Steel, steel!" Could it be that this remark is of wider applicability? Western reports that there has been a reorientation of Soviet policy toward steel and a slowdown of the industry's growth rate in 1962 would seem to indicate a belated recognition that, in the case of the Soviet Union at any rate, what is produced and how it is done may be as important as, if not more important than, how much is produced.

There are at least two substantial reasons that decisions on the rate of expansion of the steel industry and its "product mix" are of crucial importance to the rate of economic development. First, steel is still a principal input in construction and machine manufacture, both of which are essential to the formation of fixed capital in the course of development. The availability of quality steel is especially indispensable to certain machine manufacturers. Second, modern iron smelting and steelmaking are activities requiring large initial capital outlay and must be carried out on a substantial scale. The demand on available savings stemming from steel mill construction thus constitutes a matter of serious concern to poor countries.

However, the importance of steel to most underdeveloped countries is above all symbolic, because steel seems to represent power and is generally accepted as a status symbol of economic advancement. The reasoning in the last case is a simple one: First, in order to be a powerful modern nation, one must be able to assert oneself in military terms. Since steel is needed in the manufacture of arms, a country must have its own steel industry for military strength. In the second place, all modern and economically advanced nations seem to have large steel industries. An underdeveloped country must therefore

2

build up its own steel industry in order to become "developed,"--so the syllogism seems to run.

The close correlation of industrial expansion and the growth of the ferrous metallurgical sector can, of course, be shown plainly on an empirical basis. Figures 1.1 through 1.6 demonstrate quite convincingly the close correlation between the ferrous metallurgical sector and the industrial output index of three countries: the United States, the Soviet Union, and Japan. In all three cases, as the time-series charts show, the ferrous-metals series tended to fluctuate more violently than industrial production as a whole. Over fairly long periods, the average annual rate of growth was higher in the case of the Soviet Union, with Japan and the United States at comparable levels. If the growth rates are computed over somewhat shorter periods from troughs to peaks, the Soviet and Japanese data are much closer together, reflecting in both instances the effect of recovery from wartime and postwar lows.

The differential rates of growth of the ferrous sector in the three countries shown in Table 1.1 may be attributed to differences in technology and product mix, to mention only two important factors. The latter may in turn reflect different stages of industrial and economic development. But when the higher growth rates of both industrial output and steel production in the Soviet Union are taken together, it is tempting to conclude that there may be a deeper causal relationship between faster growth of the steel industry and rapid industrialization.

A serious danger arises if one misinterprets the causal factor. An industrially developed country may have a large steel output for various reasons. Not the least important is that, being developed, it may also have a large steel industry. This does not mean, however, that a large domestic steel industry is absolutely necessary before industrial development can take place to a high degree. To validate the latter statement, it would be necessary to assume autarky as a matter of national policy and to postulate on the basis of the general industrial technology that has developed in the course of the Industrial Revolution. Nor is the development of the steel industry alone a sufficient condition for economic development or even industrial growth in the narrower sense. It is

3

Table 1.1

AVERAGE ANNUAL RATES OF GROWTH OF INDUSTRIAL PRODUCTION
AND FERROUS METALS PRODUCTION IN THE UNITED STATES,
THE SOVIET UNION, AND JAPAN*
(in percent)

Country	Period	Industrial	Ferrous Metals
United States	1885-1955	4.4	5.1 (rolled steel)
	1885-1925	4.3	6.9
	1935-1955	5.9	5.7
Soviet Union	1928-1955	6.9	9.0
	1928-1940	9.9	12.8
	1946-1955	14.8	16.6 (1945-55)
Japan	1928-1954	3.7	5.1
	1928-1937	9.7	12.8 (1931-41)
	1945-1954	19.5	48.7 (1946-54)

*Sources: G. Warren Nutter, Growth of Industrial Production in the Soviet Union, National Bureau of Economic Research, Princeton University Press, Tables 53, A-32, B-2, E-1; and Nihon Keizei tôkei shû (Economic Statistics of Japan), Tokyo, 1958, pp. 27-28.

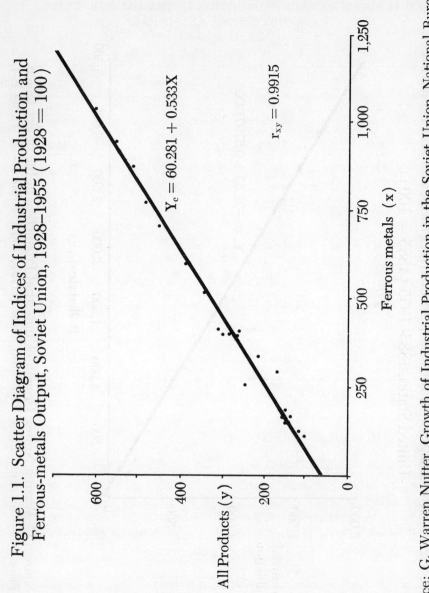

Figure 1.1. Scatter Diagram of Indices of Industrial Production and Ferrous-metals Output, Soviet Union, 1928–1955 (1928 = 100)

$Y_c = 60.281 + 0.533X$

$r_{xy} = 0.9915$

Ferrous metals (x)

All Products (y)

Source: G. Warren Nutter, <u>Growth of Industrial Production in the Soviet Union</u>, National Bureau of Economic Research, Princeton University Press, 1962, Table 53, p. 196 and Table B-2, p. 420.

Figure 1.2. Scatter Diagram of Indices of Industrial Production and Rolled Steel, United States, 1885–1955 (1885 = 100)

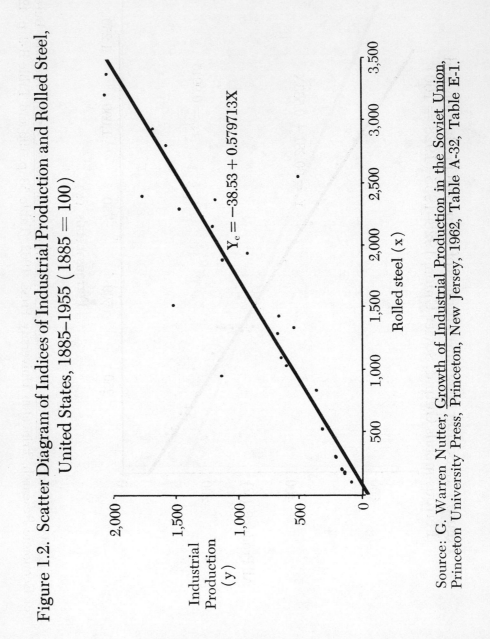

$Y_c = -38.53 + 0.579713X$

Industrial Production (y)

Rolled steel (x)

Source: G. Warren Nutter, <u>Growth of Industrial Production in the Soviet Union</u>, Princeton University Press, Princeton, New Jersey, 1962, Table A-32, Table E-1.

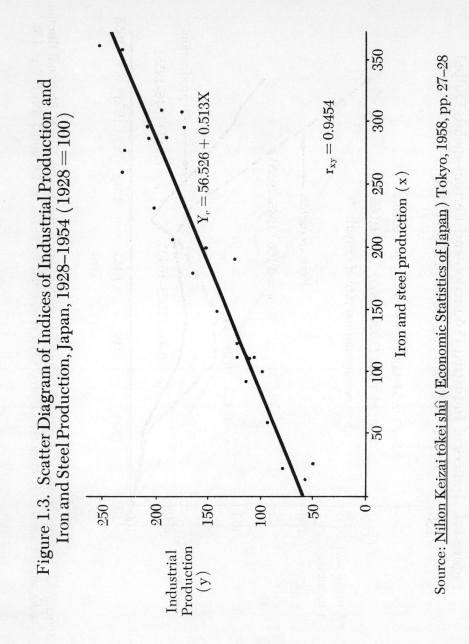

Figure 1.3. Scatter Diagram of Indices of Industrial Production and Iron and Steel Production, Japan, 1928–1954 (1928 = 100)

$Y_c = 56.526 + 0.513X$

$r_{xy} = 0.9454$

Industrial Production (y)

Iron and steel production (x)

Source: <u>Nihon Keizai tôkei shû</u> (<u>Economic Statistics of Japan</u>) Tokyo, 1958, pp. 27–28

7

Figure 1.4. Indices of Industrial Production and Ferrous-metals Output, Soviet Union, 1928–1955 (1928 = 100)

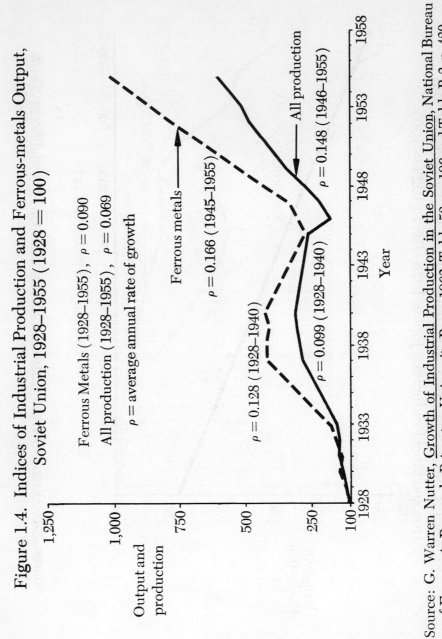

Ferrous Metals (1928–1955), ρ = 0.090

All production (1928–1955), ρ = 0.069

ρ = average annual rate of growth

Ferrous metals

ρ = 0.166 (1945–1955)

ρ = 0.128 (1928–1940)

ρ = 0.099 (1928–1940)

All production

ρ = 0.148 (1946–1955)

Output and production

1,250

1,000

750

500

250

100

1928   1933   1938   1943   1948   1953   1958

Year

Source: G. Warren Nutter, Growth of Industrial Production in the Soviet Union, National Bureau of Economic Research, Princeton University Press, 1962, Table 53, p. 196 and Table B-2, p. 420.

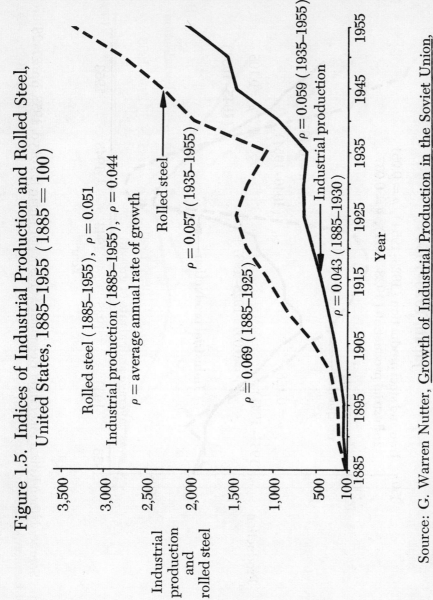

Figure 1.5. Indices of Industrial Production and Rolled Steel, United States, 1885–1955 (1885 = 100)

Rolled steel (1885–1955), $\rho = 0.051$

Industrial production (1885–1955), $\rho = 0.044$

ρ = average annual rate of growth

Rolled steel

$\rho = 0.057$ (1935–1955)

$\rho = 0.069$ (1885–1925)

$\rho = 0.059$ (1935–1955)

Industrial production

$\rho = 0.043$ (1885–1930)

Industrial production and rolled steel

3,500

3,000

2,500

2,000

1,500

1,000

500

100

1885 1895 1905 1915 1925 1935 1945 1955

Year

Source: G. Warren Nutter, Growth of Industrial Production in the Soviet Union, Princeton University Press, Princeton, New Jersey, 1962, Table A-32, Table E-1.

9

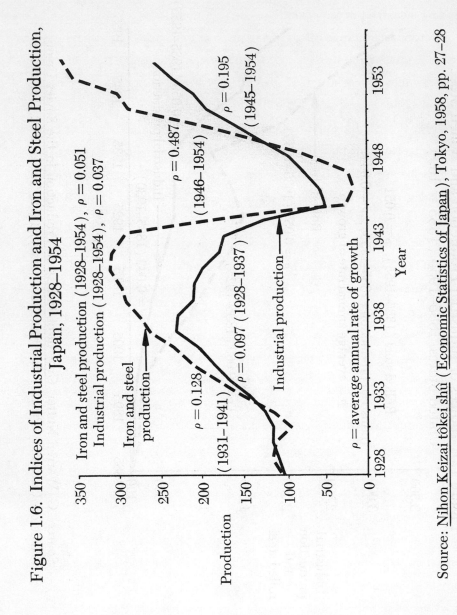

Figure 1.6. Indices of Industrial Production and Iron and Steel Production, Japan, 1928–1954

Iron and steel production (1928–1954), ρ = 0.051
Industrial production (1928–1954), ρ = 0.037

Iron and steel production

ρ = 0.128 (1931–1941)

ρ = 0.097 (1928–1937)

ρ = 0.487 (1946–1954)

ρ = 0.195 (1945–1954)

Industrial production

ρ = average annual rate of growth

Production

350
300
250
200
150
100
50
0

1928   1933   1938   1943   1948   1953

Year

Source: <u>Nihon Keizai tôkei shû</u> (<u>Economic Statistics of Japan</u>), Tokyo, 1958, pp. 27–28

10

probably true, however, that as long as production responds to market demand, the steel industry is not apt to develop unless the demand for its products is boosted by industrial development.

Yet the quantitative effect of any attempt to establish a modern steel industry on available investible funds is real enough. The importance of steel as a necessary input in construction and machine production is also very real, although it may be exaggerated in the light of the emergence of new materials, particularly if regard for heterogeneity of steels and steel products is insufficient. Exaggeration of the usefulness of steel as a general category of producers' goods plus the symbolic value of the metal may very well lead to an underestimate of the investment cost and an overemphasis on quantity. The result would be a waste of resources, unless subsequent readjustments could bring about an acceleration of the rate of economic growth in general. The ultimate benefit to be derived from readjustments to conditions of unbalanced growth and the "big push" in isolated sectors would, however, accrue mainly from the assumed condition that the industry involved would lower certain input costs to other industries so that the latter could then expand more readily. Implied here is another set of assumptions, namely, that prices would respond to increases in supply, that the quality of the products of the "overexpanded" industries would not deteriorate, and that overexpansion of the sectors concerned would not handicap the growth of other sectors through external diseconomies or other adverse effects on the economy as a whole.[2]

None of these undesirable effects of the excessive expansion of the steel industry need occur if in planning its growth their possible advent has been given due consideration, and if the day-to-day management of the industry is at a high level. The question is, of course, whether in the particular instance of Communist China the expansion of the steel industry has been properly planned and whether the plans have been adequately executed. According to an official publication of the State Statistical Bureau of Communist China,[3] the total output of iron in 1949 when the Communist regime was established on the Chinese mainland was only 158,000 tons and ranked twenty-fourth in the world. By 1957, however, Communist China's iron production was said to have risen to 5,350,000

11

tons, and its international ranking had risen to ninth. Official statistics in 1958-1960 would indicate even more rapid rates of increase. Pertinent questions include: Are these statistics meaningful? What do the actual size and state of industry seem to be? What role has the industry played in the economy as a whole and in relation to other economic sectors? Have planning and management been efficient? In particular, we may expect to learn from the steel industry the effectiveness of Communist China's economic planning as a whole and the economic influence of steel as a symbol.

Outline of the Study

The next six chapters are devoted to an analysis of Communist China's steel industry and to a search for the correct answers to the questions posed so far, as well as a number of other related questions about fact and interpretation. Chapter 2 describes the development of the infant steel industry in pre-Communist China with an analysis of both its size and its internal structure. Given this historical background, we then proceed to an analysis in Chapter 3 of the size of the industry under the Communist regime, plans of development, volume of investment entailed, results in terms of production and capacity, efficiency of equipment utilization, quality of products, and the state of intraindustry balance. The period under detailed examination spans the years between 1949 and 1960--that is, from the time the Communist regime was established to the end of the "Great Leap Forward." The absence of reliable data prevents meaningful expansion of the inquiry beyond 1960 in any detail. Chapter 4 takes us to a discussion of the meaning of the concept of "gross industrial output" as applied to the iron and steel industry, which is followed by a detailed estimate of the contribution of several subsectors of the industry to the national output, including the "native" and "semimodern" sectors of the industry in 1958-1960. The discussion includes an examination of some elements of the industry's cost structure, as well as an analysis of the distribution of the industry's product between the workers and the government. We shall also examine the correlation of the growth of the ferrous metals with that of the economy as a whole and industry in particular.

The relation between the steel industry and other sectors of the economy is discussed in Chapter 5 in terms of the distribution of finished steel by end use. One of the by-products of this discussion will be an estimate of steel consumption by the military, a problem currently of considerable interest in some quarters. The discussion further relates the domestic supply and consumption of the industry's products to external trade, thus providing some additional understanding of changes the industry has undergone since before World War II.

Chapters 6 and 7 consist of an analysis of the locational pattern of the Chinese steel industry. The former is an introductory discussion of the topic with respect to the pre-Communist period; the latter continues the discussion through 1960. Such factors as the geographical distribution of the mills, the relation of iron smelting to the relative availability of ore deposits, the regional structural balance, and the effect of the location of steel mills on the location of industry as a whole are all discussed in turn.

Chapter 8 is a summary of the findings and conclusions and is provided for the convenience of those who do not wish to concern themselves with methodology and details.

Those who have been interested in economic studies employing Communist Chinese figures need not be reminded of the difficulties and frustrations arising from the paucity and poor quality of these data. Not the least perplexing of these problems is the prevalence of data which disclose half-truths only and are therefore particularly misleading. Accordingly, considerable time and effort must be devoted to the collection and examination of relevant statistics. Some of the results of this part of our work are presented in a series of appendices. Appendix A deals with estimates of iron-ore deposits. Appendix B is concerned with the confusing statistics of the capacity and production of pig iron, ingot steel, and finished-steel products. Appendix C contains a brief discussion of an alternative estimate of finished steel. Appendix D, prepared by Ronald Hsia of the University of Hong Kong, is of a somewhat different character. It presents a description of some of the important technological changes that have been introduced into Communist China and should be read in conjunction with Chapter 3.

13

2

A HISTORICAL REVIEW OF THE MODERN CHINESE IRON AND STEEL INDUSTRY BEFORE 1949

Iron Ore Deposits

During his travels in China in the latter part of the nineteenth century, Baron von Richthofen[1] stated that Shansi was "one of the most remarkable coal and iron regions in the world" and that manufacture of iron there was "capable of almost unlimited extension." He was under the impression that these deposits would be more than adequate to supply the world market for many years to come. The exaggerated expectations were, however, in no way in accord with the facts, and subsequent explorations in the pre-Communist period tended to show that China was relatively poor in iron-ore deposits, even though the abundance of coal was substantiated. Further geological surveys following the establishment of the Communist regime have, however, again reversed the appraisal to some extent so that it is now believed that Communist China, while by no means prolific in iron-ore deposits, nevertheless possesses sufficient ore reserve to support a substantial development of the iron and steel industry. Consideration of the new discoveries and claims will be discussed in Chapter 3, and more details are given in Appendix A. For the moment, we shall concentrate on the situation as it was known in the pre-Communist period.

According to the first issue of the General Statement on the Mining Industry of the Geological Survey of China, published in 1921, discoveries prior to that time showed total ore reserves to be 678 million tons. According to the 1910 International Geological Congress, the world's iron ore reserves, including the known deposits of Europe, Asia, the Americas, Oceania, and Africa, amounted to 22,409 million tons of "actual" reserves and more than 123,377 million tons of additional "potential" reserves.[2] The same source gave the deposits of China as 100 million tons of "actual" deposits, apparently derived from rough early estimates, thus accounting for a little over 0.4 percent of the world's total. However, if instead the total of 678 million tons published in the

14

1921 issue of the General Statement were used, China's share in the world's total would be raised to 2.9 percent. Since the standards used in reporting and estimating reserves are not uniform, and since such estimates for different areas are not made at the same time, any comparison of this kind can never be expected to yield a definite result.[3] Nor is it really very meaningful. Nevertheless, it is clear that at a time when the modern iron-smelting industry was barely making its debut in China the order of magnitude thus indicated would not rank that nation among the world's iron-rich countries.

As more geological surveys and new estimates were made, both in China and elsewhere, China's relative position in the distribution of the world's known iron-ore deposits fluctuated. In particular, it was affected by the concept, coverage, and date of estimation of the data used. The preliminary figure given in the 1921 General Statement was subsequently revised to 952 million tons in 1926, 737 million tons in 1929, 1 billion tons in 1932, 1.2 billion tons in 1935, and 1.98 billion tons of verified and probable deposits plus 166 million tons of roughly estimated reserves in 1945. A later estimate based primarily on 1948 publications puts China's total reserve at 5.4 billion tons.[4] A United Nations survey published in 1950 gives the world's potential (including probable) iron reserves as 293.4 billion tons of ore, while the corresponding Chinese figure is given as 2,700 million tons. Although the publication appeared in 1950 only, this Chinese figure was derived from pre-Communist estimates so that the 0.9 percent which China's reserve represented in the world's total was still a portrayal of the relative status in the pre-Communist period, as far as the data were then known. On a per-capita basis, China stood in the 1950 United Nations report at what was decidedly the lower end of the array. Of the sixty-one areas listed, only ten had per-capita values lower than that of China. The rest were at least equal to the Chinese level or, in the majority of cases, better than the Chinese figure. A somewhat later United Nations publication, however, presented for China (including Taiwan) the revised figure of 4,180 million tons of "measured, indicated, and inferred" reserves[5] as against a world total of 79.96 billion tons. The larger Chinese figure, again derived from pre-Communist data obtained in 1948,[6] with the smaller world total resulting from application of a stricter concept than the term "potential reserve" implied in the 1950 United Nations survey,

15

gave rise to a more favorable picture. The Chinese reserve would now constitute 5.2 percent of the world's total. If we should now substitute the 5.4 billion ton estimate for China (mainland only) and compare it with the corresponding total for the world, the ratio for China would become 6.6 percent.

On the whole, the changing status of China's iron ore reserve would seem to indicate that while China could by no means account for a sizable proportion of the world's known deposits on the eve of the Communist take-over, the situation was sufficiently fluid to preclude any conclusive judgment. At any rate, of the world's large economically underdeveloped areas, China was far from being the least well-endowed in iron ore deposits. It is certain that a modern iron and steel industry of a modest size could be sustained on the basis of domestic resources alone. If the availability of domestic deposits should eventually impose a limit on the development of the Chinese iron and steel industry, such a limit would not be in sight for some time to come. In this connection it should be noted that the iron content of Chinese deposits--an average of 45 percent in the 1945 General Statement as against 37 percent in the 1921 issue--does not compare unfavorably with data elsewhere. It is only slightly below the world mean of 50 percent for probable reserves and a little above the world mean of 44 percent for potential (including probable) reserves. [7] The corresponding estimates for the United States are 45 percent and 36 percent, respectively; the U.S.S.R. figures are also comparable.

Without going into the estimates of iron ore reserves since the establishment of the Communist regime in 1949, which will be discussed in Chapter 3, it suffices to point out for the moment that even the later estimates for China were still based on rather limited geological surveys. A further increase in reported deposits should not, therefore, be surprising.

Up to 1935, however, the known deposits listed by the Geological Survey were concentrated in Manchuria, East China, Central China, and North China (including what is now Inner Mongolia). Reliable reserve figures were not available for the Northwest prior to 1935. This regional distribution conformed well with the general pattern of early industrial and commercial development in China, the lag in economic development of the interior provinces especially in the Northwest and the Southwest, and the general inaccessibility of the landbound areas not yet penetrated by railways or steamer transportation. However, enough was known about the existence of certain reserves to permit a modest beginning in ore mining and modern iron smelting, while expectations and hopes continued to be fed by dreams of future spectacular discoveries.

A Historical Review

In the following sections we shall treat developments of the modern iron and steel industry in the pre-Communist period in four separate stages: (a) the embryonic stage (1890-1920); (b) the pre-World War II nationalist phase or the interwar years; (c) expansion in World War II; and (d) the phase of postwar devastation before 1949. This will be followed by a summary of the principal characteristics during the entire period that constituted the legacy received by the Communists upon their assumption of power.

The Embryonic Phase, 1890-1920

The history of the modern iron and steel industry of mainland China dates back to 1890 when Chang Chih-tung, Governor of Hupeh province under the Manchu regime, initiated the construction of the Han-yang Iron and Steel Works at Han-yang, one of the three largest trading centers of Central China and a constituent of what is now the tri-city of Wu-han,[8] as well as the site of a new steel-industry complex being built by the Communists. Construction of this mill was completed in 1893 with the installation of two blast furnaces with a daily output capacity of 100 metric tons,[9] as well as two converters.[10] Through 1895, however, a cumulative total of 5,660 tons of pig iron only was produced; there was no recorded production of steel up to that time. Beginning in 1907, the plant began to produce standard steel, and output during the year reached 8,500 tons. Thus, it may be said that a very rudimentary basis was laid for the Chinese iron and steel industry shortly after the beginning of the twentieth century.

The Han-yang Iron Works followed what was then the normal course of Chinese government industrial enterprises: the rate of operation usually fluctuated with the vicissitudes of public financial difficulties. As governmental funds proved insufficient for operational purposes, the original works was converted in 1894 into a joint enterprise between the government and private interests. It was also merged with an iron works at nearby Ta-yeh and the coal mines of P'ing-hsiang in Kiangsi, and was renamed the Han-yeh-p'ing Iron and Steel Company. The company's increasing financial difficulties, however, led to

17

serious indebtedness to Japanese interests and virtual control was vested in the hands of the Japanese creditors during 1913-1924.

The world war brought with it a boom on the world market in ferrous metals and gave impetus to the infant iron mining and smelting industry in China, which had not been able to find in the domestic market an adequate demand for its products. (Domestic demand might have expanded much more rapidly had industrial development fulfilled the earlier promises of its proponents.) A number of iron works mushroomed at an increasing number of new locations, along with the expansion of the existing enterprises. Thus, a new Ta-yeh Iron Works was built with a Japanese loan in 1914. In 1917, an iron smelting plant was established by the Ho-hsin Company of Shanghai in the P'u-tung district of the city. Again, in the following year, the Lung-yen Iron and Steel Company was set up in Hsüan-hua of the then Chahar province in North China as a joint enterprise between government and private interests. To the East, the Japanese succeeded in acquiring the right to mine iron ore at Chin-ling-chen in Shantung province and began to produce pig iron in 1919. Also in the same year, the Yü-fan Iron and Steel Company at Fan-ch'ang of Anhwei province and the Yang-tze Machine Building Company of Hankow in Hupeh undertook to erect several iron-smelting plants of their own for the production of pig iron. In 1920 a Mining Bureau was set up by the Hupeh provincial government to take charge of iron-ore mining at the Hsiang-pi-shan mines, as well as pig iron smelting on the spot. In the then remote northern province of Shansi, the provincial government had also started out to build a small iron works at Yang-ch'üan. Construction began in 1917 and was completed in 1921. Its daily production capacity, however, was limited to 15 to 20 tons. [11]

The spate of activities in China proper noted above was accompanied by what was to turn out to be a far more portentous development in Manchuria. Here the Pen-ch'i-hu Iron Works, first of its kind in Manchuria, was founded in 1910 at Pen-ch'i-hu of Liaoning, formerly Feng-t'ien province, as a joint Sino-Japanese undertaking. Renamed the Pen-ch'i-hu Iron Manufacturing Company in 1911, it was expanded in 1914 following an increase in capitalization. [12] With the help of additional funds the company then installed several modern blast furnaces and began to produce pig iron from the deposits at nearby Miao-erh-kou.

Ore production during 1915-1925 totalled 25,000 tons while pig-iron output, which began in 1918, was at an annual rate of 30,000 to 40,000 tons.

The now famous An-shan Iron and Steel Works was first established as a project of the Japanese South Manchurian Railway Company, following the discovery of ore deposits by the geological staff of the railway in 1909. During World War I, a "partnership company" known as the Shinko Tekko Mugen Koshi was organized in 1916 on the basis of an annex to the 1915 Sino-Japanese agreement which granted Japan the right to mine iron ore in the An-shan area.[13] In April 1919, the first blast furnace of the An-shan works was blown in, and until 1933 only pig iron was produced at An-shan.

In general, it can probably be said that the primitive iron industry of China reached a peak during the initial stage of its development toward the end of World War I. Iron-ore production from modern mines reached a peak of 1,125,000 tons in China proper in 1920 and 275,000 tons in Manchuria in 1919. Pig-iron production from modern mills reached a peak of 124,000 tons in Manchuria in 1920 and was at a high of 199,000 tons in China proper in 1916.[14] These levels of output were not again attained until the mid-twenties in the case of Manchuria. Production of pig iron in China proper apparently never again reached this level until World War II, while ore production did not recover to the same height until the middle of the 1930's. The output of steel was 43,000 tons in 1913 and rose to a high of 68,000 tons in 1920 and 77,000 tons in 1921, which was also not to be exceeded again until the thirties.

The Interwar Period, 1921-1937

As will be discussed more fully later in this chapter, the mining and manufacturing of iron in China was under the strong influence of the export market, while domestic consumption played a relatively insignificant role. Accordingly, the entire industry suffered a severe setback during the post-World War I years. The drop of prices and shrinkage of the absolute volume of exports brought about a severe contraction of the entire industry and operation was interrupted in a number of the small enterprises. This was also a period of political chaos at home created by rivalry among the war lords whose activities resulted in a general interruption of economic development in China.

19

Upon the establishment of the Nationalist government in Nanking in 1927, an ambitious plan for the development of nine basic industries was proposed in 1928 under the sponsorship of the then Ministry of Industry and Commerce. Development of the iron and steel industry was accorded top priority in this scheme.[15] However, little real investment was carried out and the plans were held in abeyance. A devastating one-year war between the Central Government and local forces led by Feng Yü-hsiang and Yen Hsi-shan in 1930, ruinous floods in 1931, the occupation of all of Manchuria by the Japanese following the Mukden incident in the same year, and civil war between the Central Government and the Chinese Communists in 1932-1936 occupied virtually the entire attention and energy of the Nationalist government. The development of domestic iron and steel mills by the government in China proper was thus held back. At the same time, private interests also showed little inclination to move ahead. Their effort was instead concentrated in the light manufacturing sector such as cotton textiles, flour milling, etc.

This situation was decidedly in contrast to developments in Manchuria where, due primarily to the exploitation of local iron ore and iron smelting by the Japanese, production showed a generally much more favorable trend than inside the Great Wall.

Dichotomy of production trends in ore and iron in Manchuria and China proper. Manchuria's pig-iron production exceeded that of China proper for the first time in 1923. Three years later its iron-ore production overtook that of modern mines in China proper. These years should be regarded as outstanding landmarks in the economic history of modern China inasmuch as the subsequent industrial supremacy of Manchuria, together with all its politico-economic implications, has not yet been challenged.

The divergent production trends can be clearly seen in Figure 2.1. In the case of pig iron, production in Manchuria increased steadily from the 1922 postwar trough onward; the rate of increase began to pick up after 1932 and especially after 1934, thus reflecting the result of the expansion program[16] begun in 1934 after the occupation of Manchuria by the Japanese about two years earlier. On the other hand, pig-iron production in China proper, after some oscillation between 1918 and 1922, declined fairly steadily from 1922 to 1927

20

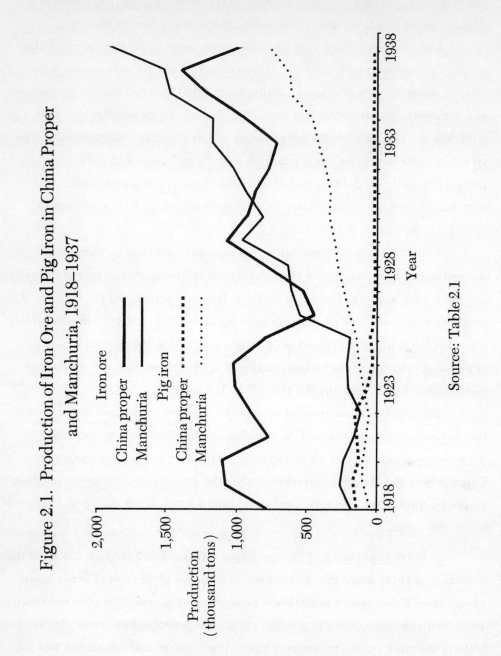

Figure 2.1. Production of Iron Ore and Pig Iron in China Proper and Manchuria, 1918–1937

Iron ore
China proper
Manchuria

Pig iron
China proper
Manchuria

Production (thousand tons)

Year

Source: Table 2.1

and remained at a very low level through 1931. From 1932 to 1937 it was at a slightly higher level, but there was no expansion of any kind to speak of.

A similar dichotomy in production trends between Manchuria and China proper can be observed in the case of iron ore, except that fluctuations were more pronounced in both regions. While the trend of Manchurian ore production was decidedly upward during this inter-war period, it was interspersed with mild dips and phases when the advance was rather sluggish. Without being precise in measurement, we can distinguish such "slow" phases in 1922-1925, 1926-1928, 1929-1931, 1933-1934, and 1935-1936. However, in China proper, there were two phases of sizable decline in ore output during these years: first in 1924-1926, and again in 1929-1933.

While the periodic slowdown of the expansion process in Manchuria seemed to be primarily phases of consolidation following sharp rises of capacity and production and was correlated with pig iron production, the fluctuations of recorded output in China proper appeared to be of a different cyclical character.[17] The wide fluctuations also stood out in sharp contrast to the general stagnation of pig-iron output in China proper, suggesting, therefore, that ore production was also much more susceptible to cyclical influences.

The greater fluctuations of ore versus pig iron output and of ore production in China proper in comparison with that of Manchuria can be explained by the sources of demand and the differential rates of economic development in China proper and Manchuria, respectively. The relative importance of the role played by foreign trade in total production offers a key to the divergent conditions in the two areas.

Relative importance of foreign trade.   Figures 2.2 through 2.4 show that beginning in 1916, there was a sharp increase in the proportion of net iron-ore export from China proper to domestic production. This situation continued through 1931, and although export did not rise continuously in absolute terms, it changed little in the later years. Dependence upon export meant that production was subject to fluctuations on the world market, which was far from being stable during the inter-war period. In contrast to the above, Manchurian ore export was a negligible part of domestic production up to 1931.[18]   Since production was for

22

Table 2.1

PRODUCTION OF IRON ORE, PIG IRON, AND STEEL INGOT, 1912–1937

(in thousand metric tons)

Year	Iron Ore				Pig Iron				Steel Ingot
	Modern Mines		Native	Total	Modern Works		Native	Total	
	China proper	Manchuria			China proper	Manchuria			
1912	721	...	...	721	178	...	...	178	3
1913	960	...	...	960	268	...	...	268	43
1914	1,005	...	...	1,005	300	...	...	300	56
1915	1,100	...	...	1,100	336	...	...	336	48
1916	629	...	500	1,129	199	...	170	369	45
1917	640	...	500	1,140	188	...	170	358	43
1918	782	193	500	1,475	139	45	170	354	57
1919	1,086	275	500	1,861	167	110	170	447	35
1920	1,125	241	500	1,866	134	124	170	428	68
1921	803	160	500	1,463	140	93	170	403	77
1922	919	140	500	1,559	164	60	170	394	30
1923	1,019	214	500	1,733	73	100	170	343	30
1924	1,046	220	500	1,766	27	134	170	331	30
1925	816	203	500	1,519	54	146	170	370	30
1926	467	566	529	1,562	12	214	179	405	30
1927	550	631	529	1,710	4	244[b]	179	427	30
1928	820	655	529	2,004	11	285	179	475	30
1929	1,061	986	583	2,630	14	295	135	444	15
1930	941	832	479	2,252	3	349	122	474	15
1931	877[a]	964[a]	496	2,337	10	342	126	478	15

Table 2.1 (continued)

| Year | Iron Ore | | | | Pig Iron | | | | Steel Ingot |
| | Modern Mines | | Native | Total | Modern Works | | Native | Total | |
	China proper	Manchuria			China proper	Manchuria			
1932	798	1,041	410	2,249	19	368	135	522	...
1933	727	1,176	410	2,313	35	433	139	607	...
1934	950	1,185	410	2,545	20	476	135	631	...
1935	1,223	1,485	427	3,135	22	608	139	729	182
1936	1,402	1,520	438	3,360	22	633	140	795[c]	414[d]
1937	992	1,950	274	3,216	30	762	128	908	340

Data for the respective years are from General Statement on the Mining Industry (hereafter referred to as General Statement), 2d issue, 1918–1925, pp. 124–135; 3d issue, 1925–1928, pp. 297–301; 4th issue, 1929–1931, pp. 121 and 126; 5th issue, 1932–1934, pp. 181–188; and 7th issue, 1935–1942, pp. 100–110.

[a] Iron-ore production for 1931 (China proper and Manchuria) was placed at 1,951 thousand metric tons in the General Statement, 4th issue, 1929–1931, p. 182.

[b] Figures for Manchuria's pig-iron production between 1926 and 1938 are from Japan–Manchoukuo Year Book, 1941, p. 712. A slightly higher figure is possible. See Appendix B.

[c] Also reported at 670,000 tons for the modern sector and 810,000 tons for the total. See Appendix B.

[d] The figure for 1936 was 350,000 tons according to the General Statement, 7th issue, 1935–1942.

Table 2.2

IRON ORE PRODUCTION AND FOREIGN TRADE
(in thousand metric tons)

Year	Production		Net Export		Net Export in Percentage of Production	
	China proper	Manchuria	China proper	Manchuria	China proper	Manchuria
1912	721	...	204.72	---	28.39	---
1913	960	...	273.88	---	28.53	---
1914	1,005	...	299.34	---	29.78	---
1915	1,100	...	305.50	3.32	27.77	...
1916	629	...	282.89	---	44.97	---
1917	640	...	267.90	0.06	41.86	...
1918	782	193	341.18	---	43.63	---
1919	1,086	275	637.31	2.90	58.68	1.10
1920	1,125	241	655.14	12.94	58.24	5.37
1921	803	160	505.26	8.52	62.92	5.33
1922	919	140	672.32	-.48	73.16	0.35*
1923	1,019	214	728.06	---	71.45	---
1924	1,046	220	849.76	---	81.24	---
1925	816	203	817.06	0.12	100.13	0.06
1926	467	566	524.67	0.60	112.35	0.11
1927	550	631	500.00	---	90.91	0.00
1928	820	655	915.06	0.24	111.59	0.04
1929	1,061	986	978.60	0.85	92.23	0.09
1930	941	832	820.56	1.39	87.20	0.17
1931	877	964	572.19	0.42	65.24	0.04
1932	798	1,041	560.01	-2.50	70.18	0.24*
1933	727	1,176	593.17	-1.84	81.59	0.16*
1934	950	1,185	857.57	-1.17	90.27	0.10*
1935	1,223	1,485	1,316.01	-1.47	107.61	0.10*
1936	1,402	1,520	1,302.70	-1.35	92.92	0.09*
1937	992	1,950	596.00	2.33	60.08	0.12

*Import Surplus.

Notes and Sources: For production, see Table 2.1. Foreign trade data for the years 1932-37 are taken from Foreign Minerals Survey, vol. 2, no. 7, Jan. 1948, p. 34. Data for the years 1912-31 are derived from Statistics of Commodity Flow of Chinese Maritime Customs and Railways, Special Series No. 7, vol. I, 1937, pp. 379-381. Data for net exports of iron ore from China proper for the years 1932-37 are data of exports in that period.

Table 2.3

PIG IRON PRODUCTION AND FOREIGN TRADE
(in thousand metric tons)

Year	Production		Net Export		Net Export in Percentage of Production	
	China proper	Manchuria	China proper	Manchuria	China proper	Manchuria
1925	54	146	28.83	121.38	44.13	83.13
1926	12	214	-9.41	170.91	78.44*	79.86
1927	4	244	-8.83	218.82	220.83*	89.68
1928	11	285	-18.23	239.87	165.72*	84.17
1929	14	295	-16.13	225.68	115.21*	76.50
1930	3	349	-18.28	220.90	609.47*	63.29
1931	10	342	-22.25	289.20	222.48*	84.56
1932	19	368	-26.76	368.80	140.84*	100.22
1933	35	433	-42.89	490.47	122.54*	113.27
1934	20	476	-44.06	439.76	220.28*	90.39
1935	22	608	-51.62	428.52	234.66*	70.48
1936	22	633	-34.38	304.85	156.28*	48.16
1937	20	762	-29.46	248.37	147.28*	32.59

*Import surplus.

Notes and Sources: For production, see Table 2.1. Foreign trade data are taken from Foreign Minerals Survey, vol. 2, no. 7, Jan. 1948, p. 41.

an expanding domestic iron smelting industry, its lesser degree of fluctuation is readily understandable.

The generally upward trend of pig iron production in Manchuria during the inter-war period coincided with heavy pig iron exports from Manchuria. Except in 1930, net pig iron export was at no time less than 75 percent of domestic production from 1925 through 1934. The sustained export was in turn a reflection of sustained demand stemming from steelmaking in Japan. In 1935, however, the relative share of export in total production fell sharply and the decline continued to the end of the period. This coincided with the expansion of domestic production in iron- and steelmaking in Manchuria and was therefore indicative of a change in the character of the Manchurian iron and steel industry. The earlier development of the fabrication stage of the iron and steel industry in Manchuria, compared with China proper, can therefore be seen first in the greater domestic consumption of iron ore, and later, in that of pig iron.

In China proper, on the other hand, there was a net import of pig iron from 1926 through 1937, the amount of import being considerably larger than domestic production in the majority of the years. At the same time, as described later in Chapter 6, most of the few modern iron mills then in existence were closed down while a few were producing below capacity. The failure of the pig iron industry in China proper to expand during this period should therefore not be attributed solely to the absence of an increasing domestic demand. It is possible, of course, that if domestic demand had been expanding as rapidly as in Manchuria, the situation would have been different. One may also speculate that had there been an active program to increase domestic steelmaking, there would also have been a larger market for domestic pig iron. However, one suspects that inefficient operation, internal financial difficulties of the mills, and an environment generally unfavorable to development during most of the period were the principal causes of the stagnation of the industry.

Expansion during World War II

The entire iron and steel industry in mainland China experienced rapid expansion during the war with Japan (1937-1945) again as a result of rising war demand and, for parts of the country at any rate, the inability to augment supply

Table 2.4

IRON AND STEEL PRODUCTION IN FREE CHINA, 1938-1945
(in thousand metric tons)

Year	Iron Ore	Pig Iron	Steel Ingot	Finished-steel Products
1938	245	41	...	0.9
1939	329	42	...	1.9
1940	348	55	...	1.5
1941	321	67	1	2.0
1942	326	78	4	5.8
1943	...	70	9	7.7
1944	...	40	12	13.4
1945	...	21	...	12.0

Source: National Resources Commission of China. The Quarterly Journal of the National Resources Commission, vol. VI, nos. 1-4, June-December 1946, pp. 102-103.

Table 2.5

PLANNED PRODUCTION CAPACITY (YEAR-END) OF PIG IRON, INGOT STEEL, AND FINISHED-STEEL PRODUCTS IN JAPANESE-OCCUPIED NORTH CHINA, 1941 TO 1947
(in thousand metric tons)

Year	Pig Iron	Ingot Steel	Finished-steel Products
1941	140	45	30
1942	140	45	48
1943	140	45	48
1944	340	170	148
1945	540	420	348
1946	940	540	448
1947	940	545	448

Source: Chang Po-p'in, Development of Natural Resources in North China during the Sino-Japanese War, Nanking, 1947, pp. 78-79.

through import. Development may be considered separately for three different areas.

First, a new though rudimentary iron and steel industry sprang up in the southwestern provinces of China which hitherto were particularly undeveloped as far as modern industry was concerned. By 1938 the area had been effectively sealed off from the rest of the world, since only the supply routes via Indo-China, Sinkiang, and, later, the Burma Road remained intermittently open for imports, and none of these was adequate for bulk shipments. Supplies for the area, therefore, had to be produced locally. In anticipation of this situation, the Nationalist government had begun to develop modern facilities for iron- and steelmaking in the Southwest shortly after the war broke out in 1937. Some of the installations at Han-yang, Liu-ho-kou, and Shanghai were dismantled and brought to the Southwest. Some of the equipment was reinstalled at Ta-tu-k'ou in the suburb of Chungking, then the wartime capital of Nationalist China. Subsequently, the Ta-tu-k'ou plant became the largest works in Free China and has since been known as the No. 101 plant under the Communist regime. It furnished the basis for the establishment of a major metallurgical center in Chungking after 1949. Other smaller wartime works were established in Szechwan, Yunnan, and elsewhere, totaling more than twenty separate enterprises. Official statistics showed that iron-ore deposits discovered in these two provinces totaled 22 million tons in Szechwan and 12.2 million tons in Yunnan up to 1942. Iron-ore production increased from 245,000 tons in 1938 to 348,000 tons in 1940 and remained at the level of 320,000 to 330,000 tons up to 1943. Pig iron production also rose from 41,000 tons in 1938 to 78,500 tons in 1942. Steel ingot production, which had not been reported up to 1940, was at the level of 12,000 tons in 1944. Finished-steel products reached the level of 13,400 tons in 1944, having risen from less than 2,000 tons before 1941. Since these statistics are derived from the National Resources Commission of China, which controlled many of the important works, the data coverage is expected to be fairly complete although some small private enterprises may have been excluded from the reports. The geographical coverage of "Free China" also fluctuated from time to time as a result of military

29

operations so that this factor should be taken into account in any evaluation of the production trend. However, the increase in all the major categories of iron and steel products during this period is quite unmistakable, and the wartime peak was apparently attained during 1943-1944 and coincided roughly with the production records in other parts of China.

Second, in addition to the expansion of a number of established mills at Shih-ching-shan, Lung-yen, T'ai-yüan, Ta-yeh, Han-yang, Chiao-tso, etc., the Japanese undertook to establish several smaller plants in other occupied areas of China proper--at T'ang-shan, Tientsin, the Hainan island, and Ma-an-shan. Long-range investment activities indicated that the Japanese occupation forces apparently intended to stay on the Chinese mainland. As a matter of fact, under two five-year plans, the Japanese aimed at the establishment of sizable iron- and steel-production facilities in North China. If the plans had been carried out, annual capacity for pig-iron smelting would have been raised from 140,000 tons in 1941 to 940,000 in 1947; for steel from 45,000 tons in 1941 to 545,000 tons in 1947; and for finished-steel products from some 30,000 in 1941 to 448,000 tons in 1947. Many of the construction projects were never completed, and installations that had been completed were subsequently in part again destroyed. Although much of the production record has not been kept, it is clear that a sizable iron and steel industry was in the making during the war years in the Japanese-occupied regions of China proper.

Lastly, in Manchuria itself, which the Japanese regarded as a major continental preserve and base for sustained military operations, a considerable expansion program was undertaken during the war in all stages of manufacturing and fabrication. There was a clear reversal of the previous Japanese policy which had intended to use Manchuria essentially, if not solely, for the production of ore and semifinished products. Shipping difficulties during the latter part of the war and plans to employ Manchuria as a base of long-term military operations prompted this change in policy. This is clearly seen in the expansion of the capacity of ingot by 224 percent over the 1936 level by the end of the war on August 15, 1945; it compares with an expansion of 215 percent both in the capacity of pig-iron making and in that of finished steel. Production statistics, however, showed increases between 1936 and 1943 of 256 percent in ore, 173 percent

30

in pig iron, 132 percent in ingot, and 260 percent in finished steel.

The hint of a change in the structure of the industry in Manchuria during the latter part of the war parallels the Japanese expansion program in North China and in the rest of China proper, even though the plans had not been realized before the war's end. The same is true in Free China, although, because of the limited supply of equipment, expansion was on a much smaller scale, and steel-making, as distinct from iron smelting, continued to lag behind. Nevertheless, wartime demand for locally produced finished-steel products had clearly made its effect felt. A second major development during this period was, of course, the geographical extension of the new iron and steel mills as well as of iron-ore mining to areas hitherto unexploited by either foreign or Chinese interests. All these effects were to be felt after the establishment of the Communist regime in 1949. Inasmuch as developments between 1945 and 1949 were primarily of a negative character, reconstruction following the Communist take-over had per-force to be limited to rebuilding on the basis of wartime developments in Manchuria and the emerging iron and steel centers of China proper. (See Chapter 5.)

Postwar Devastation (1945-1949)

The end of the war witnessed a thoroughgoing dismantling operation by Soviet occupation troops, which affected all industrial installations in Manchuria. According to the Edwin Pauley mission, which inspected a number of industrial plants in southern Manchuria, capacity loss in iron-ore mining and/or in ore-concentration facilities due to Soviet, and in part Communist Chinese, removals was at nearly 100 percent of capacity. In the case of pig iron production, blast-furnace capacity was destroyed or rendered useless by more than 70 to 80 per-cent. A 98 percent loss was suffered in the capacity of sponge-iron production. Other losses were at the levels of 57 percent in ingot making, 50 percent in semifinished steel, and 64 percent in the case of finished-steel products.[19] These data are, of course, only approximate estimates, partly because the inspectors of the Pauley mission were prevented from reaching certain areas still under Communist Chinese or Soviet occupation. Subsequent reports from Japanese sources indicate that the remnant capacities were: pig iron, 396,000 tons; ingot steel, 580,000 tons; and finished-steel products, 324,000 tons.[20]

31

Table 2.6

PRODUCTION CAPACITY AND ACTUAL OUTPUT OF IRON ORE, PIG IRON, INGOT STEEL,
AND FINISHED-STEEL PRODUCTS IN MANCHURIA, 1936 AND 1942 TO 1945
(in thousand metric tons)

Year	Iron Ore	Pig Iron	Steel Ingot	Semifinished Steel (blooms, billets, etc.)	Finished Steel (shapes and plates)	Special Steels		
						Steel	Forgings	Rolled steel
				Productive capacity				
1936	...	800	500	...	305	...	...	...
Aug. 15, 1945	8,645	2,524	1,330-1,622[a]	1,000	910-962[a]	72	6	27
Index for 1945 (1936=100)	...	315.5	324.4	...	315.4	...	...	...
				Output				
1936	1,520	633	364	...	135	...	...	...
1942	4,414	1,741	738	509	458	...	...	8
1943	5,408	1,710-1,727	844	726-774	486	...	...	8
1944	3,758	1,159	439	396	282	30	1	12
Index for 1943 (1936=100)	355.8	270.1-272.8	231.9	...	360.0	...	...	...

[a]The more recent Japanese Survey Report puts the capacity data at this time as 1,622,000 metric tons of ingot and 962,000 tons of steel products.

Source: Appendix B.

32

The total value of Soviet removals of the iron and steel industry of Manchuria was estimated at $131,000,000 according to the Pauley report, while a later investigation by a mission of twenty-one Japanese experts who had formerly held key positions in Manchuria put the value at $204,000,000.[21] These are estimates based on the then replacement value, and, as we shall see, it took the Communist regime a number of years before production capacity was restored to the 1945 "pre-Soviet removal" level. Elsewhere in China proper, no such wholesale removals took place, although dislocation through relocation of plants, close-downs due to raw material and financial difficulties, as well as transportation snarls during the period of postwar hyperinflation, and the general decline of the Chinese economy during the civil war resulted in some degree of net disinvestment in the iron and steel sector. No definite figure, however, can be placed on the quantitative losses. On the other hand, it is quite clear that in spite of supplies provided by the UN Relief and Rehabilitation Administration and some attempts to restore industrial operations where Nationalist control was firmly established, the postwar and pre-Communist period did not see any real increase in capacity.

Towar the end of 1948, only shortly before the Communist occupation of all Manchuria, the Nationalist government's reconstruction plan reportedly aimed at the rehabilitation of only one blast furnace and two open hearths at An-shan.[22] The special steel works at Pen-ch'i was then said to be in working order while a similar plant at Fu-shan was seriously handicapped by the shortage of power and essential parts. In North China, the mills of the then North China Iron and Steel Company at Shih-ching-shan, Tientsin and T'ang-shan were mostly in operation, but on a very small scale. The Shih-ching-shan operation included a pipe mill, a coking plant, and a 200-ton blast furnace, all of which were rehabilitated during 1946-1948. At T'ang-shan, production was at an annual rate of under 1,000 tons of ingot and some 600 tons of finished-steel products. At the Tientsin mill, a 25-ton open-hearth furnace was in operation during the latter part of 1948, while finished-steel products were expected to approach an annual production rate of 2,000 tons. In the rest of China, preparations were being made for the establishment of a Central China Iron and Steel Company to rehabilitate the

Hupeh mills and for the development of the iron mine on Hainan island. Finally, a 100-ton blast furnace was restored to operation at Ta-tu-k'ou (Chungking) under the joint auspices of the National Resources Commission and the Bureau of Ordnance. These activities constituted virtually the sum total of the governmental effort during the postwar and pre-Communist interlude in the iron and steel industry. Little information is available on the status of the smaller private sector of the industry during this period. But one can safely assume that these were in no better condition than the public enterprises operated by the National Resources Commission. Reconstruction of the industry was not to begin, therefore, until the establishment of Communist control over the entire mainland.

Summary of the Development of Modern Iron- and Steelmaking in China in the Pre-Communist Period

There are several major characteristics which the preceding brief description has brought to light. These may now be summarized as follows:

1. From the beginning of the modern iron and steel industry in China, when the first mill was established at Han-yang, to the end of World War II, expansion in production took place principally during the two world wars. This indicates very clearly that demand to sustain expansion on any major scale came only during wartime. However, during the First World War, expansion was primarily in ore production and, to a lesser extent, in pig iron production, both chiefly for the export market. On the other hand, the increase in investment in the industry and in production during World War II came both as a result of increase in domestic demand and because of increasing exports to Japan from the Japanese-occupied areas. However, on the whole, the increase in domestic demand both in Free China and in Japanese-occupied areas in China proper and Manchuria was probably by far the most important factor in the expansion of the market.

2. Until the Second World War the Chinese iron and steel industry was developed primarily at the stages of ore mining and iron smelting. The production of ingot steel lagged behind, while that of finished- and semifinished-steel products was even less developed. A gradual reversal of this situation had begun to emerge in Manchuria toward the end of World War II; a hint of the same

development could be observed in the rest of China, except that it was far less pronounced owing to an inadequate supply of equipment. Even in Manchuria, the turning point came at too late a stage of the war to be fully realized.

3. At the end of 1936, the last prewar year, the production capacity of finished-steel products was about 55 percent of that of ingot steel. It was too small both relatively and in absolute terms. On a national basis, after the Soviet removals, the ratio moved from a more reasonable balance of finished to ingot steel (73 to 84 percent) in August, 1945, to one that suggested a relative shortage of ingot capacity (90 percent). In Manchuria, however, the relative shortage of steel-finishing capacity was greatly accentuated. As for the relationship between iron smelting and steelmaking, the relative shortage in 1936 of steelmaking capacity in the country as a whole had been slightly reduced by the end of Soviet removals, but had by no means been eliminated. In Manchuria, however, the effect of Soviet removals was to create a relative shortage of smelting capacity. Thus, from the national point of view, there was a relative shortage of ingot capacity which would be aggravated by any expansion of capacity in steel finishing; on the other hand, in Manchuria, the shortage was relatively more acute in iron smelting and steel finishing, rather than in the capacity to produce crude steel. This geographical pattern of conflicting relative shortages in the successive stages of production presented a most perplexing problem for the industry as a whole.

4. The earlier mills were set up at a few points where large ore deposits had been discovered. They were also concentrated either in Manchuria or in a few cities where a predominant foreign-investment interest existed. Developments during World War II brought new iron and steel mills to areas which otherwise would not have seen them at the stage of economic development China had then attained. This was true in North China and even more so in parts of Free China in the Southwest such as Szechwan and Yunnan. Many of the mills, especially those in Free China, were far too small to be economical in operation. Their establishment was principally a result of wartime demand. However, once they were set up, the skilled labor that they engendered and the experience of iron- and steelmaking by modern methods which they helped develop may have proved useful in the Communist period when new iron and steel plants mushroomed, especially after the end of the First Five-Year Plan. The wider geographical distribution of iron and steel mills as a result of wartime development was

clearly a boost to later economic development in the country as a whole, even though it was itself a result of circumstances which, from the economic point of view alone, were to be greatly deplored.

5. Because of the more rapid and sustained development of the industry in Manchuria, the relative share of Manchuria in iron and steel production at all its stages was predominant in comparison with that of China proper. In the early 1920's Manchuria already had surpassed China proper in production even though the mills in Hupeh and elsewhere in China proper had been built earlier. This, of course, is both a reflection of the differential rates of economic development between Manchuria and other parts of China and a symbol of the special political and economic position that the northeastern provinces of mainland China had occupied continuously during the last decades.

6. The nature of the demand that spurred development, especially during World War II, offers a logical explanation why the Chinese iron and steel industry was developed primarily with governmental assistance. The consideration of defense as a factor was already paramount in the minds of the early sponsors of the first iron mills in China. The need for steel products for defense purposes was very clearly illustrated during World War II in Free China. The importance of steel for defense has therefore not been lost upon the Chinese, the Communists included. The subsequent adoption under the present regime of steelmaking as a symbol of industrialization and military power has therefore deep historical roots in the experience of China during the last half century. The tendency for the government to promote iron and steel enterprises under its own management may also have had the result of expanding the state sector of the economy beyond what it would have been under the Nationalist regime, thus providing one of the commanding heights of state enterprises for the Communists to take over with their assumption of power in 1949.

GROWTH OF THE IRON AND STEEL INDUSTRY SINCE 1949

Introduction

The Initial Setting

Had Manchuria not been devastated by Soviet removals and the subsequent civil war between 1945 and 1948, and had the Communist Party not seized control of the Chinese mainland, the postwar Chinese iron and steel industry would still have had a number of serious problems. Its relatively small size, its regional imbalance in spite of the appearance of a number of small mills during the war in the more remote provinces of North, Central, and Southwest China, and its "pyramidal" intraindustry structure that showed greater development in iron-ore mining and iron smelting than in steelmaking and fabrication presented a number of serious obstacles to the industry's growth. However, none of these characteristics could be regarded as peculiar to China; on the contrary, they were typical of all underdeveloped economies which had not yet embarked upon an extensive industrial development over a broad spectrum and which had not therefore found sufficient demand for the growth of the more basic capital-goods industries.

Nevertheless, given a definite industrialization program and sustained support for its implementation, the general lines of approach that should and probably would have been followed in the further expansion of the iron and steel industry would be above debate. These would have consisted of an expansion of the nation's capacity of ingot production and an increase in the capacity to produce finished products and special steels. Although the capacity shortage was more pronounced at the higher stages than in ingot making, their expansion might actually have proceeded somewhat more slowly both because of the greater technological complexities involved in making finished-steel products as compared with crude steel--which would have adverse effects on cost--and because of the need to synchronize the expansion of finished-steel production with the

37

growth of the domestic machinery industry, even allowing for the availability of an export market for the crude products. It was quite probable that the rate of domestic savings and the realizable rate of aggregate growth would have acted in this case as a brake on the expansion of the finishing stages of the steel industry.

In regional terms, the pattern of development would also have been readily predictable. Regional development of the iron and steel industry, especially of steelmaking and finishing, would have been carried out at a pace determined primarily by the relative rates of development in the different geographical and administrative regions. With the exception of the possible adoption on a small scale of integrated development plans embracing a group of related industries, in addition to iron and steel mills, the locational pull exercised by rich ore and coal deposits in remote areas would have been offset by a more powerful pull based on the market. For some time, therefore, further expansion of the iron and steel industry would still have favored the existing centers. Shanghai and Ma-an-shan, the Shih-ching-shan-T'ang-shan-Tientien complex, the Hupeh mills which were to be restored, and possibly Chungking and T'ai-yüan, would have constituted the principal beneficiaries of expansion in China proper. The Manchurian mills, on the other hand, would have borne the major portion of the responsibility of initial development, especially in the higher stages of steel finishing, just as Manchurian industry would also have had to provide the greater part of all other capital goods produced in China.

Reality, however, seemed to differ greatly from this hypothetical situation. First, the devastation of the Manchurian industrial complex complicated the problems of intraindustry as well as regional balance as we have already pointed out in Chapter 2 and as we shall discuss again in greater detail in Chapters 6 and 7. In terms of the bare essentials, ore concentration and iron-smelting capacities had been severely reduced in Manchuria during Soviet occupation so that their rehabilitation became no less urgent than the expansion of steel finishing and fabrication. At the same time, the capability of Manchurian industry to support a national industrialization program hinged upon the rapid restoration and expansion of the higher stages of steel production. But if such a development should take place, the expansion of iron smelting and ore mining would in turn have to be accelerated. While this would meet the requirement of Manchurian development, it might prove to be disadvantageous from the point of view of intraindustry balance in the entire economy. In such circumstances, should intraindustry balance for the country as a whole be given precedence over intra-industry balance on a regional basis, or should the reverse order of preference be adopted? In what manner would the rate of industrialization and over-all economic growth be affected in each case? How would the regional pattern of development be affected by these decisions through their impact on regional differentials in the rate of growth? Were the Chinese planners aware of these problems, and how did they attempt to solve them?

In the second place, the establishment of the Communist regime and the adoption of a policy of industrialization by forced draft had several important implications: (1) The highest priority was now accorded to the iron and steel industry because of its pivotal position among the capital-goods industries. The availability of savings as a constraint was likely to become less important if not inoperative as far as the sector of ferrous metallurgy was concerned. (2) Given the assurance of a sustained demand for finished-steel products, the need to maintain intraindustry balance assumed even greater importance, which was further enhanced by the clear indication that Communist China was determined to attempt to achieve industrialization along with self-sufficiency and that any protracted exportation of iron ore or pig iron, probably both necessary and desirable in the short run, would be regarded with disfavor by the planners in the long run. (3) Since the Chinese economy was now based on a central plan which supposedly would emphasize the long-term considerations much more than individual enterprises would have done under similar conditions, and since labor mobility through forced migration and government assignment of employment would be greatly increased, the locational pull of existing markets and of estab-lished iron and steel centers was correspondingly weakened. On the other hand, the burning desire, which bordered on obsession, to speed up the industrializa-tion process would continue to point to greater reliance upon the existing centers of production. Thus, the prospects and nature of the problems confronting the Chinese iron and steel industry were both drastically altered as a result of the establishment of the Communist regime in mainland China.

The ideological and political complexion of the regime also brought with it certain peculiar constraints. In the first place, barring a drastic reorientation of Western and Chinese policies, the sources of external financing and technological assistance were now essentially restricted. The course of development that the industry could follow was therefore to a large extent predicated upon the kind of assistance on which the Chinese and Soviets could agree. Soviet equipment and technology would henceforth constitute the core of Chinese development. Moreover, since Soviet removals in Manchuria were responsible for the devastation of the major portion of the Chinese iron and steel industry, the rehabilitation of the Manchurian installations with Soviet aid[1] would therefore appear to be a most natural point of departure.

In the second place, since Communist China was determined from the beginning to emphasize the military aspect of industrialization, plans for the steel industry would be affected by defense considerations in two ways: (1) The supply of finished steels suitable for ordnance purposes would have to be increased much more rapidly than in any other developing economy; (2) as a result of the orientation of Communist China's foreign policy towards the Soviet Union and the expressed enmity towards the West, the locational advantage of different steel producing centers was altered from the very beginning of the regime. The coastal areas, including Shanghai and, to a lesser extent, southern Manchuria, would now appear even less attractive than they might have been under a different foreign policy. By the same token, as far as inland provinces were concerned, to be close to the Soviet border would no longer be a serious locational disadvantage, at least from the point of view of joint Soviet-Chinese planning, as long as the two major Communist nations remained allies.

The Official Developmental Plan (1949 to 1957) in Outline

That the correlation between machine production and the production of finished steel was clear to Chinese planners will not escape the attention of any student of Communist Chinese affairs. In this regard, reference is often made to the experience of Soviet economic development which, according to a study in Planned Economy,[2] showed that with the exception of 1932 to 1937, the value of machine production in the U.S.S.R. invariably increased during the several five-year plans at a rate considerably higher than the corresponding rate of

40

increase in finished-steel production. Citing United States developments between 1929 and 1952 as an illustration, the same author also noted a much greater increase in the net value of machine production than that of finished steel. The moral of these comparisons would seem to be the implication that a high rate of machine production must be predicated upon the rapid expansion of finished-steel output and that at a given rate of increase in the latter, machine production, which is indispensable to industrialization, might be expected to rise even faster.

That such thoughts were paramount in the minds of Communist China's planners can be deduced from the allocation of investment funds. During 1949 to 1952, investment in capital construction in the metallurgical industry, i. e., primarily but not exclusively in the iron and steel industry in the narrower sense, amounted to 329. 3 million yuan or 11. 6 percent of total industrial investment in capital construction. [3] (See Table 3. 1.) The amount increased substantially during 1953 to 1957 to a planned capital construction expenditure of 2. 93 billion yuan in central-government-controlled enterprises in the metallurgical industry--i. e., the An-shan Iron and Steel Company and the enterprises of the Iron and Steel Bureau. The last figure amounted to 12. 8 percent[4] of the planned capital construction expenditure of 22. 96 billion yuan in enterprises under the jurisdiction of the industrial departments of the central authorities. [5] This was about 14 to 15 percent of planned capital construction expenditure in the production of producers' goods. Frequently compared by the Chinese planners with the allocation of about 15 percent of corresponding industrial investment expenditure in the First Five-Year Plan of the Soviet Union, it was at a level comparable to investment in machine manufacturing and the fuel and power industries. Actual investment in the metallurgical industry in 1953 to 1956 can be estimated at 2. 41 billion yuan as against the planned figure of 2. 05 billion, while actual investment in iron and steel proper in 1953 to 1956 has also been reported at 2. 06 billion yuan, or over 80 percent of the total invested in the metallurgical industry.

Industry	Percent in Planned Investment in All Industry, * 1953 to 1957
Metallurgy (central government enterprises only)	12. 8
Metal processing (including machine production)	14. 9
Coal mining and electric power	22. 4

*Source: Chao I-wen, op. cit., pp. 39, 42, 45, and 47.

Furthermore, the 2. 06 billion yuan investment in iron and steel in 1953 to 1956, which is derived from Ching Lin's article in Planned Economy quoted in Table 3. 1, amounted to 10. 4 percent of the 19. 8 billion yuan (at current prices) invested in all industry. This may be compared with an investment of 2. 55 billion yuan in the machinery manufacturing industry which constituted 12. 8 percent of total industrial investment during the period.[6] The principal point to be considered is the fact that ferrous metallurgy and machine production together accounted for about one-quarter of industrial investment during the period of the First Five-Year Plan. While an even higher percentage would not have been inconceivable, the allocation of investment noted was well in accordance with the known characteristics of forced industrialization.

A further comparison of the relative importance of investment in the iron and steel industry may be made through the estimated additions to fixed assets that are used in production. As can be seen from Table 3.2, the increment in fixed assets for production in the iron and steel industry during 1953 to 1955 was larger than that in metal processing, of which machine building is a part. It dipped considerably below that in metal processing only in 1956, which, however, might very well reflect incomplete reporting during the year, since 1956 was the last year included in the source (Major Aspects). The volume of total fixed assets for production added in metal processing and iron and steel during 1953 to 1956 was also a substantial proportion (19 and 14 percent, respectively) of the corresponding estimates for all industry.

The content of the investment program in iron and steel during the First Five-Year Plan consisted of fifteen above-norm[7] and twenty-three below-norm construction units. The former, six of which were new constructions, accounted for 27.6 percent of total investment. The remaining nine above-norm projects and all the below-norm ones were rebuilding projects and were responsible for 72.4 percent of the total investment.[8] Among the principal constructions (including rebuilding) planned were: (1) the An-shan mills; (2) the Kung-yüan plant at Pen-ch'i; (3) a special steel plant at Fu-la-erh-chi; (4) a ferrous alloy plant at Chi-lin; (5) a vanadium and titanium plant in Jehol; (6) the T'ai-yüan steel plant; (7) the Lung-yen iron mine; (8) a refractory materials plant at T'ang-shan; (9) the Ma-an-shan iron mill; (10) a major iron and steel complex at Wu-han; (11) a special steel plant at Ta-yeh; (12) another large modern complex at Pao-t'ou; (13) mills No. 101 and No. 102 at Chungking; and (14) manganese mines at Lai-pin (Kwangsi) and Tsun-i (Kweichow), the last also attached to the No. 101 plant at Chungking. In terms of regional distribution, Northeast China (five units) ranked first, followed by Southwest (three) and North China (three), Central China (two), Inner Mongolia (one), East China (one), and South China (one). Of these sixteen construction units, one of which was probably a below-norm project, the most important were the rehabilitation of the An-shan mills and the new construction planned at Wu-han and Pao-t'ou. Especially conspicuous by its omission was the group of mills in Shanghai, a major established center of the industry at the time. Only the Ma-an-shan construction, located in Anhwei province, was designed to support steel production at Shanghai. On the other hand, the most notable constructions planned were the modern complexes at Wu-han and Pao-t'ou.

Initiation, during the First Five-Year Plan, of the construction of these two iron and steel centers, the former to replace on a much grander scale the destroyed plants of the original Han-yeh-p'ing Company, has often been cited by Communist Chinese authors as an outstanding example of establishing new industries at places close to the supply of fuel, raw material inputs and markets, while satisfying the locational requirements of national defense.[9] While one may question the accuracy of this claim as far as Pao-t'ou is concerned, the

Table 3.1

ESTIMATES OF INVESTMENT IN THE METALLURGICAL INDUSTRY, 1950-1957
(in thousand current yuan)

Year	Actual Investment in the Metallurgical Industry[a]	Planned Investment in the Metallurgical Industry[a]	Actual Investment in the Iron and Steel Industry[b]
1950	86,750	...	...
1951	52,800	...	...
1952	189,684	...	...
1953	395,681	300,300	...
1954	489,853	282,200	...
1955	735,269	630,140	...
1956	787,473	832,780	...
1957	...	883,470	...
1950-52	329,234	...	...
1953-56	2,408,276	2,045,420	2,060,000
1953-57	...	2,928,890	...

[a]Central government controlled enterprises only.

[b]Ching Lin, in Planned Economy, No. 9, p. 13, September 1957.

Sources: For actual investment in 1950-52, Major Aspects, p. 11. The 1953-56 figures are derived from the following annual percentage increments in terms of the preceding years: 1953, 108.6; 1954, 23.8; 1955, 50.1; 1956, 7.1; given in Ta-kung Pao, Hong Kong, August 20, 1957. For planned investment in 1953-57, Major Aspects, p. 18.

Table 3.2

ESTIMATES OF FIXED ASSETS USED FOR INDUSTRIAL PRODUCTION, 1952-1957
(in billion yuan)

Year	(I) All Industry	(II) Metal Processing	(III) Iron and Steel	Increment in (I)	(II)	(III)
1952	13.3	1.7	1.2	...	...	...
1953	15.1	1.9	1.4	1.8	0.2	0.2
1954	17.4	2.3	2.1	2.3	0.4	0.7
1955	20.2	2.8	2.5	2.8	0.5	0.4
1956	24.1	3.8	2.7	3.9	1.0	0.2
1957	29.3	...	...	5.2	...	...

Sources: Estimated from data in Wei-ta ti Shih-nien, English translation, p. 157; Major Aspects, op. cit., pp. 23, 45, and 190.

characteristics of the industry's development plans during the latter part of the First Five-Year Plan were clearly reflected in the choice of these two major undertakings. They were both large integrated iron and steel plants designed to serve as a focus of new industrial development in what had hitherto been under-developed or underindustrialized areas--Inner Mongolia and Central China, respectively. They were both based on Soviet designs and equipment. They would both help to redress the regional imbalance of the industry as a whole, and eventually, albeit perhaps not initially, they might also add more to the industry's capacity at the finishing stages of steelmaking, even though their effect on the over-all intraindustry structure remains somewhat uncertain. On the other hand, the emphasis on restoration and rehabilitation and the apparent policy of relying to a high degree on established centers of iron- and steelmaking in order to speed up the industrialization process was clearly manifested in the overwhelming emphasis on Manchuria as a whole and the An-shan complex in particular. Although the number of construction projects in ferrous metallurgy on which work was at least begun numbered 312 during the First Five-Year Plan, the An-shan, Wu-han and Pao-t'ou constructions, each of which contained a number of construction units, set the tone for the entire plan.

Principal Features of Development in 1958-1962

According to one official report, capital construction expenditure in the iron and steel industry in 1950 to 1958 totaled 7.1 billion yuan or 15.8 percent of the corresponding expenditure in all industry. [10] Since such expenditures in 1950 to 1952 were probably close to the 329 million yuan invested in the metal-lurgical industry as a whole and 2.06 billion yuan were spent in 1953 to 1956 (Table 3.1), we may, as a rough approximation, subtract these amounts from 7.1 billion yuan and assign the remainder to the years 1957 to 1958. As one can see from Table 3.3, the volume was stepped up sharply after 1956. One may also deduce from the ensuing description that the annual average of 2.4 billion yuan for 1957-1958 would probably be a large overestimate for 1957. A very high estimate of total capital construction in iron and steel during 1953 to 1957 would probably not exceed 3 billion yuan, [11] which would leave 940 million yuan for 1957 and 3.8 billion yuan for 1958. The latter estimate would exceed the cumulative total spent during the entire 1949 to 1957 period. What this spectacular,

Table 3.3

CAPITAL CONSTRUCTION EXPENDITURE IN
THE IRON AND STEEL INDUSTRY
(in million yuan)*

Period	Total	Annual Average
1950–52	329	109.7
1953–56	2,060	515.0
1957–58	4,710	2,355.0

*Presumably at current prices.

Table 3.4

ESTIMATES OF IRON ORE PRODUCTION
(in thousand metric tons)

Year	Gross Output	50-55 Percent Iron
1949	589	...
1950	2,350	...
1951	2,703	...
1952	4,287	3,900
1953	5,821	4,800
1954	7,229	6,200
1955	9,597	7,614
1956	15,484	12,890
1957	19,370	14,900
1958	...	20,000
1959	...	40,000

*Taken from Major Aspects, op. cit., pp. 14 and 26, and other sources.

46

if at all accurate, increase in investment in one year signifies will be seen presently.

While construction of the major iron and steel complexes at Pao-t'ou and Wu-han did not really begin to show some result until the Second Five-Year Plan (1958-1962), and a number of other secondary centers also began to emerge during 1958-1960, both the rhythm and the pattern of development of the industry became confused as a result of the adoption of a new approach to industrialization by Communist China in 1958. This was the nationwide drive to establish a very large number of small production units constructed and manned by the population at large, many on a part-time basis, which would be engaged in the production of industrial goods by makeshift methods. This small industry movement was one of the twin constituent elements of the "Great Leap Forward" policy of 1958-1959, the other being the replacement of the collective farms by the all-embracing communes. [12] Many of the small production units were located in, and operated by, the rural communes, although there were large numbers of urban units as well. The original concept was to exploit the unemployed and underemployed labor resource of mainland China in order to increase industrial output by labor-intensive methods, thus enhancing sharply the rate of industrialization. In the meantime, it was planned that the small-industry movement would serve to reinforce the development of modern industry; it was not meant to supplant the latter.

The iron and steel industry was made the backbone of the small-industry movement primarily because of the symbolic significance of steel. Throughout the country, iron smelters were built during 1958. Many of the smelters have since been dubbed as "backyard furnaces" and were little more than makeshift heating plants in which ore could be melted to produce some metal. Others were described as "small blast furnaces." In 1958, when the "backyard furnace" drive first began, there were far more "native furnaces" than "small blast furnaces." But as the year ended, many "native furnaces" were abandoned and some of the "small blast furnaces" were "modernized." In this manner, distinction was made between the "small, native, mass furnaces" and the "small, modern (i.e., semimodern), mass furnaces"--or, in Communist Chinese terminology, "hsiao-t'u-ch'ün" and "hsiao-yang-ch'ün," respectively. Generally speaking, 1958 was marked by a mass movement which was more impressive in the scale of the undertaking than in the quality of the product while consolidation and technological upgrading typified developments in the following year.

The same sequence of events took place in steelmaking. Corresponding to the "small, mass, modern furnaces" in iron smelting were small side-blown converters which multiplied in large numbers in 1959, having evolved from their cruder predecessors built in 1958. The latter were often not distinguishable from iron smelters. A number of small open hearths and, on a smaller scale, some small rolling mills also came into being during 1959.

The small-industry movement dominated the scene in the first half of the Second Five-Year Plan. Furthermore, according to official claims at the end of 1959,[13] the basis of more than twenty integrated iron and steel mills and of some 300 iron-smelting plants had been established. Continued multiplication of new steel mills was also expected at the time.

However, the advance of the steel industry has been marred by the economic crisis which began in 1960. A new policy,[14] instituted in 1961 and confirmed during the Third Session of the Second National People's Congress in April, 1962, called for the reorientation of developmental policy--at least for the time being--toward the solution of the basic Malthusian problem through emphasis on agricultural production. As a part of the program, even though this particular aspect has not been openly stressed, inefficient industrial enterprises that cannot operate profitably are believed to have been closed down. Since many of the semimodern iron and steel mills may belong to this category, expansion of the semimodern sector of the iron and steel industry and its evolution into a part of the modern sector will undoubtedly be affected; since this effect will be felt more acutely by the smaller and newer mills among which we should include the many secondary centers which began to emerge during 1958 to 1959, the impact on the regional distribution of the mills may be much greater than the over-all effect on the industry or the consumers of its products.

One of the factors that compounded Communist China's economic difficulties during the second half of the Second Five-Year Plan consisted of reported difficulties and delays in obtaining Soviet equipment, a fact that should be attributed to Communist China's reduced ability to pay and inability to secure Soviet financing, not to mention any deliberate delays in shipment interposed by Soviet suppliers. To what extent the equipment shortage may have retarded the progress of construction of the larger projects, such as those at Wu-han and Pao-t'ou, is not clear. On the other hand, to conclude that new and important constructions in the steel industry have ceased altogether would be mistaken. According to the Yeh-chin Pao, [15] for instance, a large number of seamless-tube mills, several of which were imported from Hungary, were still under construction at a number of locations--including T'ai-yüan, Pao-chi, Shih-ching-shan, Ch'eng-tu, etc. --as late as 1961, although delivery of some of the equipment was not expected until 1962. A large portion of the products in question apparently consists of boiler pipes used in domestic chemical fertilizer plants being erected as a part of the new agricultural development program. The rapid growth of steel-tubing plants during a period of general economic difficulties and retrenchment is, however, also in line with the effort to improve the variety and quality of finished-steel products. While full information is not available on the details, a period of consolidation and slower quantitative expansion of the industry as a whole appears to have set in at the end of the Second Five-Year Plan.

An Analysis of the Changes in Production and Capacity

Reported Increase in Known Iron Ore Deposits and Iron Ore Production

As described more fully in Appendix A, Communist China's potential iron-ore resources in 1954 were reported at 10 billion metric tons. The estimate was raised to between 12 and 13 billion tons toward the end of the First Five-Year Plan; it was again elevated to a whopping 100 billion tons during the "Great Leap Forward."

One can safely assert that the 100-billion-ton claim is far too uncertain to serve as a basis of projection of the industry's resource base. As a working assumption we can probably accept the figure of 6.8 billion tons of "verified" reserves quoted for 1952 and 8 billion for 1958. [16] But even if the last figure were compared with an estimate of 5.4 billion tons of "measured, indicated, and inferred" reserves based on pre-Communist data, there would be substantial increase to be attributed to new discoveries through intensified geological surveying. If, on the other hand, the Communists' "verified" reserves are the

49

"measured" reserves only, the volume of new discoveries would be even greater, bordering on the spectacular in magnitude.

There has been relatively little information on the newly discovered deposits, some of which are probably extensions of earlier discoveries with revised estimates. However, from all indications, it is quite plain that the principal deposits considered immediately available for large-scale expansion are those at Ta-yeh, O-ch'eng, and Lin-hsiang in Hupeh and the Pai-yün-o-po mine at Pao-t'ou. [17] Availability of rich deposits in the two areas has clearly been a determining factor in the plan to establish the two large iron and steel complexes at Wu-han and Pao-t'ou. Other major deposits discovered appear to be located in the areas of (1) Ch'ang-yang, Pa-tung, and Chien-shih in western Hupeh; (2) P'an-chang-chuang in Szechwan; (3) western Kweichow; (4) Ching-t'ieh-shan near Chiu-ch'üan in Kansu; and (5) the P'ing-liang basin in Kansu. [18] Furthermore, it has been suggested that these deposits may form the basis of new iron and steel centers in Southwest and Northwest China, respectively. However, large-scale work on these centers does not appear to have been undertaken up to the end of the Second Five-Year Plan.

The paucity of data on iron-ore deposits is matched only by the lack of continuous information on ore production. Table 3.4 sums up what is readily available and shows, apparently incontrovertibly, that ore output has been at a high level up to the onset of the economic crisis in the second half of the Second Five-Year Plan.

Some Terminological Issues

In spite of the uncertainties surrounding the actual amount and location of major new ore discoveries it would seem that the availability of readily exploitable ore should not constitute an effective constraint to the expansion of Communist China's iron and steel industry at its present stage of development. Accordingly, we can treat the development of the manufacturing sector of the industry without serious concern on this score.

We must first clarify the terminology encountered in this study. Since in dealing with the manufacturing and fabrication part of the iron and steel industry of Communist China, the statistical data at our disposal, originating from official Communist Chinese sources, refer primarily to three items--

50

pig iron, ingot steel, and what the original Chinese term describes as kang-ts'ai or "steel materials"--a few comments on the possible interpretation of these terms are called for.

In the first place, "pig iron" is produced both from modern blast furnaces and in native smelters. In the following, we shall be concerned chiefly with the modern sector of iron smelting, since "native" iron was quantitatively unimportant until 1958. In the second place, before the "Great Leap Forward, " ingot steel was produced in the modern mills only; thus again no distinction need be made between "modern" and "semimodern" steel until 1958. In the following we shall be interested first of all in the modern sector only. Finally, the same distinction exists to some extent between modern and semimodern steel-finishing facilities, but no separate data are available. However, any output from the semimodern plants would be small in this case, and we shall consider virtually the entire published output as attributable to the modern mills.

But more important than the above distinctions is the coverage of "steel materials" in Chinese usage. Inasmuch as the same production statistics are often applied to "rolled steel"[19] in Communist Chinese publications in English, one might justifiably conclude that the two terms are used interchangeably. However, the finished products of the steel industry are not limited to rolled-steel products, even though rolled products may predominate quantitatively. The question arises therefore as to whether the production statistics of "steel materials" or "rolled steel" refer to all finished products of the steel industry or to the products of steel rolling only.

There is some evidence to support the broader interpretation. For instance, according to the Central Statistical Administration, Council of Ministers, of the U.S.S.R.,[20] the items included in the category "ferrous rolled stock" are (1) pipes produced from ingots; (2) forgings produced from ingots; (3) rolled stock for reprocessing at other plants; and (4) finished rolled stock. Accordingly, if Communist China follows Soviet practice, the term "rolled steel" or "steel materials" would have a broad coverage, including forgings and other special steel products that are not rolled.

A second problem concerning coverage is whether the "rolled steel" or "steel materials" statistics include only finished products of the steel industry or whether semifinished steel is also included. Of course, while the concept of "end products" of the industry is a much more useful one from our point of view, there is nothing illegitimate about using a gross quantity if this is made known. The trouble, of course, is that the Chinese Communists have been especially reticent about the whole matter.

Here, again, we suspect that the published official Chinese statistics correspond to the Soviet term "ferrous rolled stock" in including "rolled stock to be processed at other plants" in addition to "finished rolled stock." In other words, semifinished rolled products reprocessed in other plants may also be counted as a part of the gross output and some degree of "double counting" is present. If this is the case, the real output of finished products of the industry would, of course, be less than the published output statistics. As to whether semifinished, intermediate products that are reprocessed in different mills of the same enterprise would also be included with the final products, the situation is even less clear. While Communist China's adherence to the "factory" method[21] in recording value output would seem to suggest that intermediate products re-processed in the same factory would not be included in the final output data, there is no guarantee that this method is consistently used in dealing with physical output. Besides, the definition of the "factory" in turn raises new questions--for instance, whether the multi-plant An-shan Iron and Steel Company is treated as one "factory" in recording value and/or physical output. Moreover, consideration of the propaganda value of a large finished-steel output, especially during the "Great Leap Forward," may have provided an additional motive in reporting on a gross basis. Thus there is a distinct possibility of a much larger discrepancy between the entire "ferrous rolled stock" and what we might call "ferrous rolled stock less intermediate products" than the 8 to 10 percent[22] given in Soviet statistics.

As will be seen later in this chapter when the production and capacity statistics and the internal structure of the industry are examined, and again in Chapter 5 in connection with the distribution of the output of finished steel, there are good reasons to believe that Communist Chinese statistics of "steel materials" or "rolled steel" include semifinished goods which are further processed within the steel industry itself, possibly even when the reprocessing is done within the

52

same enterprise or "factory." However, for the time being, we shall only use the term "finished-steel products" in statistical tables in quotes to indicate that more than rolled products are included in this category and that semifinished products may also be involved.

Indices of Growth and Performance in Iron and Steel Smelting and Fabrication

After this digression let us turn to an examination of developments in iron smelting and steelmaking. In this connection, probably the most striking phenomenon that attracts our attention is the remarkable, perhaps even spectacular, rate of increase in production. If we take the production estimates developed in Appendix B which are based on various official and semioffical data, we can see that the average annual rates of increase during 1952 to 1957 (1952 as base) were 25.3 percent in iron smelting, 31.7 percent in ingot steel, and 26.6 percent in finished steel products. For the period 1957 to 1960 the corresponding annual rates of increase averaged 27 percent in pig iron, 30.9 percent in ingot steel, and 44.3 to 57.4 percent in finished steel. During the earlier years (1949-1952), when expansion of the industry consisted of the preliminary rehabilitation of existing facilities without too much new construction, the average annual rates of expansion of production were even higher--viz., 97.7 percent in pig iron, 104.4 percent in ingot steel, and 110.4 percent in finished steel. Disregarding the unusually high rates of increase in 1949 to 1952, we can nevertheless compare the remarkable expansion of the industry in Communist China with that of the U.S.S.R., where the corresponding rates of growth were slightly lower during the Second Five-Year Plan (1933 to 1937) and considerably lower during the First Five-Year Plan (1928 to 1932).

Average Annual Rates of Growth of Production

Country	Pig iron	Ingot steel	Finished-steel products
Communist China			
1952-57	25.3	31.7	26.6
U.S.S.R.*			
1927-32	15.8	10.6	9.4
1932-37	18.6	24.5	24.8

*The Soviet data are derived from Gardner Clark, The Economics of Soviet Steel, p. 10.

However, expansion of production in any industry is not by itself necessarily a virtue. Nor should it be regarded as an unadulterated index of good performance both in planning and in the implementation of plans, notwithstanding the generally accepted goal of promoting iron and steel production as a spur to industrial growth as a whole.

The increase in production may be due to an increase in capacity; or it may be due to an increase in the efficiency of utilization of existing capacity. For a poor country bent on rapid industrialization and the attainment of a low marginal capital-output ratio in order to economize the demand on savings, there is a prima facie preference for improvements in the utilization of capacity over an increase in capacity. On the other hand, it would be incorrect if one were to regard any production increase as a result of capacity expansion during a period when the level of capacity utilization has not yet reached normal technological standards attained elsewhere as a clear indication of poor performance and planning. Capacity expansion requires lead and construction time and may have to be undertaken long before the gradual increase in efficiency in production technology can reach its zenith. As stated in the People's Daily on April 4, 1957, the design and construction of an iron and steel mill with an annual capacity of 1.5 million tons would take nine years and production of iron would start in the sixth year. The corresponding period to build a mill of 160,000-ton annual capacity would take four years and production would begin in the third year. However, in both cases, the decision to build a plant cannot be implemented quickly; nor can a decision be easily altered, once construction has begun. Where imported equipment and external assistance play a large role, as they did in Communist China, the scheduling of capacity expansion may be decisively influenced by the availability of these key conditions, apart from the inflexibility inherent in the long lead time.

We, therefore, must analyze the underlying factors of the increase in production by segregating the effect of capacity expansion from that of efficiency of capacity utilization as a first step. We can then raise the question whether the performance of the industry in utilizing its capacity has been satisfactory. By inference, we shall also have raised the question whether the expansion of capacity has been necessary and manifested good judgment in the allocation of investment outlay. The last question cannot, of course, be fully answered without further examination of the return to the investment made and the distribution of the industry's output, which will be taken up in subsequent chapters.

A closer look at the capacity statistics will also cast new light on changes in intraindustry structure. Has a reasonable degree of balanced growth been maintained? Or has the principle of unbalanced growth which emphasizes the advantage of pushing one or more key industries as a stimulant to the subsequent expansion of other industries been extended to the interrelationships among different sectors of the iron and steel industry? The relationship between production and capacity statistics may also bring to light certain incongruities and possible biases in the statistics themselves, which would be an additional bonus to our efforts.

The Expansion of Capacity

The estimates of rated capacity of pig-iron, ingot-steel, and finished-steel production, taken from Appendix B (Table B-1) and the corresponding index numbers with 1949 and 1952 as base years, respectively, are given in Table 3.5. If we follow the conventional divisions of significant periods of economic development in Communist China, the following average annual rates of growth of year-end capacity may be noted in percent per year:

Period	Pig iron	Ingot steel	"Finished steel"
1949–52 (rehabilitation period)	5.9	35.8	5.5
1952–57 (First Five-Year Plan, 1953–57 inclusive)	26.3	27.3	25.8
1957–60 ("Great Leap Forward," first three years of Second Five-Year Plan, 1958–62 inclusive)	68.6	78.0	62.6

The accelerated rates of expansion shown here would seem to indicate a pro-

Table 3.5

INDEX OF GROWTH OF DESIGNED CAPACITY, MODERN SECTOR

Year	Pig Iron		Ingot Steel		"Finished-Steel Products"	
	1949=100	1952=100	1949=100	1952=100	1949=100	1952=100
1949	100	84.3	100	40.0	100	85.1
1950	100	84.3	210.8	84.2	110.1	93.8
1951	118.7	100	223.5	89.3	110.1	93.8
1952	118.7	100	250.2	100	117.5	100
1953	169.4	142.7	266.5	106.5	132.2	112.5
1954	189.2	159.5	278.2	111.2	141.0	120.0
1955	208.9	176.1	278.2	111.2	141.0	120.0
1956	264.3	222.8	549.3	220.0	145.5	123.9
1957	381.3	305.0	836.3	334.2	363.6	309.5
1958	592.2	487.4	1804.7	721.2	548.6	467.0
1959	1144.6	964.7	2895.0	1156.9	865.3	736.6
1960	1828.4	1541.0	4716.0	1884.6	1564.2	1331.5

Sources: For the original data see Appendix B, Table B-1. Where alternative data are available for any year, the slightly higher figures have been adopted to allow for the possible underestimate of rated capacity noted in the text.

Table 3.6

ANNUAL PERCENTAGE RATES OF EXPANSION OF
DESIGNED CAPACITY, MODERN SECTOR
(preceding year = 100)

Year	Pig Iron	Ingot Steel	"Finished-Steel Products"
1950	0	111	10
1951	19	6	0
1952	0	12	7
1953	43	7	13
1954	12	4	7
1955	10	0	0
1956	27	97	3
1957	44	52	150
1958	55	116	51
1959	93	60	58
1960	60	63	81

See Table B-1, Appendix B. The higher figures are used in those years in which a range is given. This is to offset possible underestimate of rated capacity in the Japanese Survey Report for the earlier years. See text, p. 61.

Table 3.7

INDEX OF GROWTH OF PRODUCTION, MODERN SECTOR

Year	Pig Iron		Ingot Steel		"Finished-Steel Products"	
	1949=100	1952=100	1949=100	1952=100	1949=100	1952=100
1949	100	13.0	100	11.7	100	10.8
1950	397.6	51.5	383.5	44.9	329.1	35.4
1951	588.6	76.2	567.1	66.4	573.0	61.6
1952	772.4	100	853.8	100	930.5	100
1953	884.1	114.5	1122.8	131.5	1244.0	133.7
1954	1204.1	155.9	1408.2	164.9	1393.6	149.8
1955	1475.6	191.1	1805.7	211.5	1776.6	190.9
1956	1941.9	251.4	2825.9	331.0	2780.9	298.9
1957	2382.1	308.4	3386.1	396.6	3021.3	324.7
1958	3874.0	501.6	5063.3	593.0	4255.3	457.3
1959	3861.8	500.0	5462.0	639.7	6524.8	701.2
1960	5162.6	668.4	7594.9	889.5	9078.0 – 11773.0	975.6 – 1265.2

Source: For the original data see Table B-1, Appendix B.

Table 3.8

ANNUAL CAPACITY ADDED IN THE PLANTS WITH LARGEST
INCREASE IN CAPACITY DURING THE YEAR
(in percent of total capacity added)

Plant	1949–1950	1950–1951	1951–1952	1952–1953	1953–1954	1954–1955
Pig iron (first three plants)	---	100	---	99	100*	100*
Ingot steel (first three plants)	97	100	93	78	100*	---
"Finished steel" (largest plant)	99	---	60	70	100	---

*One plant only.

Source: The original data in metric tons are derived from Table B-13, Appendix B.

57

gressively expanding industry, with sharp annual increases during the First Five-Year Plan and spectacular increases during the Second Five-Year Plan. In the Soviet Union, the rates of expansion were:

	First Five-Year Plan 1928-1933	Second Five-Year Plan 1933-1938
Open hearth	6.9	8.4[23]
Blast furnaces	1.3	7.5[24]

The unwary may thus be led to the conclusion that Communist China was eminently successful during the decade after 1949 in first rehabilitating and then building a large iron and steel industry surpassing all pre-Communist records. This first impression, however, must be drastically qualified for the following reasons:

First, during 1949-1952, rehabilitation of the industry by no means progressed evenly. No increase in iron-smelting capacity was registered in two out of the three years, and none was registered 1950-1951 in the case of finished-steel capacity. The acceleration in the rate of expansion between 1949 to 1952 and 1952 to 1957 did not reflect so much planned progression as a slow start in rehabilitation. While the delayed start may have been unavoidable, the rate of expansion in the later years was thus inevitably somewhat inflated.

Second, confirmation of the preceding contention that rehabilitation of the industry's productive capacity was far from being completed during the years generally designated as the "rehabilitation period" of China's economy may be found in a comparison of the rated capacity in 1945 at the end of World War II (but before the wholesale removal of industrial installations from Manchuria by Soviet troops) with the estimates during the Communist period. Such a comparison would show that the capacity reached under Japanese occupation in 1945 was surpassed only in 1956 in the case of ingot steel,[25] and in 1957 in the case of blast furnaces and steel rolling. That is to say, virtually the entire time span during the First Five-Year Plan was devoted to the replacement of capital equipment rendered useless or removed during the post-World War II

Figure 3.1. Growth of Annual Production, 1949–1960

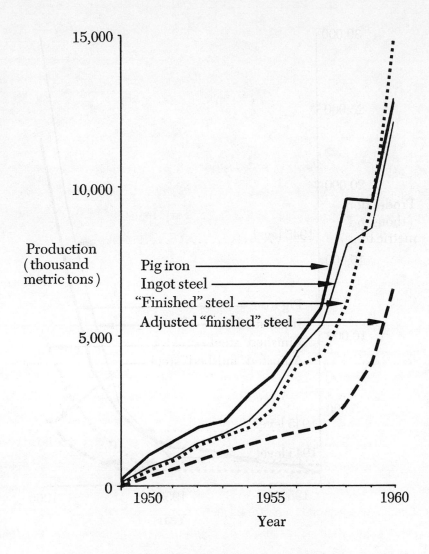

Source: Table B-1 and C-1 in Appendices B and C.

Figure 3.2. Growth of Annual Capacity, 1949–1960

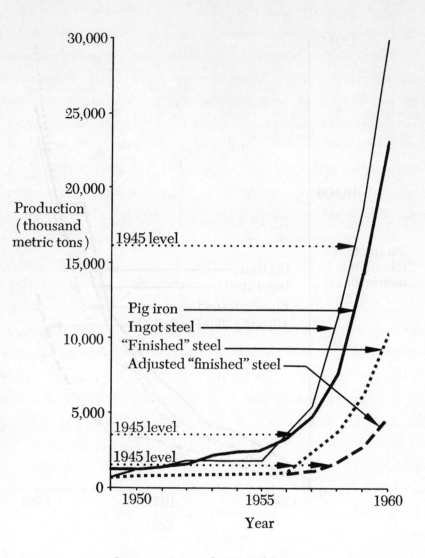

Source: Appendix B, Table B-1

Soviet occupation of Manchuria and the subsequent civil war. Communist Chinese troops were themselves active in the destruction of the steel industry in Southern Manchuria before the winter of 1948. Attention, however, should be paid to the term "replacement," for the new installations established during the 1950's were probably more advanced technologically and therefore also more productive.

Third, another factor which also tends to lead to an overestimate of the rate of capacity expansion is that the rated-capacity data of 1949 and of the first few years thereafter, when undestroyed blast furnaces and other facilities, especially at An-shan, were recommissioned, are derived from Japanese records.[26] The data on later additions, on the other hand, are obtained directly from Communist Chinese sources. According to Japanese investigators,[27] the original rated-capacity data of the various furnaces in Manchuria may have to some extent been underestimates, partly, it is said, because of the desire for secrecy and partly for the purpose of reducing the tax liability of the firms. The underestimates of designed capacity also account in part for the high ratio of actual or operating capacity to rated capacity during the Communist period as may be seen in the 1953 data in Appendix B (Table B-1).[28] As the additional new installations rose proportionately in the total, compared with the data of year-end capacities in 1949 and 1952, an upward distortion of the rate of growth would result.

Finally, the preceding comments are directed primarily at the estimates before 1957. In the case of the estimates for 1958 to 1960, additional factors must not be allowed to escape our attention. In the first place, statistics during the "Great Leap Forward" are far more inaccurate and unreliable than during the First Five-Year Plan.[29] The tendency to exaggerate and to report aspirations and plans as accomplished facts cannot be overemphasized. In the second place, in the absence of national year-end capacity estimates given by official sources, including statistics for 1957, we are forced to use the totals derived from our plant list in Appendix B (Table B-13) as the basis for our estimates of rated capacity in 1957 to 1960. Although the plant list is bound to be incomplete, it may also include some plants that do not properly belong to the modern sector; in addition, it definitely includes some planned figures. All in all, therefore, one should expect the 1958 to 1960 capacity estimates to be

61

overestimates, although the degree of overestimation cannot be ascertained at this point and is likely to vary with respect to both the regions and the commodities.

Furthermore, the rate of growth of the capacity of "finished-steel" production in 1957 to 1960 may have been exaggerated for a specific reason. For example, there is evidence that while the estimates before 1957 are based on the Japanese Survey Report and do not include mills producing semifinished steels--the large blooming mills at An-shan, for instance--the 1957 to 1960 estimates, based on the plant list in Appendix B, most probably include some of the mills producing intermediate products.

A comparison of the production and capacity estimates of pig iron and ingot steel in Table B-1, Appendix B, would readily reveal that (1) the production estimates generally tend to fall between the designed- or rated-capacity estimates and the operating-capacity estimates, or (2) they may even fall below the rated-capacity estimates as in 1959 to 1960. The first may be explained by the improved utilization of capacity without attaining the "maximum" level which is indicated more closely by "operating capacity," as well as by the possible underestimate of rated capacity mentioned earlier. The second may be explained by the overestimate of realized construction of new capacity in the last few years of our period. On the other hand, if production and capacity estimates of "finished-steel products" are compared with one another, the output series lies considerably above the two capacity series up to 1956 inclusive, but is very close to the operating capacity series in 1957 to 1959.[30] This phenomenon would be quite natural if the production series includes intermediate products throughout while the capacity series does so only during 1957 to 1960, which indeed may be the case.

Uneven Rates of Growth and Concentration of Investment in Major Plants

There are several other interesting features of the growth pattern that can be derived from the data employed in this study.

In the first place, the expansion of the industry's capacity seems to have proceeded rather jerkily from year to year. If we omit the years 1958 to 1960 when estimates are much less reliable, we can compute the standard deviations of the annual rates of capacity rehabilitation and expansion for pig iron, ingot steel, and finished steel. The average annual rates of growth[31] and standard deviations are given below in percent:

Period	Pig iron	Ingot steel	"Finished steel"
1949-57 Growth	18.2	30.4	5.5[32]
Standard deviation	16.2	42.2	4.5
1952-57 Growth	26.3	27.3	6.5[32]
Standard deviation	14.5	37.8	4.6

The exceedingly large fluctuations from year to year cannot be overlooked, and one of their effects is to vitiate any meaningful projection of future growth on the basis of an average annual rate of growth. An underlying cause of this phenomenon was probably the intermittent completion of new installations.

Using pig iron as an illustration, the increment in productive capacity in 1950 to 1951 amounted to 238,000 tons per annum on the basis of our plant list in Table B-13, Appendix B. Of this amount, 100 percent was accounted for by the first three mills where new installations were added or restored during the year. In 1953 to 1954 and 1954 to 1955 the year-end capacity of blast furnaces showed an increase at An-shan only. These examples could be easily multiplied. Table 3.8 gives an analysis of the relative shares of the first three mills with the largest increments in annual capacity of pig iron and ingot steel. In the case of finished-steel products, because of the small number of mills having steel-rolling equipment, only the relative share of the mill with the largest increment in annual capacity is used. The result also shows a very high concentration of construction activities in a small number of mills through 1955. The number of mills with additions to capacity increased later, coinciding with the acceleration of the rate of capacity expansion at the end of the real rehabilitation period of Communist China's iron and steel industry. This concentration of construction serves not only to explain the large effect on the rate of the industry's expansion of the completion of new installations in a few plants, thereby producing violent

fluctuations in the rate of growth from year to year. It also points to the tenor
of Communist China's early policy to build a small number of modern iron and
steel complexes on the basis of the mills which the Japanese and the Nationalists
had established earlier.

An-shan, Chungking, and Ma-an-shan experienced through the First
Five-Year Plan the largest increase in blast-furnace capacity; An-shan, T'ang-
shan, and Chungking enjoyed the same position in the case of steelmaking; An-
shan, Shanghai, and Mukden were among the centers where the largest increase
in steel-rolling and -finishing capacity took place. Although uncertainty regarding individual plant data may raise some questions about the ranking of certain
mills such as Fu-shun, Ta-yeh, Shanghai, and Tientsin in steelmaking, T'ang-
shan and Tientsin in steel finishing, and T'ai-yüan in iron smelting, the fact
that all these places are "household" names of the Chinese iron and steel industry indicates unmistakably the intensity of the expansion efforts at a few centers and its effect on the rhythm of growth.

There appeared to be a significant "bunching" of new constructions
which reached completion at about the same time, as can be plainly noted from
the capacity statistics toward the end of the First Five-Year Plan. The classic
example may be that of An-shan where a heavy rolling mill, a seamless-
tubing mill, a thin-plate plant, a second blooming mill, a second ingot mill,
and blast furnaces Nos. 5, 6, 7, 8, and 9 were all completed in 1956.[33] Other
major constructions represented by completely new installations and corresponding to especially high rates of annual growth of capacity were the blast furnaces
at the new iron and steel complexes of Wu-han and Pao-t'ou in 1959, the Fu-la-
erh-chi special steel works in 1958, and the Kirin ferrous alloy plant in 1957.[34]
It is probably true that "bunching" of this kind cannot be avoided in the early
stage of any large-scale economic development. Its effects on the rest of the
economy is to inject from time to time a substantially increased demand for
skilled labor and material inputs which may not be available if interindustry
and intraindustry balance has not been maintained, and if the training of workers
and technicians has not kept abreast of new constructions. On the other hand,
the "bunching" effect may also be seen in a sharp increase in real output, economic activity and employment--that is, on the assumption that the necessary

complementary inputs are available. There is also likely to be a sudden, large multiplier effect. Since, during the construction period, a major portion of the outlay was represented by imported equipment obtained on credit, the possibly inflationary effect when the "bunched" investments come into operation, in contrast to that of the construction period, may be quantitatively very large indeed. The serious shortages felt toward the end of the First Five-Year Plan may not be unrelated to this phenomenon; what happened in the iron and steel industry was no more than an important but typical example. It is also plausible to argue that the difficulties in obtaining the requisite inputs encountered by the large and sudden addition of new and technologically advanced plants may have been one, but only one, of the factors underlying the decision to build a large number of smaller iron and steel centers, aided by numerous "backyard fur-naces," all of which would operate at a lower technological level. The lesser mills might then serve as training centers for the larger enterprises and supple-ment the latter's activities.[35]

Production, Capacity, and Productivity of Equipment

The estimates of production may now be examined by relating them to the capacity estimates. If we take the estimates of year-end capacity for the period 1949 to 1960 and compute the averages for each pair of consecutive years, we arrive at what may be regarded as approximations of midyear capacity. If the latter are taken as estimates of average capacity for the successive years, we can compute output-per-unit capacity. The result of these computations, presented in Table 3.9, provides us with an index of improvement in the produc-tivity of the equipment installed. In view of the fact that Communist China is especially short of capital equipment, any index of the efficiency with which equipment is used would obviously be of key importance in evaluating the per-formance of the industry.

Starting from 1950 as the base year (=100), the index of physical-output-per-unit capacity increased steadily through 1956 in the case of steel-making and finishing. In the case of pig iron, the same upward trend existed, but the 1958 index was also almost at par with that of 1956. A rather sharp de-cline set in after the 1956 peak in the steel sector, especially in 1959 and 1960.

Table 3.9

CAPACITY, PRODUCTION, AND CAPACITY UTILIZATION:
PIG IRON, INGOT STEEL, AND "FINISHED-STEEL" PRODUCTS, MODERN SECTOR

| | I | | | II | | | III = II ÷ I | | | IV | | |
| Year | Estimated Midyear Rated Capacity (thousand tons) | | | Production (thousand tons) | | | Production per Unit Capacity (ton per ton of rated capacity) | | | Index of Production per Unit Capacity 1950 = 100 | | |
	Pig iron	Ingot steel	"Finished steel"	Pig iron	Ingot steel	"Finished steel"	Pig iron	Ingot steel	"Finished steel"	Pig iron	Ingot steel	"Finished steel"
1950	1276	993	715	978	606	464	0.767	0.610	0.649	100	100	100
1951	1395	1387	750	1448	896	808	1.038	0.646	1.077	135	106	166
1952	1514	1513	775	1900	1349	1312	1.255	0.892	1.693	164	146	261
1953	1837	1651	850	2175	1774	1754	1.184	1.075	2.064	154	176	318
1954	2287	1740	930	2962	2225	1965	1.295	1.279	2.113	169	210	326
1955	2540	1778	960	3630	2853	2505	1.429	1.605	2.609	186	263	402
1956	3019	2644	975	4777	4465	3921	1.582	1.689	4.022	206	277	620
1957	4119	4427	1733	5860	5350	4260	1.423	1.208	2.458	186	198	379
1958	6211	8433	3106	9530	8000	6000	1.534	0.949	1.932	200	156	298
1959	11080	15011	4814	9500	8630	9200	0.857	0.575	1.911	112	94	294
1960	18967	24317	8272	12700	12000	12800–16600	0.670	0.493	1.547–2.068	87	81	238–311

Sources: Averages of year-end capacity estimates from Table B-1. See also Table B-12, Appendix B.

66

The decline occurred later in the case of pig iron, but it was no less serious during 1959-1960, although the "Great Leap Forward" in the industrial sector as a whole was probably still in progress. While at their respective peaks, the index of pig-iron production-per-unit capacity was 206 (1956); that of ingot steel, 277 (1956); that of finished steel, 620 (1956).

What explanations can be offered in connection with these statistical findings--the steady increase in productivity through 1956, the high level attained then, and the reversal of the trend since the end of the First Five-Year Plan, especially in the latter part of the "Great Leap Forward"? Perhaps the last point can be explained more easily; it will therefore be dealt with first.

It is submitted that the sharp decline of the index of output-per-unit capacity in the last two to four years of the decade covered here was largely statistical. We have already alluded to the possible extension of the coverage of finished-steel capacity since 1957 to include semifinished steel. But the general decline in the case of pig iron and ingot steel, especially in 1959 and 1960, was occasioned by a much larger increase in capacity than in output, which probably means that the capacity statistics are overestimated, because some of the mills reportedly built, or planned to be built, during this period were not completed. Whether this was due to inaccurate reporting, construction delays, or lack of imported equipment cannot be ascertained. One suspects that these factors were all partly responsible for the result seen here. However, one should not rule out the possibility that there was some real decline in the efficiency with which equipment was employed in the later years. One should not be surprised if this was one of the effects when a number of new mills were completed all at once-- i.e., the effect of "bunching" noted earlier. There is also the possibility, as we shall see later, that the over-all facilities were underutilized because of the industry's inability to produce steel varieties that were in demand, in spite of excess capacity as a whole.

Turning to the question of the large increase in output-per-unit capacity through 1956 or, in the case of pig iron, 1958, one must first examine the actual level of productivity attained in order to keep the relative growth rate in its proper perspective. For this purpose we may employ some data on the "co-efficients of use" of blast furnaces and open hearths and compare them with

Soviet data in view of the predominance of Soviet technology in Chinese steel-making.

In Table 3.10, the coefficients of utilization of useful capacity of blast furnaces in Communist China, expressed in terms of tons of daily output per cubic meter of furnace space, are set alongside the corresponding data for the Soviet Union. The Chinese data, which purport to be national averages, extend through 1958 and show a steady improvement through the entire period. No national averages are available for the years 1959 and 1960, but the median values, obtained from ten and fourteen medium or large plants and individual furnaces, respectively, indicate that the coefficient may have remained during this period at a comparable level. It is also clear that by 1955-1956 the Chinese coefficient was at a comparable level with the Soviet coefficient of 1954, which would seem to indicate that Soviet technology and equipment were being profitably utilized in Communist China. As for the continued improvement at least in 1957 and 1958, there is some uncertainty because of the general deterioration of statistical reporting during this period.

On the other hand, the Chinese coefficient in the period before 1952 was comparable to the corresponding Soviet figure in the early thirties.[36] The faster advance in Communist China during the First Five-Year Plan was undoubtedly a reflection of Soviet aid and of the slower rate of progress in the Soviet steel industry, especially during the 1940's.

In the same manner, we can compare the utilization coefficients of Soviet and Communist Chinese open-hearth furnaces in terms of tons of daily output per square meter of furnace floor (Table 3.11). Here too we can see a steady progress through the years with the Chinese figure in 1956 approximating the Soviet figure of 1954. Median values based on nine and twelve furnaces, respectively, can also be derived for 1959 and 1960; they indicate the continuation of the upward trend similar to the case of the blast furnaces.

As can be seen in Figure 3.3, if the coefficients of use of blast and open-hearth furnaces are converted into index numbers (1950 = 100) and compared with the series of output-per-unit capacity given in Table 3.9, the same trends can be seen in the two series, through 1959 in the case of pig iron and through 1956 in the case of steel. This general correspondence seems to

Table 3.10

COMPARISON OF THE COEFFICIENTS OF UTILIZATION
OF BLAST FURNACES IN COMMUNIST CHINA AND
THE SOVIET UNION

(tons of daily output per cubic meter of useful space[a])

Year	Communist China[b]	U.S.S.R[c]	
		(cubic meters per ton)	(tons per cubic meter)
1949	0.62	1.00	1.00
1950	0.76	0.98	1.02
1951	0.86	0.92	1.09
1952	1.02	0.87	1.15
1953	1.03	0.85	1.18
1954	1.08	0.82	1.22
1955	1.17	0.80	1.25
1956	1.30	...	...
1957	1.32	0.74[f]	1.35
1958	1.49	0.72[f]	1.39
1959	1.46[d]	0.71[f]	1.41
1960	1.44[e]	0.70[f]	1.43

[a]According to Clark, op. cit., pp. 248-253, in Soviet practice, daily output is ordinarily computed on the basis of nominal time which excludes time spent in major repairs at the end of a campaign, as well as "cold down time," but which includes "hot down time." This practice is believed to have been adopted in Communist China at least until the time of the "Great Leap Forward."

[b]1949-56, Major Aspects, op. cit., pp. 12-13 and 35. For 1957-58, see Ten Great Years, op. cit., p. 105. The second source also gives the same figures for 1949 and 1952 as Major Aspects.

[c]Clark, op. cit., p. 254. Converted to tons per cubic meter.

[d]Median value derived from the following cases:
  1. Plant No. 1 of the Lung-yen Iron and Steel Company, 0.793.
  2. Wu-han Iron and Steel Company, 1.256.
  3. Chungking Iron and Steel Company, 1.274.

69

4. Shih-ching-shan Iron and Steel Co., 1.359.
5. Ironworks No. 1 of T'ai-yüan Iron and Steel Co., 1.422.
6. Ta-yeh Steel Works, 1.493.
7. An-shan Iron and Steel Co., 1.635.
8. Ironworks No. 1 of the Ma-an-shan Iron and Steel Co., 1.667.
9. Pen-ch'i Iron and Steel Works No. 2, 2.259.
10. Pen-ch'i Iron and Steel Works No. 1, 2.497.

Sources: <u>Yeh-chin Pao</u>, Peking, no. 4, Jan. 25, 1960, pp. 38-39.

[e]Median value derived from the following cases:

1. Lung-yen Iron and Steel Co., Plant No. 2, 0.761.
2. Pau-t'ou Iron and Steel Co., 0.883.
3. Lung-yen Iron and Steel Co., Plant No. 1, 0.958.
4. T'ai-yüan Iron and Steel Co., 0.965.
5. Shanghai Steel Plant No. 1, 1.012.
6. Wu-han Iron and Steel Co., 1.35.
7. Ma-an-shan Iron and Steel Co., 1.378.
8. Pen-ch'i Iron and Steel Plant No. 2, 1.513.
9. Shih-chia-chuang, 1.583.
10. An-shan Iron and Steel Co., 1.783.
11. Shih-ching-shan Iron and Steel Co., 1.832.
12. An-shan Iron and Steel Co., Blast furnace No. 3, 2.103.
13. Pen-ch'i Iron and Steel Plant No. 1, 2.413.
14. An-shan Iron and Steel Co., Blast furnace No. 9, 2.468.

Sources: JPRS: 5744, Jan. 12, 1961, <u>Metallurgical Industry in Communist China</u>, p. 1. U.S. Joint Publication Research Service, 1636 Connecticut Avenue, N.W., Washington 25, D.C.

<u>Hopeh Jih-pao</u>, Tientsin, Nov. 3, 1960, p. 1.

[f]<u>Promyshlennost' R.S.F.S.R., Statisticheskii Sbornik</u> (Industry of R.S.F.S.R., Statistical Compilation), 1961, p. 56.

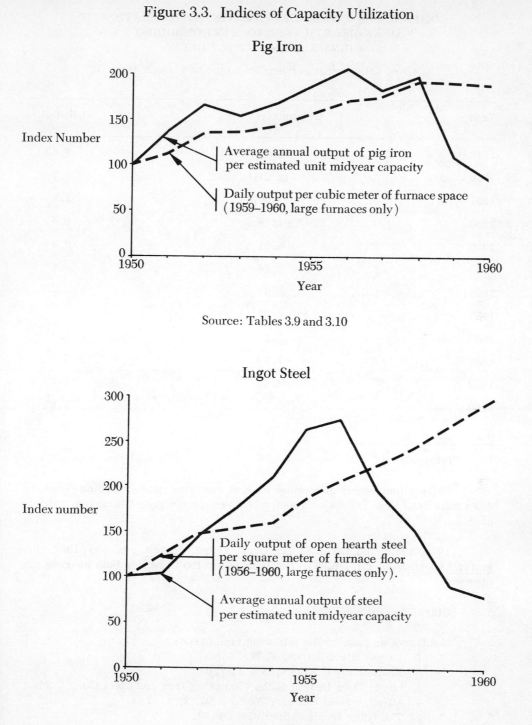

Figure 3.3. Indices of Capacity Utilization

Pig Iron

Index Number

Average annual output of pig iron
per estimated unit midyear capacity

Daily output per cubic meter of furnace space
(1959–1960, large furnaces only)

Year

Source: Tables 3.9 and 3.10

Ingot Steel

Index number

Daily output of open hearth steel
per square meter of furnace floor
(1956–1960, large furnaces only).

Average annual output of steel
per estimated unit midyear capacity

Year

Source: Tables 3.9 and 3.11

Table 3.11

COMPARISON OF THE COEFFICIENTS OF UTILIZATION OF
OPEN-HEARTH FURNACES IN COMMUNIST
CHINA AND THE SOVIET UNION

(tons of daily output per square meter of furnace floor[a])

Year	Communist China[b]	U.S.S.R.[c]
1949	2.42	5.42
1950	(3.21)*	5.7
1951	(4.00)*	5.9
1952	4.78	6.1
1953	4.91	6.4
1954	5.16	6.6
1955	6.07	...
1956	6.67	...
1957	7.21	7.1[f]
1958	7.78	7.3[f]
1959	8.64[d]	7.5[f]
1960	9.52[e]	7.6[f]

*Interpolated.

[a]Daily output based on nominal time or calender time excluding "cold down time" and time for major repairs between campaigns. Clark, op. cit., p. 252.

[b]1949, 1952, and 1957-58, Ten Great Years, op. cit., p. 105; 1952-56, Major Aspects, op. cit., p. 35. The figures for 1952 given in both sources are identical.

[c]Clark, op. cit., p. 254.

[d]Median value base on the following nine cases:
1. Ta-yeh Steel Works, 4.36.
2. Tientsin Steel Works, No. 1, 7.68.
3. Large Open Hearth of the Chungking Iron and Steel Co., 8.24.
4. An-shan Steel Refining Works, No. 2, 8.47.
5. T'ai-yüan Iron and Steel Co., 8.64.

Table 3.11 (continued)

6. An-shan Steel Refining Works, No. 1, 9.91.
7. An-shan Steel Refining Works, No. 3, 10.17.
8. Shanghai Iron and Steel Works, No. 1, 12.38.
9. Shanghai Iron and Steel Works, No. 3, 17.16.

Sources: Yeh-chin Pao, Peking, no. 4, January 25, 1960, pp. 38-39.

[e]Median value based on the following twelve cases:

1. Wu-han Iron and Steel Co., large open-hearth furnace, 7.016.
2. T'ai-yüan Iron and Steel Co., 7.219.
3. Chungking Iron and Steel Co., small open-hearth furnace, 8.509.
4. An-shan Iron and Steel Co., steel-smelting plant No. 2, 9.09.
5. Chungking Iron and Steel Co., 9.136.
6. Chungking Iron and Steel Co., large open-hearth furnace, 9.418.
7. An-shan Iron and Steel Co., steel-smelting plant No. 3, 9.62.
8. An-shan Iron and Steel Co., 9.82.
9. Tientsin First Steel plant, 10.54.
10. An-shan Iron and Steel Co., steel-smelting plant, No. 1, 10.93.
11. Shanghai Second Steel Plant, 11.856.
12. Shanghai Steel Plant No. 1, 14.117.

Sources: JPRS: 5744, Jan. 12, 1961. Metallurgical Industry in Communist China, p. 1. U.S. Joint Publication Research Service, 1636 Connecticut Avenue, N.W., Washington 25, D.C.

[f]Promyshlennost' R.S.F.S.R., Statisticheskii Sbornik (Industry of R.S.F.S.R., Statistical Compilation), 1961, p. 58.

corroborate the impression that there was a decided improvement in the utilization of capacity during the First Five-Year Plan. In each case, the divergent trends afterwards may be attributed to exaggerated capacity estimates noted earlier, improper reporting of the coefficients of use during the period of the "Great Leap," and the much lower efficiency attained in equipment utilization in the case of the smaller mills built since 1958.

In neither case, however, do the series of the coefficients of use and that of annual-output-per-unit capacity coincide completely up to 1956 or 1958. The divergence is more marked in the case of steel in some of the years, possibly for the following reasons. First, the annual-output series represents all steel production whereas the coefficient-of-use series refers to open-hearth output only. A further explanation of the divergence in both the iron and steel sectors may be found in the reduction of idleness between campaigns. Any reduction of the time spent in "cold down repairs" would increase annual output, but would have no effect on the coefficients of use which, as explained earlier, are based on "nominal time" from which "cold down repair" has been excluded. This would cause the series of annual-output-per-unit capacity to rise faster than the series of coefficients of use.

As mentioned earlier, the coefficients of use are purportedly national averages except in 1959 and 1960, when medians based on available information on a small number of furnaces and mills are presented. The data reported are presumably from the more efficient furnaces and would therefore show an upward bias. Little is known about variations in productivity both within the same mill and between large and small mills although, as far as Soviet experience goes, a wide range may exist.[37] One would expect that the same is true in the case of Communist China and that the ostensible continuation of the upward trends of the coefficients of use during the Second Five-Year Plan must be taken with a grain of salt. The reversal of the rising trends depicted by the annual-output series, though perhaps less drastic in reality than the statistics show, may yet be closer to the truth than it seems.

The Number and Size of the Mills

The rise of the efficiency of utilization of available equipment, which can be accepted as a fact for the First Five-Year Plan period at any rate, was attributable to various factors. That technology played a vital role is quite plain, and some of the technical improvements and innovations will be briefly summarized in Appendix D. Another factor was the change in the distribution of the furnaces and mills by size. A third factor was the unceasing effort to induce the workers to work harder and more efficiently, through emulation campaigns and similar devices.

Although comprehensive statistical evidence of the differences in productivity per unit capacity with respect to the size of the plant or enterprise is still wanting, the higher coefficients of use given in Tables 3.10 and 3.11 for 1959 and 1960, as well as sporadic data in the other years, can almost always be identified with some of the larger furnaces and/or larger mills. It is probably true that the larger units are always to be found in the larger mills and that they are generally newer constructions. Their newness alone would suggest that they incorporate better designs and can be used more efficiently. Thus one cannot segregate the effect of technological improvement from size.

In the following paragraphs, an attempt has been made to compare the percent distribution of the iron and steel mills by size in 1953, 1957, and 1960. Because of lack of complete information, the data are based on the plants whose year-end capacity estimates are given in Table B-13 in Appendix B. It should be noted that the original capacity estimates of steel finishing in 1957-1960 may include semifinished steel. But this is not expected to affect the present percent-distribution data too seriously.

The trend toward larger-scale production during the First Five-Year Plan period can be seen plainly both in the frequency distribution and in the increase in the mean size of the mills. On the other hand, the trend toward larger mills was halted during 1957-1960. The relative importance of the smaller mills was increased and the average capacity of the mills was either reduced or remained relatively stationary. In view of the lower efficiency of the smaller mills, a decrease in the productivity of equipment might therefore be expected on a priori grounds, official statistics of high coefficients of use in individual cases notwithstanding.

Table 3.12

PERCENT DISTRIBUTION OF IRON AND STEEL MILLS
BY SIZE OF ANNUAL OPERATING CAPACITY

Number of Tons	1953	1957	1960
Pig Iron			
100,000 or less	41.7	7.1	24.7
100,000 to under 300,000	41.7	28.6	26.0
300,000 to under 500,000	8.3	35.7	11.7
500,000 to under 700,000	---	14.3	11.7
700,000 to under 1,000,000	---	7.1	18.2
1,000,000 or more	8.3	7.1	7.8
Total*	100.0	100.0	100.0
Ingot Steel			
100,000 or less	46.2	37.5	46.5
100,000 to under 300,000	46.2	18.8	18.6
300,000 to under 500,000	---	31.3	14.0
500,000 to under 700,000	---	6.3	8.1
700,000 to under 1,000,000	---	---	4.7
1,000,000 or more	7.7	6.3	8.1
Total*	100.0	100.0	100.0
"Finished Steel"			
100,000 or less	83.3	66.7	47.1
100,000 to under 300,000	8.3	16.7	25.5
300,000 to under 500,000	---	---	19.6
500,000 to under 700,000	---	---	---
700,000 to under 1,000,000	8.3	8.3	2.0
1,000,000 or more	---	8.3	5.9
Total*	100.0	100.0	100.0

*Details may not add to 100 due to rounding.

Table 3.12 (continued)

Source: Table B-13, Appendix B. The 1953 operating capacity data are based on Survey Report, op. cit.
The number of mills included above and their average sizes are:

Number of mills	1953	1957	1960
Pig Iron	12	14	77
Ingot Steel	13	16	86
"Finished Steel"	12	12	51
Average Annual Capacity (thousand tons)			
Pig Iron	262	595	519
Ingot Steel	164	422	442
"Finished Steel"	119	322	326

Productivity and Emulation Campaigns

Finally, brief mention should be made of the close relationship of the better utilization of equipment and the introduction of new technology to the training of labor through organized emulation efforts and contests. These efforts combine the purpose of training with that of increasing production during a given span of time. They may take the form of requiring workers within a given plant to emulate the techniques and records of certain individuals or teams with notable accomplishments. In this manner, they can also be regarded as an extension of the apprenticeship practice. At the same time, however, contests and emulation drives may also be organized on an interplant basis, with the participating plants and work teams trying to outdo one another according to prior agreements. In the winter of 1955, for instance, seventy-nine mining and industrial enterprises under the jurisdiction of the Ministry of Heavy Industry took part in scheduled interplant contests involving fourteen different products and labor categories, such as open-hearth steel smelting, production of special steels, coking, iron smelting, etc. [38] Such drives have, of course, taken place regularly. The criteria adopted in judging contest results may include quantity produced, efficiency of equipment utilization, production cost, quality control, and safety standards. [39] The incentives employed consist of monetary bonuses as well as awards of special honors both to the individuals and to the plants concerned. [40]

While one cannot segregate the effect of the training function of such contests and emulation drives from that of other factors, there is no doubt that without adequate labor training much of the effect of capacity expansion and new technology would be nullified. Obviously, the more modern establishments and the better trained and more experienced workers would play a more promi-nent role in this respect. According to the Worker's Daily, this was obviously understood by the Chinese planners who envisaged in 1956 the training of 6,000 cadres and 38,000 skilled workers at An-shan during the following seven years for employment in the developing steel centers at Pao-t'ou and Wu-han. [41] A major drawback, however, lies in the frequent use of the surpassing of production norms as an objective in contests that are usually staged toward the end of a planning period. [42] This has a tendency to thwart the fulfillment of the training function, which is, of course, far more important in the long run.

Some Characteristics of an Emerging Modern Industry

If size alone were a sufficient hallmark of success, then the growth of the modern sector of the iron and steel industry described above would be strong evidence of such an accomplishment. However, preoccupation with growth viewed in terms of a few output indices may tend to divert attention from an important factor, namely, the heterogeneity of the products of the industry and the specific uses they serve. In particular, how the relationship between those products constituting successive stages of production has varied is of importance from the point of view of efficient investment allocation and the degree of vertical integration in the interest of efficient production. Some of these problems will now be considered.

The Intraindustry Balance

The continual but uneven expansion of the modern sector of the iron and steel industry and the significance of the differential rates of growth between production and designed capacity have been noted above. Together they seem to indicate that Communist China has brought about a large expansion of the industry through the concentrated development of a relatively small number of modern mills during the First Five-Year Plan while a tendency toward decentralization and the development of new centers existed during the Second Five-Year Plan. This broad picture was by and large a faithful reflection of the general features of the First Plan described in the previous section except that more reliance may have been placed on existing mills while construction of the Wu-han and Pao-t'ou complexes may have been postponed to later dates than the original plan had contemplated. There is little doubt that development under the First Five-Year Plan, with some possible modifications as the plan progressed, was also far more successful than development since the beginning of 1958. Interesting, however, is the fact that although motivated undoubtedly by the desire for speedy development--which would not have been such an overwhelmingly important criterion under a non-Communist regime--and acting without the constraints that would have severely restricted the scale and mode of activities of a non-Communist regime, in the direction of construction labor, for instance, the

79

Chinese Communists apparently found it necessary to follow a course similar to what would have been a logical course of development in a more peaceful postwar period. The single most important difference was that Communist China had had to rebuild the Manchurian iron and steel base as a result of Soviet devastation, and that this had to be done with Soviet assistance which, in turn, had to be paid for.

We turn now to another aspect of the industry, namely, the internal balance between iron smelting and steelmaking and between steelmaking and its fabrication into finished products. We have already noted the pyramidal intraindustry structure that Communist China inherited and the effect of Soviet removals from Manchuria. We must now look into the changes in the internal structure of the industry that have taken place along with the expansion of the industry as a whole.

During 1949-1955, in the Soviet Union, the ratio of pig iron to steel ingot output in tons varied from 0. 70 (1951) to 0. 77 (1955 plan) ton of pig iron to 1 ton of steel. [43] (See Table 3. 13.) In Communist China, as will be seen in Chapter 4, the pig-iron-input coefficient per ton of open-hearth steel varied from 0. 76 ton in 1955 to 1. 10 tons in 1960. In the case of Bessemer steel, the input coefficient of pig iron varied from 1. 16 tons in 1955 to 1. 36 tons in 1960. Since (1) not all the pig iron produced would go into steel production, (2) more iron may be used in steelmaking in Communist China as a substitute for scrap steel than in the U.S.S.R., and (3) the proportion of converter steel may have increased, a higher proportion of pig iron to steel should be expected in the Chinese iron and steel industry at the present stage of its development. Perhaps as a rule of thumb a ratio of 1. 1 to 1. 2 tons of pig iron to 1 ton of steel, corresponding more closely to the pig-iron-input coefficient in the Chinese Bessemer furnaces, may be regarded as an appropriate over-all ratio.

In the Soviet Union, the ratio of ingot-steel production to the output of rolled-steel products varied from 1. 27 tons (1954) of steel to 1 ton of rolled products to 1. 37 tons to 1 in 1949 during the period between 1949 and 1955. [44] Since some crude steel may be exported, one should expect the appropriate ratio in Communist China not to fall below 1. 3 to 1. 4 tons of steel ingot to 1 ton of finished-steel products.

With these general magnitudes in mind, we may take a look at the structure of the Chinese industry from the point of view both of its internal consistency and of changes brought about under the Communist regime. One of the results of such a scrutiny that strikes us immediately is the divergence of the ratio in terms of capacity from that in terms of production.

First, in terms of year-end capacity, the ratio of pig iron to crude steel in 1950-1952 showed a relatively excessive capacity to produce steel ingots. This apparently corresponded to the period when many of the large blast furnaces in Manchuria had not yet been restored. In terms of production, on the other hand, the ratio varied from about 1.6 in 1950 to 1.4 in 1952, indicating a slightly "above normal" relative output of pig iron. The divergence between the two sets of ratios may be explained by a combination of the following factors: (1) more intensive use of the blast furnaces than the steel smelters, (2) insufficient supply of suitable iron for steelmaking, (3) other possible shortages of inputs used in making steel, (4) nonoperable condition of some of the furnaces installed for making steel, and (5) the relatively late date of installation of some of the steelmaking furnaces during the year, thus creating the illusion of a larger steelmaking capacity than actually existed. One cannot be certain at this point as to the relative weights of these factors, but the conclusion that proper balance of available capacity between the two subsectors and their full utlization were not accomplished during this period seems inescapable.

In terms of rated capacity, the ratio of year-end capacity in 1953-1955 appeared to be in far better balance as the growth of blast-furnace capacity caught up with that of ingot production. This situation may have extended to 1957 in terms of operating capacity. The improvement is shown even more plainly in the production ratio which approached what we have tentatively assumed to be a proper level at the present stage of development attained by the Chinese iron and steel industry in view of the small supply of scrap steel, even though it still showed a much larger relative output of pig iron than was conventional according to contemporary Soviet standards.

Beginning in 1956, however, the rated-capacity ratio again showed an excessive development of new steelmaking facilities (the same was true for the operating-capacity ratio beginning in 1957), while the balance in terms of

81

Table 3.13

INDICATORS OF THE INTRAINDUSTRY STRUCTURE
OF THE IRON AND STEEL INDUSTRY

| Year | Ratio of Annual Capacity | | Output Ratio | | Output Ratio in the Soviet Union | |
	I Pig iron to ingot steel[a]	II Ingot steel to "finished-steel products"[a]	Pig iron to ingot steel	Ingot steel to "finished-steel products"	I	II
1949	2.00	0.94	1.56	1.12	0.71	1.37
1950	0.95	1.80	1.61	1.31	0.71	1.31
1951	1.06	1.90	1.62	1.11	0.70	1.31
1952	0.95	2.00	1.41	1.03	0.73	1.29
1953	1.27	1.89	1.23	1.01	0.72	1.29
1954	1.36	1.85	1.33	1.01	0.72	1.27
1955	1.50	1.85	1.27	1.14	0.77	1.29
1956	0.96	3.54	1.07	1.14	0.63	1.31
1957	0.91	2.16	1.11	1.26	0.60	1.31
1958	0.66	3.09	1.19	1.33	0.60	1.32
1959	0.79	3.14	1.10	0.94	0.59	1.31
1960	0.77	2.83	1.06	0.72-0.94	0.59	1.31

Sources: Figures for Communist China are derived from data in Table B-1, Appendix B. The Soviet data are computed from Clark, op. cit., for 1949-1955 and from Promyshlennost' R.S.F.S.R., 1961, p. 54, for 1956-1960. The latter are for R.S.F.S.R. only. See also Appendix C for an alternative estimate based on alternative estimates of finished-steel output.

[a]The operating-capacity ratios for 1952-1960 were:

Year	Pig Iron to Ingot Steel	Ingot Steel to "Finished-Steel Products"
1952	1.08	2.29
1953	1.47	1.50
1954	1.53	1.58
1955	1.53	1.86
1956	1.17	2.72
1957	1.23	1.75
1958	0.89	2.50
1959	1.07	2.54
1960	1.05	2.29

production was not too lopsided because some of the steel furnaces would have to remain idle in the face of an insufficient supply of iron. Since the proportion of Bessemer steel increased during this period, and with it probably the demand for pig iron, the pressure on the pig-iron supply became greater. Whether, beginning in 1958, the availability of iron from the "semimodern" furnaces offered any real relief is a moot question to which we shall return in the next chapter. But, as far as the First Five-Year Plan was concerned, development of the open-hearth and Bessemer furnaces outstripped the growth of blast-furnace capacity and production. The state of imbalance that had existed in 1950 and 1952 in terms of capacity was not ameliorated as a result of the Plan. As for the 1958-1960 period, the imbalance seemed to have continued in spite of greater uncertainties about the statistics themselves. On the other hand, the imbalance in production was less pronounced.

Next, if we look at the relationship between steel ingot and finished-steel products, an excess of ingot capacity, compared with that of finished products, appeared to exist from 1950 onward. In terms of rated capacity, the ratio remained fairly stable at about 1.8:2 between 1950 and 1955, but deteriorated considerably in 1956 and subsequent years. In terms of production, on the other hand, there was again a much smaller ratio of ingot output to that of steel products. To some extent, this may be expected in view of the limitation imposed on steel finishing by the shortage of raw material, although some withdrawal from accumulated stock of crude steel should be possible. What is interesting is that, with the exception of 1958, the ratio of ingot to finished-steel production in Communist China was consistently below that of the Soviet Union. In 1959-1960, the Chinese ratio was even below one ton of steel to each ton of finished-steel products. Since there is little reason to expect a greater degree of exaggeration of production reports at the stage of finishing and fabrication during the last stages of the "Great Leap Forward" than in 1958, one wonders again whether the output statistics of "rolled" or "finished" products, details of which have never been fully published, may not contain a certain amount of "double counting."[45] This point has been discussed before and will be raised again when we consider the uses of finished steel in Chapter 5.

If we are right in thinking that the capacity data in 1957-1960 and the production data in the entire period contain semifinished intermediate products, then a serious imbalance apparently existed between steelmaking and finishing. There was too much ingot capacity. On the other hand, if the imbalance was less serious in production, it was largely a result of the inadequate supply of quality steel to be converted into suitable finished products that were in demand and of possible "double counting" in finished-products output. Large import of finished quality steel products and absence of large steel-ingot exports both seem to point to the shortage of quality steel and its products.

Supply of New Products

That there has been excess capacity at the ingot stage seems to be a fairly well-established fact which cannot but be interpreted as an unfavorable reflection of investment planning. It has also been found that the degree of imbalance has been less pronounced in terms of production. But one possible explanation of this phenomenon is that lack of inputs of suitable quality and/or lack of demand for products of inferior quality which do not meet specifications may have been an important underlying cause. For instance, steel production may have been kept in check by the inadequate supply of good iron. At the same time, the output of both steel and finished-steel products may have been kept below full capacity because the wrong products have been produced. If this is the case, then the malaise of the industry is even more complicated than an unbalanced intraindustry structure would indicate.

The Chinese Communists seem to be quite aware of the importance of increasing the varieties of the steel industry's products. Beginning around 1954-1955 and up to 1959 there was a distinct acceleration in the number of new products reportedly brought out by the industry. As may be seen in Table 3.14, the number of new varieties of steel produced in Communist China rose from 180 in 1952 to 500 in 1959 while the varieties of steel products increased from 400 to 6,000 in the same period. The criteria used in these statistics in defining a new variety are not clear and one suspects that only minor variations in specifications may have taken place in many cases. However, the crux of the problem is whether the new products can be supplied in quantity.

At the time of the "Great Leap Forward," the official People's Daily

Table 3.14

CUMULATIVE NUMBER OF NEW VARIETIES OF STEEL PRODUCED EXPERIMENTALLY

Year	Steel		Steel Products	
	Total	Increment	Total	Increment
1952	180	...	400	...
1953	178-182	2	484	84
1954	200	18	571	97
1955	239	39	1,307	726
1956	291	52	2,089	782
1957	372	81	3,997-5,000	2,911
1958	...	...	6,000	1,000
1959	500	...	6,000	0
1960	...	...	...	...
1961	...	...	...	...
1962	...	...	119	...

Notes and Sources: Data derived from Major Aspects, op. cit., p. 36; Chin-jih Hsin-wen (Today's News), Hong Kong, December 30, 1957; Hui-huang-ti Shih-nien (The Glorious Ten Years), Peking, 1959, pp. 113-115; Wei-ta ti Shih-nien, English translation, p. 77; People's Daily, January 7, 1958; Kung-jen Jih-pao (Workers' Daily), Peking, May 23, 1957; Peking Review, October 12, 1962.

Some of the "new products" are listed below in the order of their appearance in Communist Chinese literature:

1950   Steel rails.

1954   Heat-resistant stainless steel.

1955   Steel plate (for ship construction), various shapes of steel material for automobile manufacturing, 50-kilogram heavy rail, alloy seamless tubing, silicon-steel sheet, big-angle steel, I-beam, steel plates, high-grade-carbon structural steel, silicon steel (for electrical engineering industry), narrow-gauge steel rails, abrasion-resistant nodular cast-iron rolls.

1956   High heat-resistant alloy steel.

1957   Steel plate for automobiles, cold-drawn alloy-steel products including tubes for planes, large tool steel, heavy forgings.

1958   Low-alloy high-strength structural steel, 550-millimeter-high steel I-beam.

Table 3.14 (continued)

1959	High-grade alloy structural steels, special steels for instruments and meters, seamless-steel tubing (for boilers).
1960	Seamless tubes (for chemical-fertilizer equipment), heavy and light rails, special steel shapes for the manufacture of combine harvesters, rolled steel for making coal-mine tunneling machines, special specifications of steel plates for shipbuilding, tubes with a diameter of 168 millimeters, capillary tubes, bimetallic steel plates, high-speed-drill steels containing no chromium, copper-silicon-bearing steel rails.
1962	High-strength seamless tubes.

Sources: Ten Great Years, op. cit., pp. 101-102; Far Eastern Economic Review, vol. IX, no. 4, Hong Kong, July 24, 1955; The Glorious Ten Years, pp. 113-115, Peking, 1959; New China Semi-monthly, No. 127, 1958; Chin-jih Hsin-wen, Hong Kong, December 30, 1957; Survey of China Mainland Press, November 28, 1960, p. 16; NCNA, An-shan, December 24, 1962.

stated quite openly that although the number of varieties of steel products had risen from five to six thousand, a number of items such as heavy rails, thin sheets, seamless tubing, and cables were far from being in sufficient supply to meet the demand of economic development.[46] The shortage was especially acute in the case of many special, cold rolled, and large items. The "Great Leap" has been followed by a sharp decline of economic activity, including industrial production, and a period of adjustment of policy, with far greater emphasis on the variety and quality of products. In a critical analysis of the industrial situation in the first part of 1961, when the downturn was in full swing, the Hong Kong China News Analysis[47] quoted the People's Daily as saying, "The number of products cannot be considered apart from the quality and the type of product. If attention is not paid to type and quality, quantitative figures become meaningless." Referring to steel products in particular, the Hong Kong journal pointed to a 10-percent increase in the first quarter output of eight items in 1961 over the corresponding level in 1960 although their production was still said to be grossly insufficient to meet the demand. The eight items included the four mentioned above and consisted of heavy rails, medium and thin sheets, seamless tubes, silicon-steel sheets, welded steel tubes, and other quality, as well as large, steel products. A final example of the nature of the problem may be found in a report in the official Peking Review in late 1962[48] which proudly announced the production of 119 new types of steel products in the first eight months of 1962. Some of these were said to be in quantity production. Left unsaid was the proportion of new items which, though produced experimentally, could not yet be supplied in quantity.[49]

An increasing variety of products in quantity production and the maintenance of high quality of the output are of course not easily achieved, while efforts to achieve these goals constitute the cause of the usual growth pains of a developing industry. But in the Chinese case, there may be more to these difficulties than one may normally expect. "Conservatism" among the industrial managers was said to be a major obstacle, according to the People's Daily.[50] "The Bureau of the Iron and Steel Industry and many enterprises always stressed the difficulties they would have in drawing up production plans for new products," wrote the paper. "They were unwilling to add to the number of new varieties for experimental production.... Some enterprises were unwilling to accept orders for new products...." One needs little perspicacity to note that much of this "conservatism" may be plain common sense and prudence while another part of it may be a reflection of the fear of failure--failure to produce the new products to the satisfaction of the plan with respect to quantity, quality, and cost, and failure to fulfill the output quotas of the established products due to the disruptive influence of experimentation and diversion of effort. While this "conservative" spirit was apparently broken during the "Great Leap Forward" if the increasing number of new steel varieties were used as a gauge, the degree of real success was highly doubtful as may be seen by the renewed emphasis on quality and variety since the end of the "Leap."

The Experiment That Failed

Upon the conclusion of its First Five-Year Plan, the Communist Chinese regime was seized by a determination to accelerate the rate of industrial expansion through the institution of a vast number of small industrial enterprises to be operated by part-time workers and peasants mobilized under the commune system inaugurated at the same time.[51] At the core of this industrial movement was the expansion of iron and steel production under the slogan "i-kang-wei-kang," i.e., using steel as the "moving spirit" or Leitmotiv of industrialization. On August 5, 1958, the People's Daily reported an official plan to build 200 small Bessemer converters and 13,000 iron-smelting furnaces before the end of the year. Such a program would add 10 million tons to the annual steelmaking capacity of the country and 20 million tons to its pig-iron capacity. While there are no reliable and complete statistics of the effective expansion of capacity during 1958, there was no doubt that the effort was massive.[52] It was followed in 1959 and 1960 by a process of consolidation and upgrading in the course of which many of the "native" iron and steel furnaces were either abandoned or replaced by furnaces of improved design. Some of these "modernized" and expanded mills are represented in the capacity data of the modern sector of the industry with which we have been primarily concerned in this chapter. The production data, as given in Table B-12, Appendix B, and reproduced below, also testify most vividly to the gigantic scale of the experiment.

Production in Million Metric Tons

Sector	Pig Iron		Ingot Steel	
	1958	1959	1958	1959
Modern	9.5	9.5	8.0	8.6
Native	4.2	11.0	3.1	4.7

On the basis of our analysis thus far, a massive drive to establish many small producing units and subsequently to weld these into secondary mills supplementing the large established centers like An-shan, Shanghai, Chungking, etc., would have several advantages. The new mills would expand the geographical base of the industry and give new impetus to the economic development of many more areas simultaneously. They would vastly increase the scale of industrial development. They would enable the more advanced mills to engage in

experimentation with new products. They would offer the large modern mills a greater number of sources of supply of raw materials, thus contributing to the stability of the industry's output. However, these advantages would accrue to the economy only if the underlying assumptions that the new producing units could yield products of adequate quality and at a reasonable cost and that they would not disrupt the other sectors of the economy were satisfied. Unfortunately for Communist China, these basic conditions were not present.

Admission of the poor quality of the products of the "backyard furnace" was first made in 1959, and it was instrumental in spurring the drive to stress quality improvement and technological innovation. The costliness of the mass movement, to be discussed more fully in Chapter 4, has probably led to its virtual abandonment in 1961-1962 in view of the new policy of retrenchment under which all enterprises that could not operate profitably were to cease production.[53] The immediate cause of the failure of this experiment is twofold: overestimate of the technical possibilities of the labor-intensive methods in iron and steelmaking and underestimate of the cost, plus an undue emphasis on breaking quantitative records at the expense of quality.

Perhaps the most fundamental factor in the failure is revealed in the

following passage of Chou En-lai's report to the First Session of the Second
National People's Congress on April 18, 1959:[54]

> But the most important cause of the "Great Leap Forward" in
> 1958 was our discovery in the spring of the year when we evalu-
> ated the experience of the First Five-Year Plan that an even
> better way to establish socialism, i.e., our General Line, was
> to give priority to the development of heavy industry and to use
> steel as the spearhead in an advance on a broad front. Steel is
> the most important raw material in industrial production and
> capital construction. Insufficiency of steel production has hin-
> dered the development of the entire economy. We undertook there-
> fore in 1958 to mobilize the strength of the entire population to
> increase iron and steel production, increasing the output of steel
> from 5.35 million tons in 1957 to 11.08 million tons in 1958....
> We expanded the powers of the local authorities to exercise con-
> trol over industrial construction and production, thus elevating
> greatly the activist attitude of the working masses to engage in
> industry.... In realizing the 1959 plan we should make an all out
> effort to expand the mass movement on all economic fronts....

The keynote lies in the Communists' reliance on mass movement and
their misplaced confidence both in the limitless substitutability of labor for
capital and in the regime's ability to provide sufficient ideological incentive to
sustain a prolonged drive toward industrialization. This attitude in the drive
for more steel probably contributed significantly to the management and
planning errors which brought about the sharp economic decline at the end of
the Second Five-Year Plan period.

4 CONTRIBUTION TO THE NATIONAL PRODUCT AND THE COST STRUCTURE

Gross Value Output and Value-Added of the Industry

The primary purpose of this chapter is to evaluate the role of the iron and steel industry in the production of the aggregate output of the Chinese economy by determining the amount that can be properly said to have originated in this particular sector. The indirect impact of the availability of iron and steel on the rest of the economy, especially machinery production, railway construction, building, and the manufacture of arms, will be discussed in the following chapter in conjunction with the distribution of the industry's output.

Lack of detailed data on the cost structure of the various activities subsumed under the broad description of "the iron and steel industry" makes it impossible to account in detail for the individual contributions of all the subsectors. However, it is possible to estimate the values-added in some of the principal subsectors within the manufacturing branch of the industry along with corresponding estimates of the iron and steel industry as a whole. In the following, a very rough measure of the order of magnitude of the value-added in the entire iron and steel industry will be attempted first. We shall preface this by considering the data on gross value output.

The Gross Value Output of the Iron and Steel Industry and the Value of Sales of Its Principal Products, 1952-1957

The conceptual fuzziness of the term, "the iron and steel industry," is inevitably transmitted to the statistical measurement of the industry's gross value output. For instance, in Communist Chinese literature, the terms "metallurgical industry" and "iron and steel industry" have often been used interchangeably. This is an understandable practice as long as the production and fabrication of nonferrous metals remains unimportant. It lends itself to

91

imprecision and confusion, however, when this condition is no longer satisfied. Another moot question concerns the boundary line between the iron and steel industry and the metal processing industry of which the manufacture of machinery and equipment is the principal division. It would be logical to maintain that the raw materials and products of ferrous metals used by the metal processing industry should be included in the output of the iron and steel industry, while the end products, such as machines, should be regarded as the output of metal processing. But such a distinction must be arbitrary to some extent; it cannot be, and apparently has not been, consistently maintained. According to _Major Aspects_,[1] for instance, iron and steel castings are listed among the products of the metal processing industry although their inclusion in the output of the iron and steel industry would be equally plausible, and some steel castings are undoubtedly included in the statistics of "finished-steel products" or "steel materials." Perhaps this lack of consistency owes its origin partly to differences in the scope of activities of the various iron and steel enterprises and machine manufacturers. Perhaps it is also a result of inconsistency in the reporting system. From our point of view, however, the principal objection lies in the resultant absence of precision in the concept of the gross value output of the iron and steel industry.

Nevertheless, the composition of what is doubtless the core of the iron and steel industry is quite clear. The principal products of this industry are generally grouped into two divisions: the iron and manganese mining sector and the iron- and steel-smelting and -finishing sector. Included in these divisions are also such items as ferrous alloys, coke, and refractory bricks. But official production statistics that are most commonly given cover only pig iron, crude or ingot steel, and "finished steel" or rolled products. In addition, data on iron and manganese ores and coke are also available. Thus, the production of these six major commodity groups may be regarded as the core of the "iron and steel industry," the gross value output of which is inclusive of their production even though some minor items should be added if a complete enumeration is desired.

With this understanding of the approximate scope of the iron and steel industry in mind, we may now take a look at the official statistics of its gross value output and the corresponding values of its principal constituents. The

92

official gross output data for the industry as a whole for 1952 to 1956, as given
in official sources and supplemented by our estimate for 1957, are given below
in thousands of 1952 yuan:[2]

1952	1953	1954	1955	1956	1957
1,369,594	1,871,333	2,327,556	2,896,611	4,124,915	5,201,600

Alternatively, we may list the gross value outputs of the six principal commodity
categories computed as products of their physical outputs and their respective
1952 prices.[3] As explained above, these values may also be regarded as indicative of the bulk of the production of the iron and steel industry.

Commodity	1952	1953	1954	1955	1956	1957
			(billion 1952 yuan)			
Iron Ore	0.17	0.23	0.28	0.37	0.60	0.76
Manganese Ore	0.01	0.01	0.01	0.01	0.03	0.03
Pig Iron	0.39	0.45	0.62	0.77	0.97	1.19
Crude Steel	0.93	1.22	1.54	1.97	3.08	3.69
"Finished Steel"	1.31	1.75	1.97	2.51	3.92	4.26
Coke	0.13	0.16	0.20	0.25	0.32	0.33
Total	2.94	3.82	4.62	5.88	8.92	10.26

Some interesting observations may be made immediately as we compare
the official gross value output statistics of the entire industry with the sum of
the six items constituting the bulk of the same industry. For instance, the official
figures are consistently less than the sum of the six items given above.[4] One
chief explanation may be found in the fact that the iron and steel mills are highly
integrated, even if not fully integrated in every case, and that raw materials
produced and consumed by the same enterprise would not therefore be included
in their gross value output. Thus, of the six items listed above only finished steel
and a portion of the other five items representing either the output of nonintegrated enterprises or that part of their production which is not consumed in subsequent stages of the process of steelmaking within the same enterprises[5] would
be included in the official gross value output statistics of the entire iron and
steel industry, if the "factory" method of accounting is strictly adhered to.

This explanation has both pros and cons. On the one hand, it apparently is supported by the fact that the official data are consistently larger than the estimates of the value of "finished-steel products," although the differences between the two series are not excessive, which would seem to indicate that the other end products--goods produced by nonintegrated iron and steel enterprises and goods not consumed in the manufacture of finished-steel products--may not be too large.[6] On the other hand, according to T.C. Liu and K.C. Yeh, there is some evidence that the official industrial output statistics, though based on the "factory" method, nevertheless include crude steel, iron ore, and coke.[7]

The only item in the ferrous-metals group that seems to have been excluded from the official statistics is pig iron. However, if this interpretation is correct, there would still remain an unexplained difference between the sum of the five remaining items and the official industrial output statistics.[8] Furthermore, a supplementary explanation of the discrepancy between the official value output estimate of the entire industry and the sum of the six or five principal items may lie in the exaggeration of the output statistics. In particular, the inclusion of semifinished steel, which is used up in the course of fabrication, in the statistics of "finished steel" output would account for a noticeable discrepancy.[9]

A Rough Estimate of Value-Added in the Iron and Steel Industry, 1952-1957

The foregoing discussion has stressed the element of uncertainty surrounding the various estimates of the iron and steel industry's value output. If, however, the official gross value output statistics are actually net of most of the raw materials produced and consumed within the industry, then the value-added in the iron and steel industry can be approximated quite simply by subtracting purchases from outside the industry. Moreover, approximate values derived in this manner should not show gross discrepancies from the sums of the values-added in the principal subsectors if the latter are estimated separately. Thus a cross check can be made on the reliability of the two sets of estimates.

What are the purchases that should be subtracted from the official

Table 4.1

ESTIMATES OF PRINCIPAL EXTRA-SECTORAL PURCHASES OF THE IRON AND STEEL INDUSTRY
(million 1952 yuan)

Purchases	1952		1953	1954	1955	1956		1957	
Coal[a]	64.20		70.49	90.65	104.26	125.70		144.32	
Electricity[b]	40.40		55.20	68.66	85.00	120.00		151.32	
	(a)	(b)				(a)	(b)	(a)	(b)
Transportation[c]	22.52	22.57	28.05	35.05	43.02	61.43	60.30	73.74	75.33
Repair and Maintenance[d]	30.20	30.33	38.13	48.96	61.95	92.45	90.48	111.43	114.10
	(a)	(b)				(a)	(b)	(a)	(b)
Total	157.32	157.50	191.87	243.32	294.23	399.58	396.48	480.81	485.07

Notes and Sources:

[a]Derived from Yuan-li Wu, Economic Development and the Use of Engergy Resources in Communist China, Praeger, 1963, pp. 90, 111 ff.

[b]Electricity data for 1952, 1955, and 1956 are taken from source (a). Data for 1953, 1954, and 1957 are computed under the assumption that they increased in the same proportion as the gross value output of the industry in the same years.

[c]The sum of transportation cost in pig iron, open hearth, and converter steel production. See the sectoral estimates on pages 103, 111, and 116.

[d]Repair and maintenance comprise one-half the sum of depreciation in the sectoral estimates on pages 103, 111, and 116.

Table 4.2

MATERIAL INPUT COEFFICIENTS PER METRIC TON
OF PIG IRON AND THEIR PRICES
(kilograms)

Material	1952	1953	1954	1955	1956	1957	1958	1959	1960
Iron Ore[a]	1,641	1,760	1,735	1,743	1,725	1,725	1,725	1,725	1,725
Scrap Iron[b]	250	250	250	250	250	250	250	250	250
Limestone[b]	500	500	500	500	500	500	500	500	500
Manganese Ore[b]	40	40	40	40	40	40	40	40	40
Coke[c]	1,000	941	893	804	791	751	711	733	754

Prices of Material Inputs in
Current Yuan per Metric Ton

Material	1952	1957
Iron Ore	39[d]	28[b]
Scrap Iron[f]	120	87
Limestone	5[g]	3-5/8[h]
Manganese Ore	53[i]	38[j]
Coke	44.0[k]	46.2[l]

Notes to Table 4.2

(a) For 1952-1956, Major Aspects, op. cit., p. 35, ore of 55 percent Fe. For 1957-1960, the 1956 figure has been used for lack of more recent information although the general deterioration in the quality of ores from the mines in 1958-1960 as a result of the "Great Leap" may mean that larger quantities were actually required than in 1956.

(b) Only the An-shan figure in 1949-1951 is available. See Survey Report, op. cit., p. 47. However, since the ore input figures are fairly stable during this period, it is believed that employment of a constant coefficient in this case would not do great violence to the estimates. In general, because of the greater efficiency of the An-shan blast furnaces, adoption of the An-shan figures for the entire country would tend to offset any overestimate of input requirements in the subsequent years due to improvements in material economy.

(c) Yuan-li Wu, Economic Development, op. cit., Chapter 5.

(d) Derived from the price of iron ore in 1957 under the assumption that the 1952 and 1957 prices stood in the same relationship to each other as those of pig iron. See the section on open hearth steel.

(e) Price of iron ore paid by the Shanghai No. 1 mill. See Kang-t'ieh (Iron and Steel), no. 1, January, 1958, p. 14.

(f) Estimated by assuming that the ratio between steel and scrap steel prices can also be applied to pig iron and scrap iron prices. See the section below, p. 107.

(g) Liu and Yeh, op. cit., Appendix H.

(h) See the section on input prices in steel production.

(i) Same as (g).

(j) Estimated by assuming that the change in manganese ore prices between 1952 and 1957 is in the same proportion as that of iron ore.

(k) Liu and Yeh, op. cit., Appendix F.

(l) Estimated under the assumption that the prices of coke and coal changed in the same proportion between 1952 and 1957. See the section on steel input prices below, p. 107.

gross value output because they are definitely made from outside of the iron and steel industry? Coal, electric power, and transportation input are probably among the most important of such external purchases. First, even though many of the iron and steel enterprises may own and operate their own power plants and coal mines, the fact that they are included in the statistics relating to the power and coal industries and that separate ministries are in charge of coal mines and power plants suggests that they should be treated as purchases from sources external to the iron and steel industry. Second, there is no apparent objection to treating transportation service as an external purchase. Finally, it is possible that maintenance and repairs may consist in part of outside purchases. On the other hand, any overestimate of external purchases in these four categories would probably be offset by other external purchases not accounted for, particularly purchases of mineral products used in steelmaking from some of the mining sectors. As an approximation, therefore, we may confine ourselves to these four categories only.

If these extra-sectoral purchases are subtracted from the official gross value output data, the remainder would then approximate the gross value-added in the iron and steel industry as a whole. The estimates, in millions of 1952 yuan, are:

1952		1953	1954	1955	1956		1957	
(i)	(ii)				(i)	(ii)	(i)	(ii)
1,212	1,212	1,679	2,084	2,602	3,725	3,728	4,721	4,717

If the value output estimates still contain some intermediate products, then the correct value-added in the iron and steel industry would be somewhat smaller. The question is whether the above estimates are at all reasonable. To what extent do these estimates correspond to the values that can be obtained by aggregating the estimates of the principal subsectors?

97

Value-Added in Some Principal Subsectors of
Iron- and Steelmaking, 1952-1960

Although available information does not permit us to reconstruct the cost structure of all of the principal subsectors of the iron and steel industry, it is possible to examine in some detail the input-output relationship in several parts of the industry. As a result of such an examination, we may derive estimates of both gross and net values-added in these subsectors. When combined with corresponding estimates in other subsectors which have been obtained by other students of the Chinese economy, we may arrive at some reasonable estimates for the bulk, if not the whole, of the iron and steel industry. For the 1952-1957 period, these estimates may then be compared with over-all estimates for the entire industry presented in the foregoing section.

Because of the introduction of the "backyard furnace" movement in 1958 and the consequent inflation of the reported production of "native" iron and steel in that year, which was followed by a partial consolidation and revamping of the small smelters in 1959-1960, it is necessary to proceed with our examination in two parts, dealing respectively with the modern and the native sectors of iron- and steelmaking.

The Modern Pig Iron and Crude Steel Subsectors

Pig iron. Apart from labor, the production costs of pig iron making may be divided into material inputs, fuel and power, transportation, miscellaneous expenses, and depreciation. Of the material inputs and fuel the principal items are iron ore, scrap iron, limestone, manganese ore, and coke. The approximate input coefficients per metric ton of pig iron produced may be estimated first and then converted into value terms at 1952 and 1957 prices, respectively, as shown in Table 4.2.

As for the other inputs, transportation costs are incurred in bringing some of the raw materials from a distance. However, since ore supplies are generally located near the smelters, the amount involved is unlikely to be large. Because of its bulk, coal used in the coke ovens may be an exception. But this should be considered as a part of the costs of coking. As a simple approximation, we shall estimate transportation cost at 3.5 percent of material cost in accordance with certain official instructions issued by the Communist planners for use in the railway equipment plants.[10]

In the case of electricity, consumption per ton of pig iron averaged 59 kilowatt hours at Ma-an-shan and Ta-yeh in 1953.[11] Electricity rates averaged 72.04 yuan per thousand kilowatt hours in 1952 and 59.70 yuan in 1957.[12]

Miscellaneous nonproduction expenses other than labor cost can be derived only very roughly on the basis of the number of nonproduction workers, estimated at 3.9 percent of the total number of employees in the pig iron section, and similar outlay in steelmaking. The amount involved varied from a high of 0.25 yuan per ton in 1952 to a low of 0.06 yuan in 1957. The decline between the two years reflected improvement in cost control, while no change in the estimates for the different years need be made whether 1952 or 1957 prices are used because of the insignificant variation in the official wholesale price index. Because of the dependence of this estimation in turn on estimates of the number of workers in the various branches of the iron and steel industry, a matter to which further reference will be made later, some uncertainty shrouds the issue. Fortunately, the relative magnitude involved in this case is so small that even a larger margin of error can be tolerated without serious distortion of the estimates of production cost and value-added.

Finally, little information is available on depreciation. We must therefore fall back on the assumption by Liu and Yeh that it can be approximated at the level of 5 percent of the value of production or 10 yuan per ton of pig iron valued at 200 yuan in 1952.

On the basis of the above estimates, we are finally in a position to derive the gross and net values-added in the modern sector of pig iron production, both at 1952 and 1957 prices. The estimates are presented first in terms of yuan per ton of pig iron produced, followed by aggregate estimates covering the entire iron output of the modern sector. (See Tables 4.3 and 4.4) From these estimates, we can also perceive the entire cost structure, with the exception of wage estimates to which we shall return at a later stage.

Crude steel. (1) Open hearth steel. The principal material inputs used in open hearth steelmaking in China are pig iron, a small proportion of scrap steel, iron ore, coal, and limestone. The input coefficients per metric

99

Table 4.3

PRICE, COSTS, AND VALUE-ADDED PER METRIC TON OF PIG IRON, MODERN SECTOR, 1952–1960

		1952	1953	1954	1955	1956	1957	1958	1959	1960
						1952 Yuan				
I.	Price[a]	200.00	200.00	200.00	200.00	200.00	200.00	200.00	200.00	200.00
II.	Cost of materials and fuel[b]									
III.	Iron ore	64.00	68.64	67.67	67.98	67.28	67.28	67.28	67.28	67.28
	Scrap iron	30.00	30.00	30.00	30.00	30.00	30.00	30.00	30.00	30.00
	Limestone	2.50	2.50	2.50	2.50	2.50	2.50	2.50	2.50	2.50
	Manganese ore	2.12	2.12	2.12	2.12	2.12	2.12	2.12	2.12	2.12
	Coke	44.00	41.40	39.29	35.38	34.80	33.04	31.28	32.25	33.18
	Subtotal	142.62	144.66	141.58	137.98	136.70	134.94	133.18	134.15	135.08
III.	Electricity	4.25	4.25	4.25	4.25	4.25	4.25	4.25	4.25	4.25
IV.	Transportation	4.99	5.06	4.96	4.83	4.78	4.72	4.66	4.70	4.73
V.	Other miscellaneous nonlabor cost[c]	0.25	0.23	0.15	0.11	0.08	0.05	0.06	0.05	0.05
VI.	Total cost excluding wages and depreciation	152.11	154.20	150.94	147.17	145.81	143.96	142.15	143.15	144.11
VII.	Depreciation	10.00	10.00	10.00	10.00	10.00	10.00	10.00	10.00	10.00
VIII.	Gross value-added (I-VI)	47.89	45.80	49.06	52.83	54.19	56.04	57.85	56.85	55.89
IX.	Net value-added (VIII-VII)	37.89	35.80	39.06	42.83	44.19	46.04	47.85	46.85	45.89

Table 4.3 (continued)

		1952	1953	1954	1955	1956	1957	1958	1959	1960
						1957 Yuan				
I.	Price ^{d}	145.00	145.00	145.00	145.00	145.00	145.00	145.00	145.00	145.00
II.	Cost of materials, fuel, and power									
	Iron ore	45.95	49.28	48.58	48.80	48.30	48.30	48.30	48.30	48.30
	Scrap iron	21.75	21.75	21.75	21.75	21.75	21.75	21.75	21.75	21.75
	Limestone	1.81	1.81	1.81	1.81	1.81	1.81	1.81	1.81	1.81
	Manganese ore	1.52	1.52	1.52	1.52	1.52	1.52	1.52	1.52	1.52
	Coke	46.20	43.47	41.26	37.14	36.54	34.65	32.85	33.86	34.83
	Subtotal	117.23	117.83	114.92	111.02	109.92	108.03	106.23	107.24	108.21
III.	Electricity	3.52	3.52	3.52	3.52	3.52	3.52	3.52	3.52	3.52
IV.	Transportation	4.10	4.12	4.02	3.89	3.85	3.78	3.72	3.75	3.79
V.	Other miscellaneous nonlabor cost	0.25	0.23	0.15	0.11	0.08	0.05	0.06	0.05	0.05
VI.	Total cost excluding wages and depreciation	125.10	125.70	122.61	118.54	117.37	115.38	113.53	114.56	115.57
VII.	Depreciation	7.25	7.25	7.25	7.25	7.25	7.25	7.25	7.25	7.25
VIII.	Gross value-added (I-VI)	19.90	19.30	22.39	26.46	27.63	29.62	31.47	30.44	29.43
IX.	Net value-added (VIII-VII)	12.65	12.05	15.14	19.21	20.38	22.37	24.22	23.19	22.18

101

Notes to Table 4.3

(a) Liu and Yeh, op. cit., Appendix F.

(b) All unit costs are derived from Table 4.2, except electricity, transportation, and miscellaneous nonlabor cost.

(c) These estimates are derived as follows:

Step 1. Estimate of pig-iron output per man-year on the basis of estimates for 1952 and 1957. The 1953 figure is an average of data for Pen-ch'i, Lung-yen, and T'ai-yüan, and is also used for 1952. Cf. Survey Report, op. cit., pp. 1, 47, 269, and 271. The 1957 figure of 405 tons is estimated on the basis of a general improvement of labor productivity by 138.5 percent over the 1953 level reported in Wei-tu ti Shih-nien, English translation, p. 107. The 1954-1956 figures are interpolated. The 1957 figure is also used for 1958-1960 for lack of more recent information.

Step 2. Estimate of the total number of employees from the reported output of the modern sector of pig-iron production and the man-year labor productivity derived in Step 1.

Step 3. Estimate of the number of nonproduction workers at 3.9 percent of the labor force derived in Step 2.

Step 4. Estimate of total miscellaneous nonlabor expenses in administration from the number of nonproduction workers and the estimated amount per nonproduction worker in the steel sector in 1952-60 (see below). The estimates can be made at both 1952 and 1957 prices, but the difference is insignificant.

Step 5. Derivation of miscellaneous expenses per ton of pig iron from the total and the reported output estimates.

Step	1952	1953	1954	1955	1956	1957	1958	1959	1960
1. Output of pig iron per man-year (metric tons)	170	170	229	288	347	405	405	405	405
2. Number of full-time workers in the pig-iron sector	11,176	12,794	12,934	12,604	13,767	14,469	23,531	23,457	31,467
3. Number of full-time nonproduction workers in pig-iron sector	436	499	504	492	537	564	918	915	1,227
4. Total miscellaneous nonlabor cost (million 1952 or 1957 yuan)	0.48	0.50	0.45	0.39	0.36	0.32	0.53	0.52	0.70
5. Total miscellaneous nonlabor cost per ton (yuan)	0.25	0.23	0.15	0.11	0.08	0.05	0.06	0.05	0.05

(d) See the note on pig-iron price in the section of text on open-hearth steel.

Table 4.4

VALUE OUTPUT, COSTS, AND VALUE-ADDED IN PIG IRON PRODUCTION, MODERN SECTOR

		Million 1952 Yuan*								
		1952	1953	1954	1955	1956	1957	1958	1959	1960
I.	Price [a]	380.0	435.0	592.4	726.0	955.4	1,172.0	1,906.0	1,900.0	2,548.8
II.	Cost of materials and fuel	271.0	314.6	419.4	500.9	653.0	790.8	1,269.2	1,274.4	1,721.5
III.	Electricity	8.1	9.2	12.6	15.4	20.3	24.9	40.5	40.4	54.2
IV.	Transportation	9.5	11.0	14.7	17.5	22.9	27.7	44.4	44.6	60.3
V.	Other miscellaneous nonlabor cost	0.5	0.5	0.5	0.4	0.4	0.3	0.5	0.5	0.7
VI.	Total cost excluding wages and depreciation	289.1	335.3	447.2	534.2	696.6	843.7	1,354.6	1,359.9	1,836.7
VII.	Depreciation	19.0	21.8	29.6	36.3	47.8	58.6	95.3	95.0	127.4
VIII.	Gross value-added	90.9	99.7	145.2	191.8	258.8	328.3	551.4	540.1	712.1
IX.	Net value-added	71.9	77.9	115.6	155.5	211.0	269.7	456.1	445.1	584.7

*All figures rounded to one-tenth million.

[a]See note to second part of this table.

103

Table 4.4 (continued)

						Million 1957 Yuan*				
		1952	1953	1954	1955	1956	1957	1958	1959	1960
I.	Production value [a]	275.5	315.4	429.5	526.4	692.7	849.7	1,381.9	1,377.5	1,847.9
II.	Cost of materials and fuel	222.7	256.3	340.4	403.0	525.1	633.1	1,012.4	1,018.8	1,379.0
III.	Electricity	6.7	7.7	10.4	12.8	16.8	20.6	33.5	33.4	44.9
IV.	Transportation	7.8	9.0	11.9	14.1	18.4	22.2	35.4	35.7	48.3
V.	Other miscellaneous cost	0.5	0.5	0.5	0.4	0.4	0.3	0.5	0.5	0.7
VI.	Total cost excluding wages and depreciation	237.7	273.5	363.2	430.3	560.7	676.2	1,081.8	1,088.4	1,472.9
VII.	Depreciation	13.8	15.8	21.5	26.3	34.6	42.5	69.1	68.9	92.4
VIII.	Gross value-added	37.8	41.9	66.2	96.1	132.0	173.5	300.1	289.1	375.0
IX.	Net value-added	24.0	26.1	44.7	69.8	97.8	131.0	231.0	220.2	282.6

*All figures rounded to one-tenth million.

[a]The pig-iron-output series employed in the computation is as follows (thousand metric tons):

1952	1953	1954	1955	1956	1957	1958	1959	1960
1,900	2,175	2,962	3,630	4,777	5,860	9,530	9,500	12,744

The above series excludes native iron. See Table B-12, Appendix B. For unit-price and –cost estimates, see Table 4.3

104

ton of steel produced are tabulated in Table 4.5.

The corresponding "ex-factory" prices of these inputs, some of which have already been given before, both in 1952 and 1957, are presented in Table 4.6.

From these prices and input coefficients the corresponding material costs, both at 1952 and 1957 prices, can be readily derived.

In order to estimate the gross value-added in open hearth steelmaking, it is necessary then to account for the three remaining principal, deductible items--transportation of material inputs, electricity consumed, and other miscellaneous nonlabor expenses in administration.

(a) As in the case of pig iron production, transportation cost is again estimated at 3.5 percent of total material cost.

(b) Electricity consumption is based on the number of kilowatt hours consumed per worker and the estimated number of workers in open hearth steelmaking. The former is given for the years 1952 and 1956;[13] linear interpolation takes care of the intermediate years while no change from the 1956 level is assumed in 1957-1960. The number of workers, on the other hand, is derived indirectly from some piecemeal information on labor productivity. Thus, in 1953, according to Survey Report,[14] an average of 211 tons of open hearth steel was produced per man-year. In 1957, however, labor productivity was said to have increased by 92.9 percent above the 1952 level,[15] which was probably not appreciably different from the 1953 level. This would put the 1957 output per man-year at 407 tons. Estimates for 1954-1956 may then be interpolated, while no change from the 1957 level during 1958-1960 is assumed. The number of workers in full-time equivalents is then obtained by dividing the estimated open hearth output by the quantity of steel produced per man-year.[16]

(c) Other miscellaneous nonlabor costs are estimated for 1957 on the basis of 572 yuan yearly per nonproduction worker, which was apparently the official norm.[17] The number of nonproduction workers is in turn estimated at 3.9 percent of the total number of workers obtained under (b) (10,000 persons in 1957). In 1952, the corresponding administrative expenses are estimated at 1,103 yuan per nonproduction worker. For the 1953 to 1956 period estimates are interpolated, while no change is assumed after 1957. No distinction again need be made between 1952 and 1957 prices because of the small magnitudes involved.[18]

105

Table 4.5

MATERIAL INPUT COEFFICIENTS PER METRIC TON OF INGOT STEEL, OPEN HEARTH
(in kilograms)

Material	1952	1953	1954	1955	1956	1957	1958	1959	1960
Pig iron[a]	769	769	784	763	783	783	815	846	1097
Scrap steel[b]	354	354	309	305	264	264	264	264	264
Iron ore[c]	231	231	225	201	206	206	206	206	206
Coal[d]									
Standard coal	175	175	175	175	175	175	214	214	214
Raw coal	245	245	245	245	245	245	300	300	300
Limestone[e]	40	40	40	40	40	40	40	40	40

[a] For 1953-1956, the quantity of pig iron consumed per ton of open hearth steel is given in T'ung-chi Kung-tso (Statistical Work), no. 18, September, 1957, p. 33. The 1953 figure is also used for 1952, and the 1956 figure used for 1957. The 1959 figure of 846 kilograms is obtained by subtracting the 264 kilograms of scrap steel from the approximate national norm of metal consumption in 1959 or 1,110 kilograms, which is given in Chi-hua yü T'ung-chi (Planning and Statistics), no. 2, January, 1959, p. 6. The 1958 figure is interpolated on the basis of the 1957 and 1959 figures. The 1960 figure is obtained from total metal consumption in the same way as the 1959 estimate. The total metal consumption of 1,361 kilograms is a simple unweighted average of five mills, including the No. 1, No. 2, and No. 3 mills of Shanghai, the No. 1 mill of Ma-an-shan and one mill in Tientsin. The data are taken from various issues of Kung-jen Jih-pao (Workers' Daily), Chieh-fang Jih-pao (Liberation Daily), and Ho-pei Jih-pao (Hopei Daily) in 1961.

[b] For 1953-1956, the amount of scrap steel input is given in Chi-hua Ching-chi (Planned Economy), no. 4, April 1957, p. 15. No data are available for the other years. In the table we have used the 1953 and 1956 figures for 1952 and 1957-1960, respectively. Although a steady decline in scrap steel was noted during 1953-1956 along with a concomitant drop in pig iron consumption, it is doubtful that this gradual improvement in material consumption was continued after 1958, as may be seen in the general increase in metal input (including both pig iron and scrap steel) reported in 1959-1960.

A cross-check of scrap steel and pig iron consumption may also be made by comparing their total weight with the quantity of metal consumed per ton of open hearth steel reported in Major Aspects, op. cit., p. 35.

	1953	1954	1955	1956
	kilograms			
Total weight of pig iron and scrap steel	1,123	1,093	1,068	1,047
Metal consumption reported in Major Aspects	1,180	1,164	1,130	1,119

The small discrepancy between the two series may be due to the inclusion of the iron content of the ore under "metal consumption."

[c] For 1953-1956, see Yeh-chin Pao (Metallurgical Bulletin), no. 1, January 2, 1958, p. 34. No data are available for the remaining years. In the table we have used the 1953 and 1956 figures for 1952 and 1957-1960, respectively.

[d] Taken from Yuan-li Wu, Economic Development, op. cit., Chapter 6.

[e] The only information on limestone consumption is derived from Survey Report, op. cit., p. 660.

Table 4.6

INPUT PRICES IN STEEL MAKING
(current yuan per metric ton)

Material	1952	1957
Pig iron	200[a]	145[b]
Scrap steel	414[c]	300[d]
Iron ore[e]	39	28
Coal[f]	12.84	13.49
Limestone	5.00	3.63[g]

[a]Liu and Yeh, op. cit., Appendix F.

[b]Mean of 140 yuan and 150 yuan. Yeh-chin Pao, no. 1, January 2, 1958, p. 34.

[c]The price of steel in 1957 was 500 yuan per ton (Standard Railway Design and Budget Handbook, JPRS No. 10913, October 31, 1961, p. 33, rounded estimate) while that of scrap steel was 300 yuan. For 1952, the price of crude steel is therefore estimated at 690 yuan a ton under the assumption that the drop in its price in 1957 from the 1952 level was proportionately the same as that of pig iron (from 200 yuan to 145 yuan or 27.5 percent). It is then assumed that the relation between the prices of steel and scrap steel remained unchanged between 1952 and 1957.

[d]Yeh-chin Pao, no. 1, January 2, 1958, p. 35.

[e]See the estimates in the preceding section on pig iron.

[f]See Yuan-li Wu, Economic Development, op. cit., Chapter 6.

[g]Derived from the 1952 price by multiplying the latter by (1-0.275). See (c) above.

Finally, since no information is available on depreciation, this is simply taken to be 5 percent of the price per ton.

Tables 4.7 and 4.8 present the assembled information on the cost structure of open hearth steelmaking developed thus far and the corresponding gross and net value-added at 1952 and 1957 prices, respectively.

(2) Converter steel. According to some reports, the proportion of converter steel in Communist China's total steel output has risen steadily through the years. This would seem to be true if we consider the entire steel output, including that of the modified native furnaces such as the small side-blown converters prevalent since 1958. On the other hand, if these semimodern and native sectors are excluded, the increase in the share of converter steel in total output would not be as significant. In 1956, for instance, 14.5 percent of total steel production came from the converters, according to one source.[19] This is only slightly higher than the proportion of 12 percent based on operating-capacity estimates.[20] As far as the modern sector of steelmaking is concerned, therefore, converter steel played a subordinate role before 1958, and has probably played only a slightly more important part since that time.

The estimates of value-added in converter steelmaking considered here are confined to the modern sector only. The input coefficients in physical and value terms are tabulated in Table 4.9. Estimates of aggregate costs and values-added are given in Tables 4.10 and 4.11. With the exception of a few items explained in notes appended to the tables, the procedures followed in the individual estimates are the same as those employed in the preceding sections.

The Native and Semimodern Iron and Crude
Steel Subsectors

On the basis of what we have done in estimating the value-added in the modern iron and steel mills, we may now attempt to assess the corresponding values in the native and semimodern subsectors, which played an extremely important role in the spectacular quantitative increases in reported output during 1958-1960. Two steps must be taken in this connection. First, an adjustment must be made to allow for the poorer quality of the products, which was extremely serious in 1958 and only slightly less so in 1959-1960. Second, the

Table 4.7

PRICE, COST, AND VALUE-ADDED PER METRIC TON OF OPEN HEARTH STEEL, MODERN SECTOR[a]

1952 Yuan

		1952	1953	1954	1955	1956	1957	1958	1959	1960
I.	Price	690.00	690.00	690.00	690.00	690.00	690.00	690.00	690.00	690.00
II.	Cost of materials and fuel									
	Pig iron	153.80	153.80	156.80	152.60	156.60	156.60	163.00	169.20	219.40
	Scrap steel	146.56	146.56	127.93	126.27	109.30	109.30	109.30	109.30	109.30
	Iron ore	9.01	9.01	8.78	7.84	8.03	8.03	8.03	8.03	8.03
	Limestone	0.20	0.20	0.20	0.20	0.20	0.20	0.20	0.20	0.20
	Coal	3.15	3.15	3.15	3.15	3.15	3.15	3.85	3.85	3.85
	Subtotal	312.72	312.72	296.86	290.06	277.28	277.28	284.38	290.58	340.78
III.	Electricity	1.43	1.75	1.68	1.64	1.60	1.41	1.41	1.41	1.41
IV.	Transportation	10.95	10.95	10.39	10.15	9.70	9.70	9.95	10.17	11.93
V.	Other miscellaneous nonlabor cost	0.20	0.19	0.13	0.10	0.08	0.06	0.06	0.05	0.05
VI.	Total cost excluding wages and depreciation	325.30	325.61	309.06	301.95	288.66	288.45	295.80	302.21	354.17
VII.	Depreciation	34.50	34.50	34.50	34.50	34.50	34.50	34.50	34.50	34.50
VIII.	Gross value-added (I-VI)	364.70	364.39	380.94	388.05	401.34	401.55	394.20	387.79	335.83
IX.	Net value-added (VIII-VII)	330.20	329.89	346.44	353.55	366.84	367.05	359.70	353.29	301.33

[a]Derived from Tables 4.5 and 4.6. See also text.

109

Table 4.7 (continued)

					1957 Yuan					
		1952	1953	1954	1955	1956	1957	1958	1959	1960
I.	Price	500.00	500.00	500.00	500.00	500.00	500.00	500.00	500.00	500.00
II.	Cost of materials and fuel									
	Pig iron	111.51	111.51	113.68	110.64	113.54	113.54	118.18	122.67	159.07
	Scrap steel	106.20	106.20	92.70	91.50	79.20	79.20	79.20	79.20	79.20
	Iron ore	6.47	6.47	6.30	5.63	5.77	5.77	5.77	5.77	5.77
	Limestone	0.15	0.15	0.15	0.15	0.15	0.15	0.15	0.15	0.15
	Coal	3.31	3.31	3.31	3.31	3.31	3.31	4.05	4.05	4.05
	Subtotal	227.64	227.64	216.14	211.23	201.97	201.97	207.35	211.84	248.24
III.	Electricity	1.19	1.45	1.40	1.36	1.33	1.17	1.17	1.17	1.17
IV.	Transportation	7.97	7.97	7.56	7.39	7.07	7.07	7.26	7.41	8.69
V.	Other miscellaneous nonlabor cost	0.20	0.19	0.13	0.10	0.08	0.06	0.06	0.05	0.05
VI.	Total cost excluding wages and depreciation	237.00	237.00	225.23	220.08	210.45	210.27	215.84	220.47	258.15
VII.	Depreciation	25.00	25.00	25.00	25.00	25.00	25.00	25.00	25.00	25.00
VIII.	Gross value-added (I-VI)	263.00	262.75	274.77	279.92	289.55	289.73	284.16	279.53	241.85
IX.	Net value-added (VIII-VII)	238.00	237.75	249.77	254.92	264.55	264.73	259.16	254.53	216.85

110

Table 4.8

VALUE OUTPUT, COSTS, AND VALUE-ADDED IN OPEN HEARTH STEEL PRODUCTION*

Million 1952 Yuan[a]

	1952 (a)	1952 (b)	1953	1954	1955	1956 (a)	1956 (b)	1957	1958	1959	1960
I. Production value	716.2	765.9	942.5	1,182.0	1,515.9	2,372.2	2,215.6	2,842.8	4,250.4	4,585.1	6,337.0
II. Cost of materials and fuel	324.6	347.1	427.2	508.5	637.3	953.3	890.3	1,142.4	1,751.8	1,930.9	3,129.7
III. Electricity	1.5	1.6	2.4	2.9	3.6	5.5	5.1	5.8	8.7	9.4	12.9
IV. Transportation	11.4	12.1	15.0	17.8	22.3	33.4	31.2	40.0	61.3	67.6	109.5
V. Other miscellaneous nonlabor cost	0.2	0.2	0.3	0.2	0.2	0.3	0.3	0.2	0.4	0.3	0.5
VI. Total cost excluding wages and depreciation	337.7	361.0	444.9	529.4	663.4	992.5	926.9	1,188.4	1,822.2	2,008.2	3,252.6
VII. Depreciation	35.8	38.3	47.1	59.1	75.8	118.6	110.8	142.1	212.5	229.3	316.9
VIII. Gross value-added (I-VI)	378.5	404.9	497.6	652.6	852.5	1,379.7	1,288.7	1,654.2	2,428.2	2,576.9	3,084.4
IX. Net value-added (VIII-VII)	342.7	366.6	450.5	593.5	776.7	1,261.1	1,177.9	1,512.3	2,215.7	2,347.7	2,767.5

*All figures rounded to one-tenth million.

[a]See note which appears in the continuation of this table.

Table 4.8 (continued)

	Million 1957 Yuan											
	1952		1953	1954	1955	1956		1957	1958	1959	1960
	(a)	(b)				(a)	(b)				
I. Production value	519.0	555.0	683.0	856.5	1,098.5	1,719.0	1,605.5	2,056.0	3,080.0	3,322.5	4,592.0
II. Cost of materials and fuel	236.3	252.7	311.0	370.2	464.1	694.4	648.5	832.1	1,277.3	1,407.7	2,279.8
III. Electricity	1.2	1.3	2.0	2.4	3.0	4.6	4.3	4.8	7.2	7.8	10.7
IV. Transportation	8.3	8.8	10.9	13.0	16.2	24.3	22.7	29.1	44.7	49.3	79.8
V. Other miscellaneous nonlabor cost	0.2	0.2	0.3	0.2	0.2	0.3	0.3	0.2	0.4	0.3	0.5
VI. Total cost excluding wages and depreciation	246.0	263.0	324.2	385.8	483.5	723.6	675.8	866.2	1,329.6	1,465.1	2,370.8
VII. Depreciation	26.0	27.7	34.2	42.8	54.9	86.0	80.3	103.0	154.0	166.1	229.6
VIII. Gross value-added (I-VI)	273.0	292.0	358.8	470.7	615.0	995.4	929.7	1,193.8	1,750.4	1,857.4	2,221.2
IX. Net value-added (VIII-VII)	247.0	264.3	324.6	427.9	560.1	909.4	849.4	1,090.8	1,596.4	1,691.3	1,991.6

[a]The open hearth output series employed in the above computation is as follows (thousand metric tons):

1952		1953	1954	1955	1956		1957	1958	1959	1960
(a)	(b)				(a)	(b)				
1,038	1,110	1,366	1,713	2,197	3,438	3,211	4,120	6,160	6,645	9,184

The data, except those indicated by (b) are estimated at 77 percent of the total steel output for 1952–1959. Cf. Survey Report, Chart 5. See also Chapter 2. The (b) figures are derived on the basis that 82.3 percent of total crude steel production in 1952 and 71.9 percent in 1956 were from open hearth furnaces. See Yeh-chin Pao, no. 1, January 2, 1958, p. 35.
For unit price and cost data, see Table 4.7.

112

Table 4.9

MATERIAL INPUT COEFFICIENTS PER METRIC TON
OF CONVERTER INGOT STEEL
(in kilograms)

Material	1952	1953	1954	1955	1956	1957	1958	1959	1960
Pig iron[a]	1,230	1,184	1,172	1,159	1,179	1,179	1,239	1,299	1,359
Scrap steel[a]	78	75	75	74	75	75	79	83	87
Limestone[b]	30	30	30	30	30	30	30	30	30
Lime[b]	4	4	4	4	4	4	4	4	4
Coke[c]	150	150	159	143	144	144	144	144	144

[a]The pig iron and scrap steel inputs are derived from total metal consumption per ton of converter steel by employing the ratio obtained between the two items at Ta-yeh in 1953, where 1,075 kilograms of pig iron and 70 kilograms of scrap steel--a ratio of 94 percent to 6 percent--were used in combination. Cf. Survey Report, op. cit., p. 647. The data of total metal consumption, in kilograms, are:

1952	1953	1954	1955	1956	1957	1958	1959	1960
1,308	1,259	1,247	1,233	1,254	1,254	1,318	1,382	1,446

Of these, the figures for 1953-1956 are taken from Major Aspects, op. cit., p. 35. The 1956 figure is also used for 1957. The 1960 figure is an average of 24 plants, taken from Yeh-chin Pao, no. 9, March 4, 1960, pp. 43-44, and the April 11, 1960 issue of the same journal, pp. 14-15. The 1958-1959 estimates are interpolated from the 1957 and 1960 figures. It may also be noted that the corresponding total metal consumption figures in mills under the Ministry of Metallurgical Industry in 1953-1956 were somewhat lower than the preceding national averages given in this note. This is as one would expect, inasmuch as mills not under the Ministry were the smaller and less efficient ones. For comparison, the figures of the mills under the Ministry were as follows (in kilograms):

1953	1954	1955	1956
1,190	1,185	1,161	1,160

Cf. Yeh-chin Pao, no. 1, January 2, 1958, p. 34.

[b]The only figures of limestone and lime inputs available are those at Ta-yeh. See Survey Report, op. cit., p. 660.

[c]T'ung-chi Kung-tso, no. 18, September 1957, p. 33. For details, see Yuan-li Wu, Economic Development, op. cit., on the use of energy resources.

Table 4.10

PRICE, COST, AND VALUE-ADDED PER METRIC TON OF CONVERTER STEEL

		1952 Yuan								
		1952	1953	1954	1955	1956	1957	1958	1959	1960
I.	Price	690.00	690.00	690.00	690.00	690.00	690.00	690.00	690.00	690.00
II.	Cost of materials and fuel[a]									
	Pig iron	246.00	236.80	234.40	231.80	235.80	235.80	247.80	259.80	271.80
	Scrap steel	32.29	31.05	31.05	30.64	31.05	31.05	32.71	34.36	36.02
	Limestone	0.15	0.15	0.15	0.15	0.15	0.15	0.15	0.15	0.15
	Lime[b]	0.22	0.22	0.22	0.22	0.22	0.22	0.22	0.22	0.22
	Coke	6.60	6.60	7.00	6.29	6.34	6.34	6.34	6.34	6.34
	Subtotal	285.26	274.82	272.82	269.10	273.56	273.56	287.22	300.87	314.53
III.	Electricity	1.98	2.44	2.32	2.28	2.24	1.96	1.96	1.96	1.96
IV.	Transportation	9.98	9.62	9.55	9.42	9.57	9.57	10.05	10.53	11.01
V.	Other miscellaneous nonlabor cost	0.31	0.28	0.19	0.15	0.11	0.08	0.07	0.08	0.08
VI.	Total cost excluding wages and depreciation	297.53	287.16	284.88	280.95	285.48	285.17	299.30	313.44	327.58
VII.	Depreciation	34.50	34.50	34.50	34.50	34.50	34.50	34.50	34.50	34.50
VIII.	Gross value-added (I-VI)	392.47	402.84	405.12	409.05	404.52	404.83	390.70	376.56	362.42
IX.	Net value-added (VIII-VII)	357.97	368.34	370.62	374.55	370.02	370.33	356.20	342.06	327.92

[a]For prices and input coefficients, see Tables 4.6 and 4.9.

[b]The price of lime was 55.2 yuan per ton in 1952 and 40 yuan per ton in 1957 under the assumption that the change in price between 1952 and 1957 was in the same proportion as that of pig iron. Cf. Kang-t'ieh, no. 1, January 1958, p. 14.

114

Table 4.10 (continued)

| | | 1957 Yuan | | | | | | | | |
		1952	1953	1954	1955	1956	1957	1958	1959	1960
I.	Price	500.00	500.00	500.00	500.00	500.00	500.00	500.00	500.00	500.00
II.	Cost of materials and fuel									
	Pig iron	178.35	171.68	169.94	168.06	170.96	170.96	179.66	188.36	197.06
	Scrap steel	23.40	22.50	22.50	22.20	22.50	22.50	23.70	24.90	26.10
	Limestone	0.11	0.11	0.11	0.11	0.11	0.11	0.11	0.11	0.11
	Lime	0.16	0.16	0.16	0.16	0.16	0.16	0.16	0.16	0.16
	Coke	6.93	6.93	7.35	6.61	6.65	6.65	6.65	6.65	6.65
	Subtotal	208.95	201.38	200.06	197.14	200.38	200.38	210.28	220.18	230.08
III.	Electricity	1.67	2.02	1.95	1.90	1.85	1.62	1.63	1.62	1.62
IV.	Transportation	7.31	7.05	7.00	6.90	7.01	7.01	7.36	7.71	8.05
V.	Other miscellaneous nonlabor cost	0.31	0.28	0.19	0.15	0.11	0.08	0.07	0.08	0.08
VI.	Total cost excluding wages and depreciation	218.24	210.73	209.20	206.09	209.35	209.09	219.34	229.59	239.83
VII.	Depreciation	25.00	25.00	25.00	25.00	25.00	25.00	25.00	25.00	25.00
VIII.	Gross value-added (I-VI)	281.76	289.27	290.80	293.91	290.65	290.91	280.66	270.41	260.17
IX.	Net value-added (VIII-VII)	256.76	264.27	265.80	268.91	265.65	265.91	255.66	245.41	235.17

Table 4.11

VALUE OUTPUT, COSTS, AND VALUE-ADDED IN CONVERTER STEEL PRODUCTION

Million 1952 Yuan

	1952 (a)	1952 (b)	1953	1954	1955	1956 (a)	1956 (b)	1957 (a)	1957 (b)	1958	1959	1960
I. Production value	111.78	66.93	146.97	184.23	235.98	369.84	447.12	442.98	549.93	662.40	714.84	987.39
II. Cost of materials and fuel	46.21	27.67	58.54	72.84	92.03	146.63	177.27	175.63	218.00	275.73	311.70	450.09
III. Electricity	0.32	0.19	0.52	0.62	0.78	1.20	1.45	1.26	1.56	1.88	2.03	2.81
IV. Transportation	1.62	0.97	2.05	2.55	3.22	5.13	6.20	6.14	7.63	9.65	10.91	15.76
V. Other miscellaneous nonlabor cost	0.05	0.03	0.06	0.05	0.05	0.06	0.07	0.05	0.06	0.07	0.08	0.11
VI. Total cost excluding wages and depreciation	48.20	28.86	61.17	76.06	96.08	153.02	184.99	183.08	227.25	287.33	324.72	468.77
VII. Depreciation	5.59	3.35	7.35	9.21	11.80	18.49	22.36	22.15	27.50	33.12	35.74	49.37
VIII. Gross value-added (I-VI)	63.58	38.07	85.80	108.17	139.90	216.82	262.13	259.90	322.68	375.07	390.12	518.62
IX. Net value-added (VIII-VII)	57.99	34.72	78.45	98.96	128.10	198.33	239.77	237.75	295.19	341.95	354.38	469.25

Table 4.11 (continued)

Million 1957 Yuan

	1952 (a)	1952 (b)	1953	1954	1955	1956 (a)	1956 (b)	1957 (a)	1957 (b)	1958	1959	1960
I. Production value	81.00	48.50	106.50	133.50	171.00	268.00	324.00	321.00	398.50	480.00	518.00	715.50
II. Cost of materials and fuel	33.85	20.27	42.89	53.42	67.42	107.40	129.85	128.64	159.70	201.87	228.11	329.24
III. Electricity	0.27	0.16	0.43	0.52	0.65	0.99	1.20	1.04	1.29	1.56	1.68	2.32
IV. Transportation	1.18	0.71	1.50	1.87	2.36	3.76	4.54	4.50	5.59	7.07	7.99	11.52
V. Other miscellaneous nonlabor cost	0.05	0.03	0.06	0.05	0.05	0.06	0.07	0.05	0.06	0.07	0.08	0.11
VI. Total cost excluding wages and depreciation	35.35	21.17	44.88	55.86	70.48	112.21	135.66	134.23	166.64	210.57	237.86	343.19
VII. Depreciation	4.05	2.43	5.33	6.68	8.55	13.40	16.20	16.05	19.93	24.00	25.90	35.78
VIII. Gross value-added (I-VI)	45.65	27.33	61.62	77.64	100.52	155.79	188.34	186.77	231.86	269.43	280.14	372.31
IX. Net value-added (VIII-VII)	41.60	24.90	56.29	70.96	91.97	142.39	172.14	170.72	211.93	245.43	254.24	336.53

Notes and Sources: The converter output series employed in the above computation is as follows (thousand metric tons):

	1952 (a)	1952 (b)	1953	1954	1955	1956 (a)	1956 (b)	1957 (a)	1957 (b)	1958	1959	1960
	162	97	213	267	342	536	648	642	797	960	1,036	1,431

The (a) figures and those without notation are estimated at 12% of total steel output. Cf. Survey Report, Chart 5.
The (b) estimates are derived from the following:

Year	Converter Output as Percent of Total	Source
1952	7.18	Note (a), Table 4.8
1956	14.50	Same
1957	14.90	Same

117

generally far less efficient operation of the semimodern furnaces and the grossly inefficient performance of the native furnaces must be considered. Some reasonable approximation may then be expected in estimating the net contribution of the native and semimodern subsectors of the iron and steel industry to the national product. This will also serve to cast light on the effectiveness of the entire "backyard furnace" movement of the "Great Leap Forward" of 1958-1959, the general economic effect of which has already been described elsewhere.[21]

Pig iron. (1) Question of quality. Starting with pig iron, the focal point of the "backyard furnace" movement in 1958, we should note immediately that there is an unusual paucity of statistical data relating to the usefulness and quality of native iron produced in that year. Of course, the poor quality of the native iron--its brittleness and unsuitability for steelmaking--has not been disputed even by official Chinese sources. Segregation of the native iron component in 1959 from the total output reported in 1958 was itself informal recognition of the inferior and unreliable quality of the product. There have also been many officially inspired reports on measures to improve quality.[22] On the other hand, reports by non-Chinese visitors have sometimes gone so far as to suggest that the entire native iron output was useful only as ballast, which is to say that it was completely useless for further fabrication. Yet the fact that some of the native smelters of 1958 were converted into semimodern blast furnaces in 1959 and that some of the pig iron was used by the modern mills in steelmaking would argue against such a wholesale dismissal of the native iron output. The problem here, therefore, is to measure the average proportion of this off-grade material that can be used for one purpose or another and its equivalent value in terms of the output of the modern mills.

Writing in 1960 and referring to prevailing conditions at the time and probably also in the latter part of 1959, K. P. Wang stated that more than 80 percent of the small-scale simple furnaces of 6 to 30 cubic meters met quality specifications.[23] Sporadic official reports occasionally offer an even more favorable picture. For instance, a "red banner" small furnace at Ch'ang-ning (Hunan) was said to have met standard specifications in over 90 percent of its product in mid-1960.[24] Other small furnaces in Szechwan were also reported to have topped the target ratio of 90 percent at about that time.[25] Furthermore, of seven efficient semimodern furnaces mentioned in a <u>Metallurgical Bulletin</u> report around the first quarter of 1960, six reported 100-percent compliance with grade specifications, while 81 percent was reportedly attained by the seventh.[26] From the above, it seems that 90 percent was a target rate reached only by furnaces that won special mention in emulation contests and that even 80 percent was probably well above the average accomplishment.

Still more arguments can be marshalled that would point to even lower proportions of up-to-grade material in the total output of the semimodern furnaces, and, <u>a fortiori</u>, in that of the native furnaces in 1958. First, in view of the generally lower technological level of the semimodern mills, the quality of their output is more likely to be comparable to that of the least efficient units among the modern mills than to that of the more efficient modern mills. In this respect, again according to the <u>Metallurgical Bulletin</u>,[27] of ten modern blast furnaces observed during 1959, the lowest ratio of grade-level output was 73.55 percent reported at the No. 1 mill of the Lung-yen Iron and Steel Company. A somewhat later report[28] of the same journal gave 77.03 percent for the T'ai-yüan Iron and Steel Company in March, 1960, and 69.22 percent for the same No. 1 mill at Lung-yen. The data suggest that an even lower ratio may have been obtained at the No. 2 mill of Lung-yen. In contrast, the best up-to-grade ratio reported for the large blast furnaces at the end of 1959 was 99.66 percent at the Pen-ch'i No. 2 Iron and Steel Works. This compares with a record of nearly 100 percent at the Shih-ching-shan mill in the first quarter of 1960. At first glance, it is hard to believe that the small semimodern furnaces of 1959 and later vintage, not to mention the native makeshift installations of 1958, could even approach the performance of the least efficient modern furnaces in 1959-1960. In round numbers and giving the Chinese native and semimodern mills every benefit of the doubt, we should probably assume that no more than 70 percent of the output of the semimodern mills of 1959 and 1960 was up to grade and that, therefore, a minimum 30-percent discount of the reported pig iron output of the semimodern mills beginning in 1959 should be taken as an allowance for inferior quality.

Of course, one could argue against such a treatment by assuming that off-grade iron from the semimodern furnaces can still be used for certain purposes. While this may be true in the case of off-grade products of the large

119

modern mills, serious doubt must be entertained in dealing with that of the semimodern mills. By the same token, a minimum discount of 30 percent should be applied to the native iron output of 1958. In the latter case, we can only err in being too conservative.

An additional consideration lending support to the contention that ours is still a conservative estimate is that no allowance has been made so far for a possible drop of the standard of the original specifications. If the up-to-grade ratio is to be meaningful, the grade itself must remain constant. This may not have been the case as far as the output of the semimodern mills was concerned; it was in all probability not the case during 1958 when only native iron was produced.

(2) Cost estimates. Turning now to the question of the cost of producing iron in the small native and semimodern furnaces, we may note the following points. First, in the case of most native furnaces operated in 1958, proper cost accounting was almost certainly nonexistent. When part-time labor was used to tend these furnaces, absence of additional monetary payment might easily result in not accounting for some of the labor cost. The same consideration applies to some of the raw materials obtained "free" such as the pots and pans, railings, and door frames, etc., taken from the population as raw materials. On the other hand, mining was in some instances undertaken simultaneously with smelting by the same work teams so that some of the mining cost may have been included in that of iron making.

More cost figures, however, are available in the case of the semi-modern mills initiated later, thus indicating the existence of at least a rudimentary accounting system. However, such production cost statistics as are available exhibit wide variations. This is partly to be explained by the lack of uniform accounting practices. Discrepancies in scale and in the degree of continuity of operation, as well as wide differences in technical standards and in the quality and kind of the raw materials and fuels used, also contribute to a high variability. In the absence of data on the capacity and output of individual plants corresponding to the individual cost figures on hand, any estimate of a representative figure for the entire native and semimodern iron-making industry is subject to greater uncertainty than is usually the case in dealing with Communist Chinese statistics.

In a discussion on the production cost of native furnaces in the Wan-hsien Special District, Szechwan, in 1958,[29] the per ton cost of native iron was given at around 115 yuan in the case of furnaces possessing a daily capacity exceeding one ton. Furnaces of one-half to one-ton daily capacity reported per ton costs varying from 170 to 250 yuan. In both instances, however, operation was "normal." On the other hand, if operation was intermittent, the unit production cost was in general higher than 450 yuan; in individual cases, it even reached a high of 1,400 yuan.

Certain pledges to keep production cost down were given at a national conference of the operators of small blast furnaces held in September, 1959. These cost ceilings, which are reproduced below, again exhibit a wide range extending from a low of 120 yuan to a high of 300 yuan per ton.[30]

Area	Cost ceiling pledges in current yuan per metric ton
An-shan, Wu-han, and Lung-yen (small blast furnaces only)	120
Yunnan	180
Hunan and Kweichow	200
Hopeh, Kiangsu, Shansi, and Szechwan	220
Anhwei, Honan, Shantung, and Inner Mongolia	250
Chekiang, Fukien, Hupeh, Kiangsi, Kwangsi, Kwangtung, Liaoning, and Ningsia	280
Heilungkiang, Kansu, Kirin, Shensi, Sinkiang, and Tsinghai	300

The median value of these seven pledges is 220 yuan, while the mean of the twenty-eight areas reporting, disregarding their differences in size and hence in blast furnace capacity, is 245 yuan. If we exclude An-shan, Wu-han, and Lung-yen, where performance of the small furnaces probably benefited from the availability of skilled labor with technical know-how in the large modern mills and other external economies, the mean, weighted by provinces, would then be about 252 yuan. As an indicator of the average per ton cost of the small native furnaces which by 1959 were still in operation, though they probably represented the more efficient and at least partially improved models, we may perhaps take the 245-yuan figure as representative.

Additional unit cost data applicable to the semimodern mills in operation in late 1959 and early 1960 present a far more favorable picture. According to the Metallurgical Bulletin,[31] forty-eight such iron works, excluding a model "Leap Forward" furnace which purportedly had a unit cost of 76. 80 yuan only, reported in March, 1960, unit production costs that ranged from 94 to 150 yuan. The mean is 129. 7 yuan; the standard error of estimate is 2. 37 yuan; at 95-percent-confidence interval, the range may be placed between 125 and 134 yuan. The order of magnitude involved in this instance is substantially lower than the 220 (median) or 245 (mean) yuan of the pledged maximum costs for the native furnaces. Until more accurate estimates can be made, we shall tentatively use these figures as the unit costs of producing pig iron in the semimodern furnaces in 1959 and 1960. We shall also use 245 yuan as the representative unit cost of native pig iron in 1958. Since no significant price changes in the inputs involved have been reported in 1957-1960, we shall assume that these figures, given in current prices, may also be treated as if they were 1957 prices.

According to a Szechwan report, the cost structure of a small native furnace of one-ton daily capacity, in normal operation from June 1 to October 20, 1958, included the following:[32]

Item	Percent
Raw materials	52
Fuel	27
Production workers' wages	15
Supplementary payments	0. 17
Workshop expenses	5

If the last item is regarded as entirely deductible in computing value-added, the total deductible cost, excluding depreciation, which is probably not allowed for, would be 84 percent of production cost. Depreciation, however, was quite rapid in such cases, since the native furnaces were not durable. Thus 84 percent of the total cost would probably underestimate deductible cost in arriving at net value-added. Since the less efficient furnaces consumed more fuel and raw materials, explaining the high total costs, the proportion of deductible cost in total cost would be even higher for the native furnaces as a whole. It would not be unreasonable, therefore, to employ 84 percent as a minimum estimate of deductible cost in terms of the total production cost for both the native furnaces in 1958 and the semimodern furnaces in the later years. Applied to the cost figures discussed earlier, the deductible costs would be as follows:

Native furnaces, 84% of 245 yuan = 206 yuan
Semimodern furnaces, 84% of 125-134 yuan = 105-113 yuan

3. Value-added in native pig iron production. The above discussion has brought us to the point at which a rough estimate of value-added by the native pig iron sector since 1958 can be made. This is done by (a) discounting the unit price--145 yuan at 1957 prices--by 30 percent to allow for the useless portion of the output and (b) subtracting from the above 206 yuan in 1958 and 113 yuan in 1959-1960. As may be noted, we have discarded the lower estimate of 105 yuan for 1959-1960, since it is significantly below the estimated cost for modern mills in the same period. This procedure then gives us a gross value-added estimate per ton of pig iron of minus 104.5 yuan in 1958, and a corresponding value per ton of semimodern iron of minus 11.5 yuan in 1959-1960.

It will be recalled that the total production cost in 1958 per ton of pig iron, excluding wages and depreciation, has been estimated at about 113 yuan at 1957 prices and 142 yuan at 1952 prices. If the same ratio between the 1952 and the 1957 input costs for modern mills is used to inflate the estimated production costs of the native and semimodern furnaces so as to arrive at 1952 price base, the adjusted deductible costs at 1952 prices would be 142 yuan in 1959-1960 and 258 yuan in 1958. The corresponding gross value-added per ton would be minus 118 yuan in the case of the native iron of 1958 and minus 2 yuan in the case of the semimodern iron of 1959-1960. In any event, the contribution of the backyard furnace movement to national income was therefore worse than nil.

123

<u>Steel</u>. The question may now be raised as to whether the same nega-
tive result existed in the case of steelmaking in the native open hearth furnace
and the side-blown converters introduced since 1959. The following conflicting
considerations may be presented.

1. According to one report in <u>T'ung-chi Kung-tso</u>,[33] for each ton of
native steel it should be possible to use no more than 1.15 ton of pig iron. A
similar optimistic report published in the <u>People's Daily</u> of September 19, 1958,
stated that in an experimental small open hearth furnace, constructed by the
Northeast Industrial Engineering Institute, it was possible to produce a ton of
steel with not more than a ton of metal input. On the other hand, a different report at about the same time[34] stated that it was, on the whole, not possible to
produce steel ingot by native methods, since the latter could not provide high
enough furnace temperatures. Furthermore, as late as March, 1960,[35] it was
reported that the pig iron consumption of converters in fourteen provinces, presumably in 1959 and the first quarter of 1960, ranged from 1,365 kg. to 1,744
kg. per ton of steel, the median being 1,569 kg., i.e., considerably higher than
the average pig iron consumption of the converters in modern mills only. Again,
during 1960, according to Po I-po,[36] the unit input of pig iron required by converters ranged from 1,100 kg. in the more advanced enterprises to 1,500 kg. in
the technically backward enterprises, or even a little higher. From these reports, it would appear that the more optimistic statements of 1958 were either
sheer exaggeration or limited to experimental cases only, and that perhaps even
the 1960-1961 input estimates would be too low for 1958-1959.

The inadequacy of information on cost in steelmaking from the native
and semimodern furnaces leaves us with little choice. Some arbitrary, but
plausible, assumptions must therefore be made:

(1) For the semimodern furnaces, the deductible cost per ton in 1959-
1960 would be higher than that of the modern converters by a fraction not less
than that by which pig iron consumption by the semimodern furnaces exceeded
that by the modern converters--21 percent in 1959 and 15 percent in 1960,
using 1,569 kg. (median for 1959-60) as the pig iron input coefficient of the
semimodern furnaces.[37]

(2) For the native furnaces, the deductible cost per ton in 1958 would

124

be higher than that of the modern converters by a fraction not less than that by which the least efficient average pig iron consumption of the fourteen provinces in 1960 (1,744 kg.), reported earlier, would exceed that of the modern converters (1,239 kg. in 1958). The last figure was 41 percent.

It is also necessary to make an arbitrary decision on the extent of the off-grade portion of the output that was so useless that it was discarded completely. The position we propose to take requires the following additional assumptions:

(3) In 1958-1960, the portion of waste in the output of the native and semimodern converters was not less than that of the semimodern blast furnaces, that is, 30 percent. (4) The output of the native furnaces in 1958, though nominally described as steel, was actually indistinguishable from iron and should therefore be treated as such with respect to its price.

The preceding four assumptions provide us, therefore, with the following cost and gross value output figures:

Year	Price per Ton Produced		Deductible Cost (Excluding Depreciation)
1958	1952 price:	70% of 200 yuan or 140 yuan	1952 prices: 141% of 299.30 yuan or 422.0 yuan
	1957 price:	70% of 145 yuan or 101.5 yuan	1957 prices: 141% of 219.34 yuan or 309.3 yuan
1959	1952 price:	70% of 690 yuan or 483 yuan	1952 prices: 121% or 313.44 yuan or 379.3 yuan
	1957 price:	70% of 500 yuan or 350 yuan	1957 prices: 121% of 229.59 yuan or 277.8 yuan
1960	Same as in 1959		1952 prices: 115% of 327.58 yuan or 376.7 yuan
			1957 prices: 115% of 239.83 yuan or 275.8 yuan

The gross value-added estimates may now be derived as follows:

Year	1952 Prices	1957 Prices
	(yuan per metric ton)	
1958	-282.0	-207.8
1959	103.7	72.2
1960	106.3	74.2

The aggregates.   The preceding separate estimates of gross value-added in the native iron and steel subsectors in 1958-1960 may now be aggregated, simply by multiplying the per ton estimates by the output data given in Appendix B. The latter are:

Year	Output of Native (1958) and Semimodern (1959-60) Furnaces (in million metric tons)	
	Pig iron	Crude steel
1958	4.16	3.08
1959	11.00	4.72
1960	14.80	6.45

The corresponding gross value-added estimates are, in rounded values:

Sector	1952 Yuan (millions)			1957 Yuan (millions)		
	1958	1959	1960	1958	1959	1960
Native and semimodern pig iron	-491	-22	-30	-435	-127	-170
Native and semimodern steel	-869	490	687	-640	341	479
	-1,360	468	657	-1,075	214	309

It is not possible, however, to derive from the above figures estimates of net value-added by subtracting some simple estimate of depreciation. The

126

reason lies in the great variance of the types of furnaces built during the initial period and lack of construction cost data throughout the entire three-year period. For instance, in iron smelting, a simple Ying-ch'ao type furnace of 1- to 2-cubic-meter capacity with a daily "designed" output of 1 to 2 tons was said to cost only 400 yuan to build[38] while a more "mechanized" type, also of no more than 1 to 3 cubic meters in capacity, would cost 3,000 yuan in construction cost.[39] At the other extreme, however, an 8-cubic-meter semimodern furnace at Chou-k'ou-tien cost as much as 100,000 yuan to build.[40] In steelmaking too, similar illustrations can be cited. Thus, a very small converter (load capacity, 100 kg. only) was built in Shansi in 1958 at 5,000 yuan while the most primitive types, which consisted of a simple brick structure equipped with a one-half horsepower blower, were obviously one-man construction jobs that could be accomplished in a few hours at the most and would cost very little.[41] On the whole, however, the cheaper constructions probably dominated the field, at least through most of 1959, while the low initial investment was partly offset by a very short useful life. One might, however, assume that on balance the net result would be a rather low depreciation per ton which, when compared with the much higher total production cost, can perhaps be safely disregarded for 1958. On the other hand, for 1959-1960, we shall continue to use the same depreciation rate as in the case of the modern mills, i.e., 5 percent of the product price. If our assumption is in error, the result would be an overestimate of the already negative net value-added in 1958. In this manner, we arrive at the estimates given in Table 4.12.

An Appraisal and Some Conclusions

A Second Look at Value-added in the Iron and Steel Industry

What would happen if we were to aggregate our incomplete estimates for the various subsectors of the iron and steel industry and combine them with approximate estimates of the remaining subsectors, most of which can be derived from the study by Liu and Yeh? The subsectors that have been discussed in detail are:

(1) pig iron produced by modern mills, 1952-1960

127

Table 4.12

GROSS AND NET VALUE-ADDED IN NATIVE IRON AND STEEL, 1958-1960

| | 1952 Yuan, millions | | | 1957 Yuan, millions | | |
	1958	1959	1960	1958	1959	1960
Gross Value-added						
Iron	-491	-22	-30	-435	-127	-170
Steel	-869	490	687	-640	341	479
	-1,360	468	657	-1,075	214	309
Depreciation						
Iron	---	110	148	---	80	107
Steel	---	163	223	---	118	161
		273	371		198	268
Net Value-added						
Iron	-491	-132	-178	-435	-207	-277
Steel	-869	327	464	-640	223	318
Total	-1,360	195	286	-1,075	16	41

(2) crude, open hearth, and converter steel produced by modern mills, 1952-1960

(3) native and semimodern pig iron and steel, 1958-1960

The other major subsectors for which additional information is needed are:

(4) crude steel produced in electric furnaces

(5) iron ore

(6) coke

(7) finished-steel products

(8) native iron, 1952-1957

(9) manganese ore

For simplicity we shall estimate value-added in the production of electric furnace steel at the average rate of open hearth and converter steel, and adopt for the present the estimated deductible costs in percent of gross value output developed by Liu and Yeh in estimating items (5), (6), and (7), except that in the case of item (7) the adjusted figures based on Appendix C will be presented as an alternative. Item (9) is taken from the same study by Liu and Yeh. In the case of item (8), the unit value-added estimates of the modern mills will be tentatively used for 1952-1957, inasmuch as the native works of the pre-1958 period were more efficient than those during and after 1958 and the quantities involved were too small to warrant a more precise estimate. In this manner, the aggregate estimates of the six principal commodity groups would amount to the data in Table 4.13.

Several comments may be made immediately on the aggregate estimates of the values-added in the iron and steel industry as represented by the six commodity groups listed:

First, the totals are remarkably close to the estimate made earlier in this chapter on the basis of the official gross value output of the iron and steel industry and the principal purchases made from other sectors of the economy. Moreover, the discrepancies between the two sets of estimates are smaller when the finished-steel output is not adjusted for possible double counting due to the inclusion of semifinished products.[42] One may therefore use the "unadjusted" aggregate estimates as a reasonable approximation of the contribution of the iron and steel industry to the national product. The differences between the relevant series are given in Table 4.14.

Table 4.13

VALUE-ADDED IN THE IRON AND STEEL INDUSTRY, 1952–1957

(in million 1952 Yuan)

	Gross Value-added					
	1952	1953	1954	1955	1956	1957
I. Pig Iron						
(1) Modern	90.9	99.7	145.2	191.8	258.8	328.3
(2) Native	1.4	2.7	7.5	12.8	2.7	4.3
II. Ingot Steel						
(1) Open hearth	(a) 378.5 (b) 404.9	497.6	652.6	852.5	(a) 1,379.7 (b) 1,288.7	1,654.4
(2) Converter	(a) 63.6 (b) 38.1	85.8	108.2	139.9	(a) 216.8 (b) 262.1	(a) 259.9 (b) 322.7
(3) Electric	(a) 56.4 (b) 53.8	74.8	96.3	125.1	(a) 180.1 (b) 244.2	(a) 237.1 (b) 174.6
III. Finished Steel[a]						
(1) Unadjusted figures[b]	485.4	649.0	727.1	926.9	1,450.8	1,576.2
(2) Adjusted figures[c]	297.9	415.9	478.4	609.8	642.0	697.1
IV. Iron Ore[d]	140.5	190.1	231.4	305.8	495.9	628.1
V. Manganese Ore[e]	10	10	10	10	30	30
VI. Coke[f]	65.4	82.4	103.9	130.2	163.8	170.7
Total[g]						
(1) including III-1	(a) 1,292.2 (b) 1,290.4	1,692.1	2,082.1	2,695.0	(a) 4,178.6 (b) 4,197.0	(a) 4,889.0 (b) 4,889.2
(2) including III-2	(a) 1,104.6 (b) 1,102.8	1,459.0	1,833.5	2,377.9	(a) 3,369.8 (b) 3,388.2	(a) 4,009.8 (b) 4,010.1

Table 4.13 (continued)

				Net Value-added			
		1952	1953	1954	1955	1956	1957
I. Pig Iron							
	(1) Modern	71.9	77.9	115.6	155.5	211.0	269.7
	(2) Native	1.1	2.1	5.9	10.4	2.2	3.5
II. Ingot Steel		(a) (b)				(a) (b)	(a) (b)
	(1) Open hearth	342.7 366.6	450.5	593.5	776.7	1,261.1 1,177.9	1,512.3
	(2) Converter	58.0 34.7	78.5	99.0	128.1	198.3 239.8	237.8 295.2
	(3) Electric	51.3 48.9	68.1	87.8	114.3	180.9 223.3	216.8 159.6
III. Finished Steel							
	(1) Unadjusted figures	419.8	561.3	628.8	801.6	1,254.7	1,363.2
	(2) Adjusted figures	257.6	359.7	413.8	527.4	555.2	602.9
IV. Iron Ore		132.0	178.6	217.4	287.3	465.9	590.1
V. Manganese Ore		10	10	10	10	20	30
VI. Coke		59.1	74.5	93.9	117.7	148.1	154.3
Total[h]						(a) (b)	(a) (b)
	(1) including III-1	1,145.9	1,501.4	1,851.9	2,401.6	3,742.2 3,742.8	4,367.6 4,377.9
	(2) including III-2	983.7	1,299.8	1,636.9	2,127.3	3,042.7 3,043.3	3,607.3 3,617.6

131

Notes to Table 4.13

(a) Figures for finished steel represent 37 percent of the value output. See Liu and Yeh, op. cit., p. 644, and the first section of this chapter.

(b) Appendix B.

(c) Appendix C, adjusted.

(d) Figures for iron ore represent 82.6 percent of value output. Cf. Liu and Yeh, op. cit., p. 736, and the first section of this chapter.

(e) Liu and Yeh, op. cit., p. 741.

(f) Figures for coke represent 52 percent of 44 yuan per ton times coke output of the given years.

(g) For further comparison the gross value output of the same six categories is as follows (million 1952 yuan):

	1952	1953	1954	1955		1956		1957
Gross value Output								
(1) Unadjusted	2,940	3,820	4,620	5,880		8,920		10,260
(2) Adjusted	2,440	3,190	3,940	5,020		6,740		7,880
Total (1), in percent of gross value output	(a)	(b)			(a)	(b)	(a)	(b)
(1)	44.0	43.9	44.3	45.1	45.8 46.8	47.1	47.7	47.7
Total (2), in percent of gross value output								
(2)	45.3	45.2	45.7	46.5	47.4 50.0	50.3	50.9	47.9

For unadjusted gross value output, see the first section of this chapter.

The adjusted gross value output is derived from this chapter and Appendix C where the adjusted finished-steel output is given.

(h) For further comparison, the gross value output of the same six categories is as follows (million 1952 yuan):

	1952	1953	1954	1955		1956		1957
Gross value Output								
(1) Unadjusted	2,940	3,820	4,620	5,880		8,920		10,260
(2) Adjusted	2,440	3,190	3,940	5,020		6,740		7,880
Total (1) in percent of gross value output (1)	(a) 39.0	(b) 38.9	39.3	40.1	(a) 40.8 42.0	(b) 42.0	(a) 42.6	(b) 42.7
Total (2) in percent of of gross value output (2)	40.3	40.2	40.7	41.5	42.4 45.1	45.2	45.8	45.9

132

Table 4.14

COMPARISON OF THE ESTIMATES OF THE GROSS VALUE-ADDED
OF THE IRON AND STEEL INDUSTRY, 1952-1957
(million 1952 Yuan)

Year	I Based on the Official Gross Value Output	II Based on Six Commodity Groups, "Finished-Steel" Output Unadjusted		III Based on Six Commodity Groups, "Finished-Steel" Output Adjusted		$\frac{\text{I-II}}{\text{I}}$	$\frac{\text{I-III}}{\text{I}}$
						(percent)	
1952	1,212	(a)	1,292	(a)	1,105	-6.6	8.8
		(b)	1,290	(b)	1,103	-6.4	9.0
1953	1,679		1,692		1,459	-0.8	13.1
1954	2,084		2,082		1,834	0.1	12.0
1955	2,602		2,695		2,378	-5.8	8.6
1956	(a) 3,725	(a)	4,179	(a)	3,370	-12.2	9.5
	(b) 3,728	(b)	4,197	(b)	3,388	-12.6	9.1
1957	(a) 4,721	(a)	4,889	(a)	4,010	-3.6	15.1
	(b) 4,717	(b)	4,889	(b)	4,010	-3.6	15.0

Source: Data derived from Table 4.13 and page 97 of Chapter 4.

Second, a comparison may be made between the percent ratio of the gross value-added in the value output of Communist China's iron and steel industry and the corresponding ratios in the Soviet Union and the United States, respectively. During 1952-1957, the Chinese ratio was between 44 and 48 percent;[43] the corresponding ratio in the Soviet Union, including both ferrous metallurgy and the mining of ferrous ores, was between 44.4 and 45.2 percent.[44] For the United States during 1946-1961, the ratio was about 55 percent.[45] Discrepancy between the ratios would reflect not only technological differences, but also different relative prices between outputs and inputs and different product mixes.

For some individual commodities, the Chinese ratios are very close to those of the United States. For instance, in the case of pig iron, the Chinese ratio varied from 22.9 percent in 1953 to 28.9 percent in 1960 (based on 1952 yuan); the United States 1954 census ratio cited by Nutter was 22.62 percent.[46] For steel ingot and castings, the 1954 United States ratio was 63.8 percent; the corresponding Chinese ratio varied from a low of 48.7 percent for open hearth steel in 1960 to 58.2 percent in 1957. The ratios for converter steel fluctuated between 52.5 percent in 1960 and 59.3 percent in 1955. The ratios for iron ore were again close: 79.62 percent in the United States in 1954; 82.6 percent in Communist China. Thus one principal reason for the lower over-all Chinese ratio for the entire industry seems to be the lower ratios at the more advanced stages of production. One suspects that this phenomenon is largely a result of the greater weight of ordinary- and low-quality products in the Chinese product mix, aggravated by inefficiency in the use of raw materials.

Wages and Productivity

A number of other interesting conclusions may be deduced from our findings. One of these is the relative importance of wages as a measure of the workers' share in the output of such a key industry which, according to official statistics, accounted for 8 percent of the country's modern industrial output in 1957. For 1952-1956 the number of workers in the iron and steel industry and their annual wages in yuan can be obtained from Major Aspects. The total wage bill can therefore be computed and expressed as a percent of the gross value-

Table 4.15

THE SHARE OF WAGES IN THE PRODUCT
OF THE IRON AND STEEL INDUSTRY

	Percent of Wages in Gross Value-added	
Year	(a) Series with unadjusted finished steel	(b) Series with adjusted finished steel
1952	9.6	11.3
1953	10.2	11.8
1954	8.6	9.8
1955	7.1	8.0
1956	5.8	7.2

Notes and Sources: The values-added are derived from Table 4.13. The wage bill estimates are obtained from the following employment and annual wage per worker (Major Aspects, op. cit., p. 45):

	1952	1953	1954	1955	1956
Number of workers in the iron and steel industry	211,587	254,109	261,521	276,902	304,269
Annual wage in yuan	587.4	679.2	686.2	691.3	797.8
Total wage bill in million yuan	124.3	172.6	179.5	191.4	242.7

added. Disregarding the fact that the wages are in current yuan--price changes during the period were small for wage goods--we see that the wage bill was a declining proportion of the gross value-added. If the "unadjusted series" is used, the proportion would fall from 9.6 percent in 1952 to 5.8 percent in 1956. If the "adjusted series" is employed, the ratio would decline from 11.3 percent in 1952 to 7.2 percent in 1956.

In contrast, if we take the Soviet Union at the beginning of the First Five-Year Plan, for ferrous metallurgy alone, the gross value-added was 42.4 percent of the gross value output.[47] Deductible cost would therefore account for 57.6 percent of value output. At the time, according to Clark,[48] wages were 28 percent of total cost. The share of wages in gross value output, W, can therefore be found from $W/57.6 + W = .28$, and W equals 22.4. The share of wages in gross value-added would be 22.4/42.4, or 52.8 percent. In the case of the United States, during 1946-1961, for the steel industry as a whole, employment cost averaged 64.9 percent of the gross value-added. For individual companies during 1961 and 1962, the corresponding ratio was frequently well above 70 percent.

If we employ Marxian economic terminology, the "rate of exploitation" as expressed by the ratio of "surplus value" to "variable capital" would be equal to 690 percent in 1952 and 1150 percent in 1956.[49] It is rather ironic that Communist China should allow its workers such a small share of the fruit of their own labors.

One may also express the gross value-added per worker as an index and compare it with an annual wage index. With 1952 as the base year, the former series rose by 126 percent in 1956 against a 36-percent increase in the annual wage rate. Even if the "adjusted series" of value-added estimates were used, the increment in value-added per worker between 1952 and 1956 would still be at least 112 percent. The growing discrepancy between the increase in money wages and the improvement in productivity is graphically presented in Figure 4.1.

The real explanation of this situation is not far to seek. It lies in the policy of the Communist Chinese authorities to restrain consumption by depressing the workers' income. Chinese planners have chosen to keep the prices of essential consumers' goods at a relatively low level, partly because of their

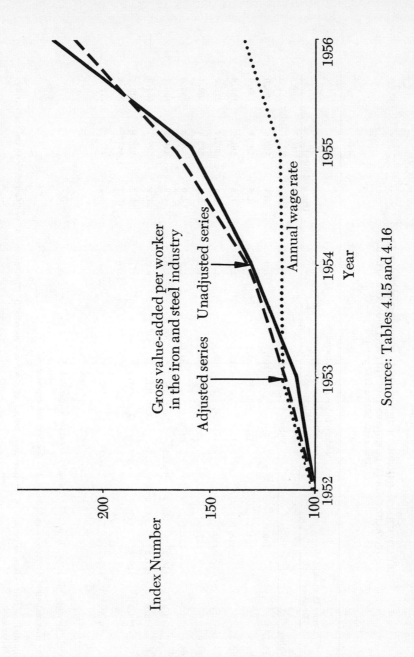

Figure 4.1. Comparison of Indices of Gross Value-added per Worker and Annual Wage Rate in the Iron and Steel Industry, 1952–1956

Source: Tables 4.15 and 4.16

Table 4.16

RELATIVE RATES OF GROWTH OF THE GROSS DOMESTIC PRODUCT AND
OF VALUES-ADDED IN MODERN INDUSTRY AND IRON AND STEEL

(values in billion 1952 yuan)

Year	Gross Domestic Product[a]		Modern Industry[a] (including manufacturing, mining and utilities)		Iron and Steel[b]			
	Value	Index	Value	Index	Unadjusted[c] (a)	Adjusted[c] (b)	Index (a)	Index (b)
1952	75.7	100.0	9.4	100.0	1.3	1.1	100.0	100.0
1953	78.9	104.2	11.8	125.5	1.7	1.5	130.8	136.4
1954	82.3	108.7	13.8	146.8	2.1	1.8	161.5	163.6
1955	86.1	113.7	15.1	160.6	2.7	2.4	207.7	218.2
1956	96.6	127.6	19.6	208.5	4.2	3.4	323.1	309.1
1957	100.0	132.1	21.9	233.0	4.9	4.0	376.9	363.6
1958	110.7[d] / 112.4	146.2[d] / 148.5	27.1[d] / 28.8	288.3[d] / 306.4	5.8	4.5	446.2	409.1
1959	119.1 / 123.4	157.3 / 163.0	37.7 / 42.0	401.1 / 446.8	9.2	7.2	707.7	654.5
1960	120.7 / 129.2	159.4 / 170.7	45.3 / 52.4	481.9 (a) / 557.4 (b)	12.1 / 13.8	9.3 / 10.1	930.8 / 1,061.5	845.5 / 918.2
1961	82.1	108.5	17.1	181.9	...	...	...	...

[a]Y. L. Wu, et. al., op. cit., vol. I, p. 241, Table 51, revised estimates.

[b]Figures for iron and steel derived from Table 4.13. See text for explanation.

[c]The "unadjusted" series refers to the use of finished-steel output as given in Appendix B. The "adjusted" series refers to the tentatively adjusted data in Appendix C.

[d]The lower series of gross domestic product and value-added in modern industry are traceable to a somewhat lower series of estimates for modern manufacturing and are not entirely independent of the steel industry estimates. See the discussion in the source cited in Note (a) above. The higher estimates are based on estimates of gross industrial output derived from power consumption alone without reference to steel output.

138

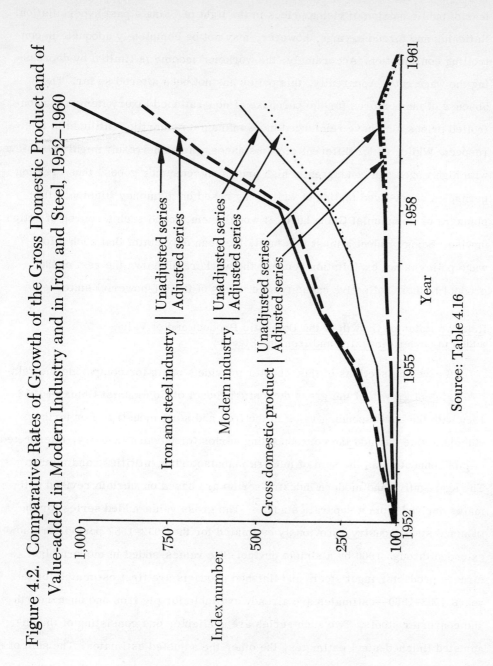

Figure 4.2. Comparative Rates of Growth of the Gross Domestic Product and of Value-added in Modern Industry and in Iron and Steel, 1952–1960

Source: Table 4.16

fear of public opinion of rising prices in the light of China's past hyperinflation. Rationing and forced savings, however, may not be completely adequate in controlling consumption. Accordingly, the workers' income is limited by depressing the wage rate. Apparently, this policy has not been altered so far. The absence of many stores for the purchase of non-rationed luxury items at uncontrolled prices may have reinforced the Communist authorities' attitude in this respect. While, under different circumstances, the same result might be achieved with high wages and concurrently high prices on consumer goods, thus creating perhaps a short-lived feeling of well-being based on a "money illusion," the planners of Communist China have, it would seem, found such a course of action unwise. Being prudent almost to a fault, they can only claim that such a low-wage policy is not exploitation because the workers also own the rest of the product in their collective capacity as citizens of the all-powerful state.

Relative Rates of Growth of the Domestic Product and of Value-added in Modern Industry and Iron and Steel

Preceding sections of this chapter provide a basis for comparing the relative rates of growth of the gross domestic product of Communist China in 1952-1960 with the corresponding rates in the iron and steel industry. For further elucidation we can add the corresponding series for modern industry, interpreted in this connection as the sum of modern manufacturing, utilities, and mining. The aggregative and modern industry series are based on certain revised estimates derived from a separate study.[50] The gross value-added series for the iron and steel industry, previously estimated for the 1952-1957 period, are now extended through 1960 by a simple device. The values-added in modern blast furnace products, ingot steel, and finished products are first estimated for the years 1958-1960--estimates are already available for pig iron and open hearth and converter steels. Two such series are available, one consisting of the unadjusted finished-steel estimates, the other the adjusted estimates. The sum of the values-added in pig iron, ingot steel, and finished products is then divided by 83 percent and 80 percent, respectively, to yield an "unadjusted" as well as an "adjusted" series of gross value-added for the entire industry. These percentage figures represent the virtually constant proportions which the sum of

140

the values-added of pig iron, ingot steel, and finished steel products occupied in the industry total in 1952-1957. The results are then adjusted by including the "contributions" of the native iron and steel movement of the last three years (1958-1960). The final results and the index numbers (1952 = 100) are presented in Table 4.16. They are illustrated further in Figure 4.2.

As one might expect, the iron and steel series rose fastest, followed by the modern industry series, and then the gross domestic product series. This is perfectly consistent with the Communist regime's policy during the period to emphasize the development of the industrial sector and, with it, especially the metallurgical industry, as a symbolic rallying point and central focus of all industrial developmental efforts. It is also noteworthy that the fast rate of growth of the iron and steel industry has been accomplished in spite of the miserable failure of the "backyard furnace" drive. But other less apparent points should be considered.

In the first place, there is a causal relation between development in ferrous metallurgy and in the rest of the economy. This is true especially within the modern industrial sector and the production of machines in particular. While one may marvel at the high rate of growth of the industrial sector of the economy given the concomitant and even more rapid advance of the ferrous metals, there is still the contrary question of why the industrial sector has not expanded more, given such a rapid advance of the production of ferrous metals. Has the entire modern industrial sector actually developed to its fullest extent, given the rate of growth of the iron and steel industry as represented by the value-added index estimated above? Or is it possible that the estimated expansion of the iron and steel industry has not been as effective as it might have been in stimulating development in other industries?

Attention has already been called to the imbalance between the successive stages of fabrication.[51] The limited variety of steel products has also been pointed out earlier. If we may anticipate some of our findings in the next chapter, the apparently large build-up of inventory beyond the planned quantities may find at least partial answer in the possibility that too much of the wrong kinds of steels has been produced. The continued import of substantial quantities of finished steels testifies to the inadequate supply of the right kinds of steels. Our

141

discussion on the native iron and steel sector in the preceding sections would seem to point to a strong possibility that defective products may have been an important cause of the unduly large inventories accumulated outside the native sector of the industry as well. Even the State Statistical Bureau[52] has found it expedient to admit that "the quality of the products is low, particularly the quality of high-grade steel. For example, not one of the six steel mills in China which produce high-grade steel fulfilled the quality plan in types of steel (in 1956); moreover, goods for household use were frequently returned. In 1955, a total of 840 metric tons of high-grade steel materials was returned. " Products of cold rolling, cold drawing, heavy forging, and vacuum refining were among the most deficient. Developments in 1958-1960 in the light of an overwhelming emphasis on quantity as a result of the "Leap Forward" program did little to improve the situation. Withholding of aid and technical assistance by the Soviet Union aggravated it further. Thus, much of the success indicated by the rapid rate of advance has a rather hollow ring.

In the second place, since ferrous metallurgy is a part of the modern industrial segment of the economy, the latter's estimated rate of growth was favorably affected by the higher growth rate of the former. If this fast growing part were removed from the whole, the remaining industrial sector would show a lower rate of advance. The extent of the difference may be seen in Table 4.17.

A crucial methodological point is raised here. Without even questioning the extent to which defective products have been included in the reported output, if there is an excessive supply of certain steels which cannot be disposed of either at home or abroad, we may legitimately raise the question of whether it is at all meaningful to continue evaluating these products at a constant price. Statistically, valuation at a constant price would lead to an exaggeration of the rate of growth as long as products in excess of demand continue to accumulate. Since such products have not been used and therefore do not contribute to the further expansion of production, while capital goods that are utilized would, there would eventually be a decline in the marginal output-investment ratio. But as long as production of the unwanted goods continues to expand, recognition of this readjustment would be postponed. It is quite possible, however, for this situation to be concealed if our statistical series measuring the growth of the industrial sector is not long enough.

142

Table 4.17

ANNUAL GROWTH RATES OF MODERN INDUSTRY--INCLUDING MODERN MANUFACTURING, MINING, AND UTILITIES
(value-added in percent of the preceding year)

Year	Unadjusted		Exclusive of the Iron and Steel Industry			
			Unadjusted		Adjusted	
1953	25.5		24.6		24.1	
1954	16.9		15.8		16.5	
1955	9.4		6.0		5.8	
1956	29.8		24.2		27.6	
1957	11.7		10.4		10.5	
1958	23.7	31.5	25.3	35.3	26.3	35.8
1959	39.1	45.8	33.8	42.6	35.0	43.2
1960	20.1	24.8	(a) 16.5	22.9	18.0	23.9
			(b) 10.5	17.7	15.4	21.6

Source: Derived from Table 4.16

<u>The Investment Effort and Its Result</u>

The year 1960 signalled the end of a period of rapid growth of the Communist Chinese economy. The sharp decline that followed, according to at least one interpretation,[53] was in part a result of the high rate of growth registered during the First Five-Year Plan, grossly exaggerated in official reports because of certain statistical peculiarities. The decline was "triggered" partly by the sectoral disproportion built into the plan, and faulty cost accounting and abuse of labor mobility under the commune system introduced in 1958. Since the steel industry contributed significantly to the high growth rate reported, since the heavy emphasis on the metallurgical industry was an important cause of sectoral imbalance in investment, and since the "backyard furnace" movement was itself one of the most notorious cases of faulty cost accounting and mismanagement of labor, errors committed in the planning and development of the iron and steel industry were thus responsible in no small way for the economic crisis of 1961-1962.

The last statement fairly sums up the indirect, destructive effects of the policy pursued by Communist China in the relatively excessive development of iron and steel before the severe crisis of 1961-1962. To these broad, indirect costs must be added the depletions and disruptions of ore deposits as a result of the indiscriminate mass drive to produce iron and steel during the "Great Leap Forward," as well as the investment costs incurred in the regular program of development. The last item, as reported in Chapter 3, amounted to 2 billion yuan in 1953-1956 and 4.7 billion yuan in 1957-1958.[54] The sum 4.7 billion yuan was equivalent to nearly the entire amount of the gross value-added in the iron and steel industry in 1957 and more than 30 percent of the steel industry's cumulative output during the First Five-Year Plan.[55] That such a prodigious investment effort should yield such a devastating immediate effect must have been discouraging to Communist China's planners. What the future will bring and what can be salvaged out of the suspended or abandoned constructions once the crisis is over would depend on the extent of capital consumption and obsolescence during the crisis years.

An Estimate of the Value Output of Modern Industry

A final constructive note may be struck at this point. Since the lack of
a reliable output series of modern industry in Communist China during the
"Great Leap" has always plagued students of the Chinese economy, any projection
of industrial production for this period would be of interest. Our preceding
estimates have put us in a position to make a guess at the figures by correlating
the value output of modern industry with that of the ferrous metals sector.

As given in Table 4.16, the unadjusted series of value-added in the iron
and steel industry [column (a) in the last part of the table] in 1952-1957 would
average about 92.6 percent[56] of the official value output series given earlier
in this chapter. If we take 92.6 percent of the gross value-added estimates of
the modern sector of the iron and steel industry in 1958-1960, the derived value
output estimates would be 7.66 billion 1952 yuan in 1958, 9.50 billion in 1959,
and 12.4 to 14.2 billion in 1960. Substituting these estimates into a regression
equation of the form[57]

$$\log Y_c = 1.28025 + 0.59737 \log X$$

in which Y_c denotes the estimated modern industry output and X the value output of the iron and steel industry, we can estimate modern industry output (unadjusted for the "native" and "semimodern" iron and steel subsectors) as
follows:

Year	Billion 1952 yuan
1958	64.34
1959	73.17
1960	85.83 - 93.22

These estimates are somewhat below earlier estimates based on electric-power
input in industry.[58] A number of reasons for this discrepancy may be advanced,
such as the possible overestimate of power consumption by industry and other
inaccuracies in both present and earlier estimates. A more plausible explanation
may lie in the instability of the relationship between industrial output and its

145

Table 4.18

ESTIMATES OF MODERN INDUSTRY OUTPUT, 1952–1960
(billion 1952 Yuan)

Year	Modern Industry Output*
1952	22.05
1953	28.44
1954	32.98
1955	35.59
1956	44.98
1957	49.70

	Estimates Based on Power Input	Estimates Based on Value Output of the Iron and Steel Industry
1958	65.05	64.34
1959	89.70	73.17
1960	111.55	85.83–93.22

*Adjusted for "new product effect." See Yuan-li Wu, Economic Development, op. cit., Appendix C.

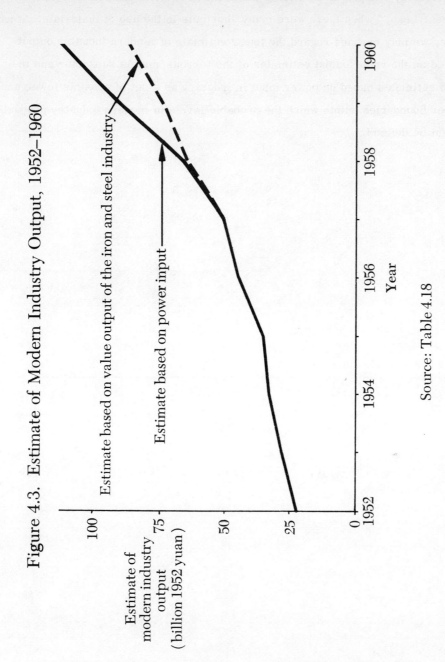

Figure 4.3. Estimate of Modern Industry Output, 1952–1960

Source: Table 4.18

147

subsectors, due primarily to changes in the production function during the "Great Leap," when there were many shortcuts in the use of materials. At any rate, we may perhaps regard the lower estimate of modern industry output based on the value output estimates of the ferrous metals subsector and the high estimates based on power input in industry as a set of possible lower and upper boundaries within which the probable levels of modern industry production might be defined.

5

DEMAND AND SUPPLY IN THE IRON AND STEEL INDUSTRY

Introduction

As we have tried to show in the preceding chapters, rapid growth was attained within the iron and steel industry in the first decade of Communist rule, although the advance was accomplished at a cost that was not always commensurate with the result. We now turn to the companion question of whether the iron and steel industry has been developed in proper relation to the rest of the economy. On the one hand, the question is whether the industry has been developed to the extent required by development in the rest of the economy. On the other hand, we must not overlook the possibility that it may have been overdeveloped, since sectoral imbalance may manifest itself in both ways and one cannot readily generalize on the relative disadvantage of oversupply versus unsatisfied demand without reference to the particular economic conditions in question.

The effect of oversupply would of course be felt in an excessive demand on certain inputs which would in turn impinge on the development of other sectors. The effect of undersupply, on the other hand, would be felt in the distribution of the output among the various categories of consumers and the rate of their development. Any interindustry imbalance and/or structural imbalance within the industry would point to serious planning errors unless it can be demonstrated that such imbalance is somehow beneficial from a dynamic point of view, for instance, in the impetus it gives to the rate of economic growth or some other accepted goal of public policy.

Supply and Demand of Iron Ore and Pig Iron

The problem of intraindustry balance with respect to the productive capacity and estimated output of pig iron, ingot steel, and finished steel has already been explored in Chapter 3. It is sufficient to point out at this juncture the relative magnitudes of (1) iron ore production and the consumption of ore in producing pig iron and (2) pig iron production and the consumption of iron in producing steel. Such a comparison will permit us to draw some interesting conclusions.

First, we may take the coefficients of iron ore input in producing pig iron given in Table 4.2 and multiply them by the pig iron output estimates of the modern and native sectors, respectively. The ore consumption estimates may be aggregated and the sum then subtracted from the ore output estimates given in Table 3.4. The residual was positive for 1952-1959, with the exception of 1958. The positive residuals in 1952-1957 were also large enough, it would seem, to allow for waste, ore at mine head not shipped out, some accumulation of inventory at the iron mills, and the withdrawal from stock in 1958. However, the deficiency in 1958 has most assuredly been underestimated and the surplus in 1959 overstated because of the possible deterioration of the quality of the ore during the "Great Leap Forward" and the undoubtedly greater ore consumption per ton of iron in the native pig iron sector. Also, iron production in the native sector exceeded that of the modern sector for the first time in 1959. This probably explains some of the reports from Communist China that ore supply has failed to match the progress of processing and fabrication.

Second, we may take the input coefficients of pig iron in steelmaking given in Tables 4.5 and 4.9 and multiply them by the corresponding steel output estimates given in Tables 4.8 and 4.11.[1] The total pig iron consumption of the modern steel mills is then subtracted from the output of the modern furnaces. Similarly, a comparison of pig iron production in the native and semimodern sector with iron consumption in the native steel sector may be made for 1958-1960.[2] These comparisons would show a surplus of output in the modern sector except in 1960, thus indicating the availability of iron for purposes other than steelmaking, waste, and addition to inventory. There was already, however, a deficiency of production in 1958 in the native iron sector. The deficiency would be even greater and probably extended to 1959-1960 if we bear in mind the heavy discount that should be made in the output statistics discussed in Chapter 4. If correct, these statistics would imply that far from being a useful supplement to the modern sector, the native sector, including perhaps even the semimodern

150

Table 5.1

IRON ORE PRODUCTION AND CONSUMPTION
(in thousand metric tons)

	1952	1953	1954	1955	1956	1957	1958	1959	1960
Iron ore production	4,287	5,821	7,229	9,597	15,484	19,370	20,000	40,000	...
Ore consumption in producing pig iron									
Modern sector	3,117.9	3,828.0	5,139.1	6,327.1	8,240.3	10,108.5	16,439.3	16,387.5	21,983.4
Native sector	47.6	103.8	263.7	421.8	84.5	131.1	7,176.0	18,975.0	25,530.0
Total	3,165.5	3,931.8	5,402.8	6,748.9	8,324.8	10,239.6	23,615.3	35,362.5	47,513.4
Residual	1,121.5	1,889.2	1,826.2	2,848.1	7,159.2	9,130.4	-3,615.3	4,637.5	...

Table 5.2

PIG IRON PRODUCTION AND CONSUMPTION
(in thousand metric tons)

	1952	1953	1954	1955	1956	1957	1958	1959	1960
Pig iron production (modern iron sector)	1,900	2,175	2,962	3,630	4,777	5,860	9,530	9,500	12,744
Consumption (modern steel sector)	(a) 1,146 (b) 1,115	1,492	1,896	2,374	(a) 3,806 (b) 3,872	(a) 4,560 (b) 4,591	7,113	7,986	13,721
Residual	(a) 754 (b) 785	683	1,066	1,256	(a) 971 (b) 905	(a) 1,300 (b) 1,269	2,417	1,514	-977
Production (native iron sector)	29	59	162	242	49	76	4,160	11,000	14,800
Consumption (native steel sector)	...	...	...	...	...	...	5,372	7,406	10,120
Residual	29	59	152	242	49	76	-1,212	3,594	4,680

Source: See Text and Appendix B.

151

segment, actually detracted from the former and undermined the usefulness of the modern mills--another sad commentary indeed to the mass industrialization program during the "Great Leap Forward"!

The relation between ingot production and consumption in steel fabrication hinges upon the interpretation of the finished-steel output estimates, a question already fully discussed in Chapter 3 and Appendix C.

Demand and Supply of Finished Steel

Since there are numerous types of finished-steel and fabricated steel products, we shall content ourselves with the category of "finished steel" as a whole, disregarding for the most part the heterogeneity of its constituent items. For the moment, we shall also disregard the probable inclusion of semifinished steels in the total reported output. This is the method by which the production estimates in Chapter 3 and Appendix B were developed. Later we shall consider the effect of excluding the semifinished steels from both the demand and the supply side.

Our principal task now is to determine the major categories of finished-steel consumption and to relate them to the available supply. Since available information does not permit us to identify all the categories of consumption or to estimate their magnitudes, we shall identify those that we can and then consider whether the unidentified uses can reasonably be expected to account for the residual obtained by subtracting consumption in the identified sectors from the reported supply.

In the first place, we shall look upon the demand for finished steel from the point of view of end use, embracing the categories of (1) investment, (2) government consumption, and (3) personal consumption. In terms of these categories, it is quite plain that there are very few consumer goods in Communist China at her present stage of economic development that would require significant quantities of finished steel as input. Such consumer durables as passenger automobiles and refrigerators are a negligible factor in the present Chinese consumption pattern. In the place of automobiles, only bicycles may represent an important source of personal consumption of finished steel. The canning industry may constitute another major portion of demand in the same category. Some household utensils may account for another part. However, with the exception of bicycle manufacturing, it has not been possible to determine the magnitude of finished steel used in personal consumption in terms of specific commodity categories.

Under the category of government consumption, the main factor is, of course, steel consumption in the production of military equipment and in the erection of military installations. There is, however, no information on the size of this factor as all military data in Communist China are highly classified. We shall therefore have to treat this category as a residual.

Under the category of investment, finished steel may be absorbed in two ways. First, it may be absorbed without prior conversion as an addition to inventory. Second, it may be absorbed by investment in other forms--principally in the form of machinery and construction of plants and buildings, including public buildings which may also be legitimately included in "government consumption." The term "machinery" should be interpreted in the broad sense so as to include such items as trucks, buses, pedicabs, etc., which, in Communist China, should be regarded as capital equipment instead of consumer durables.

Given the above division of end uses, an approximate picture of the distribution of finished-steel output can now be worked out. For clarity, this is presented schematically as follows:

A. Finished steel absorbed by investment

    1. Addition to inventory

    2. Steel used in the production of other capital goods (assumed to be equal to the amount used in capital construction), including the amount used for repairs, spare parts, etc.

        a. Finished steel used in machine production less the amount used in the manufacture of certain consumer durables included in "machine production" in official statistics

        b. Finished steel absorbed in construction plus all other steel products absorbed by investment but not otherwise accounted for (residual obtained by subtracting category "a" from category 2)

B. Finished steel absorbed by personal consumption

C. Finished steel absorbed by military use plus statistical errors (residual equal to production less "A" and "B" plus net import)

153

The following sections will be devoted to a more detailed study and estimate of the above items.

Addition to Inventory

Since the size of the inventory is directly related to the demand for finished steel, two obvious factors in determining it are: (1) it should not be so small as to endanger the fulfillment of the production plans of the domestic users and scheduled exports; and (2) it should not be so large as to create an excessive surplus, which would be an admission of poor planning in the allocation of resources. In practice, however, the level of inventory in Communist China appears to be directly related to the amount of production, rather than the demand of the users, thus making the maintenance of an appropriate inventory only an indirect result of the proper coordination between current production and demand.

In the case of finished steel, the permissible range of the size of the inventory is fixed at a minimum of 5 percent and a maximum of 10 percent of the year's output. That is to say, addition to inventory during any year should not allow the year-end inventory either to fall below the prescribed minimum or to exceed the maximum. On the basis of this general rule and the production estimates of finished steel, the permissible range of both the year-end inventory and the annual addition to inventory can be computed as follows in thousand metric tons:

Year	Production	Inventory Norms at Year End		Permissible Addition to Inventory	
		minimum	maximum	minimum	maximum
1951	808	40	81	...	...
1952	1,312	66	131	26	50
1953	1,754	88	175	22	44
1954	1,965	98	197	10	22
1955	2,505	125	251	27	54
1956	3,921	196	392	71	141
1957	4,260	213	426	17	34
1958	6,000	300	600	87	174
1959	9,200	460	920	160	320
1960	12,800-16,600	640-830	1,280-1,660	180-370	360-740

According to Planned Economy,[3] however, finished-steel inventory at the end of 1955 was as high as 1,640,000 tons. It increased by 88,000 tons to 1,728,000 tons at the end of 1956. If these figures are correct, since the existence of a very large initial stock was improbable, it would seem that there had been large additions to inventory in excess of the planned amounts. The existence of such huge "unplanned" additions to inventory, if not fictitious, would point to considerable overproduction through 1956 or, one might safely add, through the First Five-Year Plan.

If the rule governing inventory had been strictly applied, there should not have been any addition to it during 1956 and production should have been kept at a reduced level during the year. Since practice diverged widely from this ostensible rule, one might surmise that with the expansion of production after 1956, annual additions to inventory were at least as high as the rate in 1956, or about 2.2 percent of the reported annual outputs. For the years before 1956, we might tentatively assume that the maximum annual additions to stock developed above could represent the real "planned" additions, while the difference between the reported year-end inventory in 1955 (1,640,000 tons) and the maximum norm of 251,000 tons, or 1,389,000 tons, would constitute excess inventory carried. As an approximation, this amount may be treated as the accumulated "unplanned" additions in 1952-1955 to be distributed among the four years in the same proportion as the reported outputs.[4] On this basis, both the "planned" and "unplanned" additions to inventory can be computed for 1952-1955, together with the "planned" additions in 1956-1960 (see estimates in Table 5.3).

Finished Steel Absorbed in the Production of Other Capital Goods

According to a 1957 study on the relationship between machine building and the iron and steel industry,[5] total direct and indirect consumption of finished steel averaged 250 kilograms for every thousand yuan of capital construction expenditure. The latter, including expenditures both within the state plan and outside the plan, can be estimated and an approximate order of magnitude of finished steel absorbed in capital construction arrived at. The relevant data are given in Table 5.4.

155

Table 5.3

INVENTORY CHANGES IN "FINISHED-STEEL"
(in thousand metric tons)

Year	"Planned" Addition to Inventory	"Unplanned" Addition to Inventory	Total
1952	50	242	292
1953	44	323	367
1954	22	362	384
1955	54	462	516
1956	88	---	88
1957	94	...	94*
1958	132	...	132
1959	202	...	202
1960	282–365	...	282–365

*Total for 1957 through 1960 represents "planned" additions only.

Notes and Sources: For "planned" additions, 1952-1955, see Table in text; 1956, actual figures; 1957-1960 figures based on 2.2 percent of production. For "unplanned" additions in 1952-1955, see text, page 155.

Table 5.4

"FINISHED-STEEL" ABSORBED IN CAPITAL CONSTRUCTION, 1952-1961

Year	Capital Construction Expenditures (in billion 1952 yuan)			"Finished-Steel" Consumption (in million metric tons)
	Within state plan	Outside state plan	Total	
1952	3.71	0.65	4.36	1.09
1953	6.11	1.40	7.51	1.88
1954	7.35	1.54	8.89	2.22
1955	8.92	0.69	9.61	2.40
1956	15.40	0.97	16.37	4.09
1957	13.90	1.40	15.30	3.83
1958	...	...	19.50*	4.88
1959	...	...	28.70	7.17
1960	...	...	40.10	10.02
1961	...	...	13.40	3.35

*Estimates of fixed investment are used for 1958 through 1961.

Sources: The capital construction expenditures are derived from Yuan-li Wu et al., The Economic Potential of Communist China, 1962-1967, Chapter XIII. "Finished-steel consumption is estimated by multiplying "Total" column by 250 kilograms per thousand yuan. See text, page 155.

In estimating the use of finished steel (Table 5.4), it was assumed that the coefficient of 250 kilograms of steel per thousand yuan of capital construction expenditure includes finished-steel products accumulated as a necessary adjunct of the activities of the construction units. However, finished steel held in steel warehouses or in the mills is assumed to be outside of this amount and should therefore be included in the total absorbed in investment. This is a somewhat arbitrary and subjective interpretation; it is plausible, however, especially since the volume of inventory held is probably geared to the total demand for steel products, not to demand for investment in capital construction alone. The stability of the coefficient of finished-steel input is obviously only a rough approximation and is tentatively accepted here for want of a more reliable estimate.

Within the sector of capital construction it is not possible to identify the amount of steel products absorbed in the various sectors such as coal mining, power installations, etc. The only subsector in capital construction for which finished-steel consumption can be readily estimated at this time is railway construction. Although the estimate would not account for more than a minor portion of the total, a brief account will probably be of some interest.

An estimate of steel consumption by railways is made by applying different coefficients of finished-steel input to the volume of rail laying and other railway installations, respectively. The former is further divided into two classes: heavy, standard rails for trunk lines; and lighter rails for branch, spur, and industrial tracks. One figure given in an official publication[6] states that 130 tons of rolled steel are needed to lay 1 kilometer of rails. When steel needed for other installations such as stations, culverts, water towers, bridges, etc., is included, the total rises to 200 tons per kilometer of a single-track trunk line. This coefficient for rail laying appears reasonable and quite conservative when the following comparisons are made.

First, both the main lines and the major branch lines in Communist China have been built with heavy rails weighing 50 kilograms per meter. The minimum for a single-track line would therefore be 100 tons per kilometer even if the tracks were laid in a straight line. The total weight of rolled steel used, including auxiliary tracks and accessory equipment such as fish and base plates,

158

bolts and nuts, dog spikes, etc., will therefore easily account for a total of 130 tons per kilometer of tracks laid. Second, in formulating their post-World War II railway construction plans, the Nationalist Chinese planners used a unit consumption estimate of 110 to 120 metric tons for rails and accessories per kilometer of a single-track railway.[7] The latter figure is, however, based on rails of 90 pounds per yard, or approximately 45 kilograms per meter. The heavier rails now used in Communist China would lead to an increase above the lower Nationalist estimate, although not necessarily proportional to the increase in the weight of rails. These reasons all point to the relative credibility of the Communist figure of a total of 200 tons of finished-steel consumption per kilometer of rail tracks or 130 tons for rails and accessories only. As for light rails used in the construction of spur lines and industrial tracks, finished-steel consumption is estimated at 80 tons per kilometer.[8]

When these input coefficients are applied to the volume of railway construction, total finished-steel consumption in rail construction can be estimated as in Table 5.5. If the estimates in this table are then subtracted from the amount of steel products absorbed in capital construction as a whole, the residual would correspond to all the other unidentified sectors in capital construction.

Finished-Steel Consumption in Machine Production

Another approach to the further subdivision of finished-steel consumption in capital construction is to estimate the amount of steel absorbed in the manufacture of the largest component of investment in fixed assets, namely, machines and equipment. By subtracting the amount of steel used in the production of machines from the total absorbed in capital construction, we can obtain a residual which would correspond approximately to steel used in construction.

For machine manufacture, the amount of finished-steel input per 1,000 yuan of the gross value output of machines has been estimated at 276 kilograms in 1953, 255 kilograms in 1954, 225 kilograms in 1955, 166 kilograms in 1956, and 150 kilograms in 1957.[9] The data refer to the output of the First Ministry of Machine Building, which in 1956 had 437 industrial plants under its jurisdiction[10] and produced virtually all the machines and equipment for the civilian sector of the economy. The input coefficients given above indicate a gradual

159

Table 5.5

"FINISHED-STEEL" CONSUMPTION BY RAILWAYS
(in thousand metric tons)

Year	New Construction							Repair and Maintenance[g]	Total Steel Consumed[h]
	Main and Branch Lines		Light Spur Lines		Other Installations[e]	Total New Construction[f]			
	kilometers[a]	steel consumed[b]	kilometers[c]	steel consumed[d]					
1952	1,233	160	236	19	103	282		38	320
1953	706	92	494	39	84	215		39	254
1954	1,132	147	283	23	99	269		40	309
1955	1,406	183	458	37	130	350		42	392
1956	2,242	291	866	69	218	578		45	623
1957	1,166	152	569	46	121	318		46	364
1958	2,376	309	1,188	95	249	653		48	701
1959	3,136	408	1,568	125	329	862		49	911
1960	7,344*	955*	1,045*	84*	587	1,626*		52	1,678

*Plan.

(a) For the years 1952-1958, see Ten Great Years, Foreign Language Press, Peking, 1960, p. 69. The total length of rails laid in 1959, estimated at 32% more than that of 1958, amounted to 3,136 kilometers of heavy rails and 1,568 kilometers of light rails (People's Daily, April 9, 1960). According to the same source, quoting Lü Cheng-ch'ao in his report to the National People's Congress, planned rail laying in 1960 was 8,389 kilometers. The New China News Agency had reported at an earlier date that 1,045 kilometers of light-rail spur lines were included in the 1960 planned total (NCNA, March 30, 1960). The difference of 7,344 kilometers therefore represented heavy rails.

(b) (a) multiplied by 130 tons per kilometer. (See text and Ta-kung Pao, Hong Kong, May 12, 1959.)

(c) Same as (a).

(d) (c) multiplied by 80 tons per kilometer. (See text and People's Daily, Oct. 17, 1959.)

(e) Steel consumption in other rail installations per kilometer of line built has been estimated by subtracting 130 tons from the total of 200 tons required for all construction purposes. (People's Handbook, Vol. II, 1959, p. 465.)

(f) (b) + (d) + (e) = (f).

(g) Repair and Maintenance: The total quantity of steel required for maintenance in railways in Communist China can be estimated by using the average number of rails replaced per kilometer of the major railways in operation during the prewar Nationalist period. The official statistics of average annual replacement were as follows:

Railway	Average number of rails annually replaced per kilometer in operation 1932-1934
Peiping-Hankow	1.73
Peiping-Liaoning	1.71
Nanking-Shanghai	1.83

Sources: Railroad Year Book, 1932-1933, pp. 686-688; 1933-1935, pp. 720-738.

In view of the increased turnover of freight and passenger traffic in recent years, the present maintenance requirements should be greater. It is therefore safe to assume an annual replacement of 2 rails per kilometer with an average weight and length of 50 kilograms per meter and 10 meters per rail. This amounts to 1 ton of steel per kilometer per year, or 0.77% of the total rail requirement of 130 tons. This percentage is applied to the figure of 200 tons in order to include the maintenance requirement of other installations. The total requirement for maintenance thus amounts to 1.54 tons a year per kilometer of railways in operation.

Notes to Table 5.5 (continued)

The length of railways in operation in 1952-1960 were:

Year	Kilometers
1952	24,518
1953	25,072
1954	25,873
1955	27,171
1956	29,237
1957	29,862
1958	31,193
1959	32,000
1960	33,678

Sources: 1952-58, Ten Great Years, p. 144; 1959, People's Handbook, 1960, p. 43; 1960, Chiao-t'ung Yen-chiu-so (Communications Research Bureau), Fei-ch'ü T'ieh-lu She-shih Hsien-K'uang (Railways in Communist China), Taipei, 1961, p. 17.

Steel consumption at 1.54 tons per kilometer may therefore be estimated at:

Year	Thousand tons
1952	38
1953	39
1954	40
1955	42
1956	45
1957	46
1958	48
1959	49
1960	52

(h) (f) + (g) = (h).

Table 5.6

ALTERNATIVE ESTIMATES OF "FINISHED-STEEL" CONSUMPTION
IN THE MACHINE-BUILDING INDUSTRY IN 1958-1960
(in thousand metric tons)

Year	(i)	(ii)	(iii)*
1958	1,548	1,629	1,100
1959	2,568	2,442	1,300
1960	...	2,565	1,500

*Estimates in column (iii) are taken from an unpublished study by Yuan-li Wu et al., The Economic Potential of Communist China.

162

reduction in the weight of steel per unit value of output. This is to be explained both by technological improvements which gradually reduced the excessive weight of machines made in Communist China, and by the increasing unit value of the machines produced through the years in consequence of the increasing complexity of the types of machines manufactured and the overpricing of new machine products. The amount of finished steel absorbed by the machine-building industry in 1952-1957 can thus be easily computed on the basis of the input coefficients and gross value output of the machine-manufacturing industry.

For 1958-1960, steel consumption in machine making can be estimated in several ways (see Table 5.6). (i) On the one hand, according to the New China News Agency,[11] finished steel supplied to the machinery industry increased by 67 percent in 1957-1958 and 65.9 percent in 1958-1959. Total consumption estimated on this basis would amount to 1,548,000 tons in 1958 and 2,568,000 tons in 1959, respectively. (ii) On the other hand, the gross value output of the machinery industry in 1958, 1959, and 1960 has also been estimated at 10,857, 16,285, and 17,098 million 1952 yuan, respectively.[12] If the 1957 input coefficient of 150 kilograms of finished steel for every thousand yuan of machinery produced is applied to these machine output estimates, a second series of finished-steel consumption can be deduced. The estimates for 1958, 1959, and 1960 are 1,629,000 tons, 2,442,000 tons, and 2,565,000 tons, respectively. However, for the period in question, the two series are both suspect inasmuch as the machine output reports of the "Great Leap Forward" period were probably exaggerated while steel supplied to the machine-building industry may not have been actually converted into machines. Accordingly, a third series (iii) of estimates may be derived by correlating finished-steel production with steel consumption in machine building. Estimated elsewhere, these consumption statistics are given in column (c) of Table 5.6. These estimates are lower than the first two series for the years 1959-1960 and are probably closer to the truth even though they are not derived independently of the steel production series.

Table 5.7 presents a complete series of estimates of finished-steel consumption in machine building in 1952-1960. If we subtract from these estimates the corresponding data of steel consumed in manufacturing bicycles, which

163

Table 5.7

"FINISHED-STEEL" CONSUMPTION IN THE MACHINE BUILDING INDUSTRY
(in thousand metric tons)

Year	Gross Value Output of Machine Building Industry (billion 1952 yuan)[a]	"Finished Steel" (kg) Consumed per Thousand yuan[b]	"Finished Steel" Consumption[c]	"Finished Steel" Consumed in Manufacturing Bicycles[d]	Remainder[e]
	(i)	(ii)	(iii)	(iv)	(v)
1952	1.41	276	389	2	387
1953	2.17	276	599	4	595
1954	2.66	255	678	7	671
1955	3.04	225	684	8	676
1956	5.75	166	954	14	940
1957	6.18	150	927	18	909
1958	...	...	1,100–1,629*	26	1,074–1,603*
1959	...	...	1,300–2,568	26	1,274–2,542
1960	...	...	1,500–2,565	26	1,474–2,539

*First figures given for 1958–1960 are believed to be the more accurate of the two.

Notes to Table 5.7

(a) Wei-ta ti Shih-nien, English translation, p. 84, and Major Aspects, p. 193.

(b) For 1953–1956, see Planned Economy, No. 3, March, 1957, p. 10; for 1957, see Chung-kuo Kung-jen (The Chinese Worker), No. 23, 1959, p. 6. The 1953 figure is also used for 1952.

(c) For 1952–1957, (i) multiplied by (ii); for 1958–1960, see Table 5.6.

(d) The annual output of bicycles and the quantity of steel needed to manufacture a bicycle are reported to be as follows:

Year	Output (Unit = 1,000)	Steel Used per Bicycle (kg)	Total (Thousand Metric Tons)
1952	80	25	2
1953	165	25	4
1954	298	25	7
1955	335	24	8
1956	640	22	14
1957	806	22	18
1958	1,174	22	26
1959	...	...	26
1960	...	...	26

Source: For unit steel consumption see T'ung-chi Kung-tso (Statistical Work), No. 18, 1957, p. 33. The 1953 and 1956 figures are used for 1952 and 1958–1960 respectively. For bicycle output in 1952–1958 see Ten Great Years, p. 99; the 1958 figure is also used for 1959–1960.

(v) Column (iii) — Column (iv) = (v).

probably represent the major consumer durable using steel produced by the machine-building industry, we may treat the remainder as being entirely devoted to investment use.

Machine Manufacture and the Production of Weapons

One point that requires some attention at this juncture concerns the fact that the machine output data published in official sources, as well as other non-Chinese estimates, refer to the civilian sector only. Consequently, the amount of steel consumed in the production of weapons and various military "hardware," though carried out under the jurisdiction of government ministries which nominally deal with machines, is not included in the present estimate. This permits us to treat government absorption of finished steel in the manufacture of weapons as a part of the residual that can be obtained by deducting all the identifiable uses of finished steel from the total available supply.

On the other hand, it is more than likely that steel consumed in military constructions, such as fortifications, aircraft hangars, etc., would be included under "capital construction." It would therefore be a part of the residual in the investment sector.

There is some circumstantial evidence pointing to the exclusion of steel consumed by the arms industry from the machine sector. While the exact division of functions among the several Ministries of Machine Building cannot be fully ascertained with clarity, partly because of continual organizational changes, a general outline can be gleaned from the accompanying chart. In August, 1952, there were two such ministries (known respectively as the First and Second Ministries of Machine Building), of which the Second was probably also in charge of ordnance plants. In April, 1955, a Third Ministry of Machine Building was set up; it was temporarily abolished in May, 1956, together with the Ministry of Heavy Industry, and a new Ministry of Electrical Equipment Manufacturing was established at this time. This situation continued through November of the same year when a new Third Ministry came into being. Then in February, 1958, the then Second Ministry of Machine Building and the Ministry of Electrical Equipment Manufacturing were absorbed by the First Ministry, which remained in full charge of the entire sector of machine production

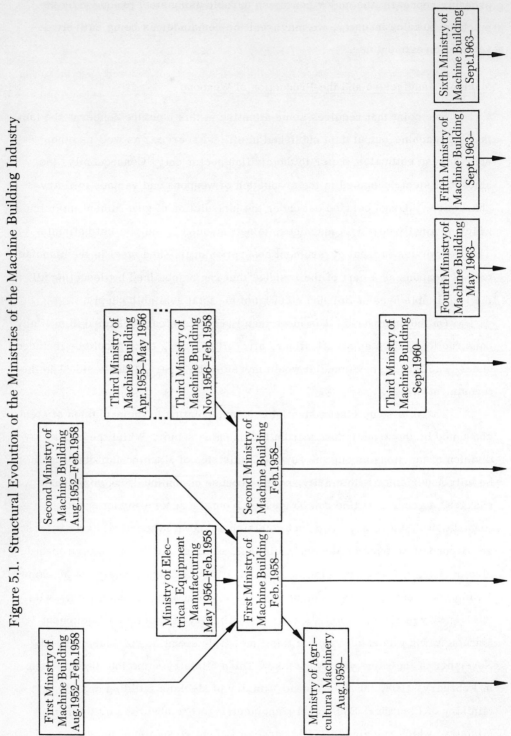

Figure 5.1. Structural Evolution of the Ministries of the Machine Building Industry

for civilian use until August, 1959. Again in February, 1958, the then Third Ministry (established in November, 1956) was renamed the Second. Then, in September, 1960, a new Third Ministry was established.

Additional reorganization took place in August, 1959, when a Ministry of Agricultural Machinery was set up; it presumably evolved from a division of the First Ministry. A Fourth Ministry for machine making was set up in May, 1963, presumably responsible for electronic equipment. A Fifth Ministry and a Sixth Ministry then came into being in September, 1963. [13] These were presumably offshoots of the then established departments and were put in charge of the missile industry and shipbuilding, respectively.

In spite of these confusing alternations in the numbering of the ministries prior to 1963, there appears to have been a general principle of keeping the functions of the Second and Third Ministries apart from those of the First. This phenomenon, it would seem, is a reflection of a distinctive divergence of fields of responsibility and interest between the First Ministry of Machine Building on the one hand and the Second and Third Ministries on the other. One may not be far wrong in surmising that the Second and Third Ministries as constituted before 1963 were intimately connected with arms production. This relationship may be in part inferred from the personnel of the ministries. For instance, before 1963 the present Second Ministry was headed by a former Vice-Minister of the Ministry of Geology who, as such, led Communist China's delegation to the Joint Nuclear Conference of the Soviet Bloc at Duvna near Moscow. He was in turn assisted by a Vice-Minister who also came from the Ministry of Geology. Moreover, it was in November, 1956, that a Third Ministry, which corresponded to the Second Ministry in 1958 to May, 1963, perhaps even the present Second Ministry, was established for the second time. This was the year when Communist China began to promote nuclear developments, including presumably a nuclear-weapons program. Before 1963, the present Third Ministry (established since September, 1960) was staffed by persons some of whom were connected with either the Army or the Navy, as well as with the ordnance bureau of the former Ministry of Heavy Industry. Although the above discussion includes a highly speculative element, circumstantial evidence indicates quite unmistakably that the Second and Third Ministries of Machine Building were concerned with the production of weapons and nuclear-power developments before May, 1963, and that the published statistics of the machine industry's output through 1960 refer to the civilian sector production only. (After May, 1963, a part of the weapons production function may have been reassigned to the newer ministries, as pointed out in the preceding paragraph.) We make this categorical assertion. Communist China's addiction to secretiveness more or less assures us that such an assumption can be safely made. From this premise it then follows that the estimated finished-steel consumption in machine production presented above does not include government consumption of finished steel for military use in arms manufacturing, other than possibly military constructions.

Personal Consumption of Finished Steel

According to the T'ung-chi Kung-tso,[14] 13.9 percent of the total volume of finished steel allocated by the Communist government in 1953-1956 went to the Ministry of Commerce for distribution through the market in contradistinction to direct allocation to factory steel users. The total amount for the four-year period was reported to be 1,660,000 tons. At the same time, the relative share of the annual distribution made in this manner was said to have declined steadily from 28.6 percent in 1953 to 24.5 percent in 1954, 9.7 percent in 1955, and 2.8 percent in 1956.[15] The absolute quantities given for the last two years were: 1955, 280,000 tons; 1956, 120,000 tons. Since steel was purchased through the distributive channels of the Ministry of Commerce only by (1) civilian consumers and (2) productive enterprises for purposes outside of their plans, the gradual diminution of the relative importance of this method to acquire steel between 1953 and 1956 was clearly an indication of the extension of the scope of planned uses by productive enterprises. Thus the small amount of 120,000 tons registered in 1956 may be regarded as an approximation of the amount of steel used in personal consumption during that year. To this we should add some 14,000 tons used in manufacturing bicycles as this amount was probably allocated directly to the manufacturers within the plan, as well as an undetermined amount for other consumer goods industries receiving direct allocation, while another undetermined amount should be subtracted from the 120,000 tons in order to allow for such steel as might still be used by the nonconsumer goods industries for purposes

168

outside of the plan. On balance, we may not be far wrong if we take 134,000 tons (sum of 120,000 and 14,000) as the approximate amount of finished steel used for personal consumption purposes in 1956. On a per capita basis, the amount would be 0.21 kilogram a year, given a midyear population of 621.2 million.[16]

This exceedingly small amount is nevertheless not unreasonable as one might think at first glance. As a basis of comparison, we could take the estimate of civilian steel consumption in Manchuria in 1944. This was reported to be no more than 5,000 tons according to the Pauley Report.[17] The corresponding per capita value in this case would be about 0.12 kilogram only,[18] or even less than the estimate for 1956 given above. In view of the wartime shortage in Manchuria in 1944, the relatively easier supply situation in Communist China, and the expansion of certain light industries for export,[19] we might take the per capita figure of 0.21 kilogram as applicable to "personal consumption" in the entire period. The total estimates of annual consumption of finished steel in the production of consumer goods could therefore be approximated by multiplying 0.21 kilogram with the midyear population estimates. The result is shown in Table 5.8.

Foreign Trade in Finished Steel

According to the T'ung-chi Kung-tso,[20] finished steel allotted to the Ministry of Foreign Trade for export in 1953-1956 totaled 320,000 tons or 2.7 percent of the cumulative total allotment of 11,910,000 tons. The yearly allotments may be estimated from index numbers with 1953 as base as follows:

Year	Index	Thousand Tons
1953	100	10
1954	170	17
1955	930	93
1956	2020	200*
Total		320

*Also given as 210,000 tons in Chi-hua Ching-chi, no. 9, 1957, p. 13.

169

Table 5.8

PERSONAL CONSUMPTION OF "FINISHED-STEEL"

Year	Midyear Population (million)	Steel Consumption (thousand tons)
1952	569	119
1953	581	122
1954	595	125
1955	608	128
1956	621	130
1957	637	134
1958	654	137
1959	668	140
1960	682	143

Notes and Sources: For the midyear population, see Yuan-li Wu et al., op. cit. The consumption estimates are based on a per capita consumption of 0.21 kg and the above midyear population estimates. Figures are rounded to nearest one-tenth.

Table 5.9

IMPORTS AND EXPORTS OF "FINISHED-STEEL"
(in thousand metric tons)

Year	Imports[a]	Exports[b]	Import Balance
1952	506	...	506
1953	850	...	850
1954	836	1	835
1955	865	21	844
1956	634	34	600
1957	630	44	586
1958	1,950	92	1,858
1959	940	139	801
1960	823	116[c]	707

[a]Chukyo: Tekko Suryo Chosa, 1950-1960 (Communist China: Survey of the Iron and Steel Production, 1950-1960), by the Investigation Committee of the Overseas Iron and Steel Market Affairs, Tokyo, October 1962, p. 20. Chinese imports of finished steel in 1953-1957 are from Planned Economy, no. 9, September 1957, pp. 13 and 16.

[b]Chukyo: Tekko Suryo Chosa, 1950-1960, op. cit.

[c]Average of 1958 and 1959.

170

However, it appears that the export allotments did not necessarily coincide with exports, which together with the import statistics can be found in the Chukyo: Tekko Suryo Chosa (Communist China: Survey of Iron and Steel Production, 1950-1960), as presented in Table 5.9. These statistics, based on Japanese sources, are considerably lower than the allotment data.

As for imports, estimates can also be made from the 1953 figure given in Planned Economy, together with index numbers for 1954-1957.[21] For 1958-1959, only the trade returns of the partner countries are available. A similar figure based on the export statistics of seventeen partner countries can also be found for 1960. The details are again given in Table 5.9.

A Tentative Estimate of the Military Use of Steel

The total amount of finished steel available from current production and imports can now be aggregated and compared with the end uses identified thus far (including exports). Since addition to inventory, including estimated unplanned additions, has already been accounted for as one of the identified uses, the residual unidentified consumption cannot be regarded as change in inventory. Since the principal unidentified use would be government consumption for the manufacture of ordnance products (presumably under the present Second and Third Ministries of Machine Building), that is, steel used in military construction and the building of arms factories being presumably already included under "capital construction," the residuals (Table 5.10, last line) may therefore be viewed as an approximation of the amount of steel absorbed by arms production. This would seem to be a plausible explanation for the years through 1956.[22]

Reference may be made at this point to Gardner Clark's estimate of the amount of steel products consumed in the production of munitions and in the construction of ordnance plants in the Soviet Union during the 1930's.

U.S.S.R. Steel Consumption (in Million Tons)

Year	Munitions Manufacturing	Construction of Ordnance Plants
1933	1.2	0.1
1934	2.0	0.2
1935	2.4	0.3
1936	2.1	0.7
1937	3.2	0.8
1938	4.1	0.9

Source: Clark, op. cit., Appendix B.

According to Wraga,[23] the Soviet Army, excluding security troops, totaled 1.9 million men in 1936. If we should add 20 percent to this figure to allow for the security troops, the navy and the air force, the armed forces would total approximately 2.3 million men. The volume of steel used in munitions would correspond to .91 ton per man in 1936. In contrast, Communist China had in 1957 about 3.5 million men under arms, not counting the militia, while the amount of steel products consumed in the manufacture of military items has been estimated at 820,000 tons[24] in the four-year period between 1953 and 1956. On an annual per capita basis, only .06 ton of steel products was therefore absorbed in this manner. The much lower equipment and maintenance levels of the present Communist Chinese armed forces, even in comparison with the Red Army of 1936, are therefore quite apparent.

Allocation and Consumption of Finished Steel and
Some Tentative Conclusions

A complete summary of the various end uses of finished steel and their availability can be gleaned from Table 5.10. Whether or not the total consumption estimates are reasonable can be partly checked against Communist official statistics of steel allotment by industry under the unified allocation program for

Table 5.10

BALANCE BETWEEN PRODUCTION AND CONSUMPTION OF "FINISHED STEEL" BY END USE

(in thousand metric tons)

Item	1952	1953	1954	1955	1956	1957	1958	1959	1960
Production	1,312	1,754	1,965	2,505	3,921	4,260	6,000	9,200	12,800–16,600
Imports	506	850	836	865	634	630	1,950	940	823
Total Available Supply	1,818	2,604	2,801	3,370	4,555	4,890	7,950	10,140	13,623–17,423
Domestic Consumption (Identified) and Exports	1,501	2,369	2,730	3,065	4,342	4,102	5,241	7,651	10,561–10,644
Investment	1,382	2,247	2,604	2,916	4,178	3,924	5,012	7,372	10,302–10,385
Capital construction	1,090	1,880	2,220	2,400	4,090	3,830	4,880	7,170	10,020
Railway	320	254	309	392	623	364	701	911	1,678
Machine building (civilian sector)	387	595	671	676	940	909	1,074–1,603	1,274–2,542	1,474–2,539
Other (residual)	383	1,031	1,240	1,332	2,527	2,557	3,105–2,576	4,985–3,717	6,868–5,803
Addition to Inventory	292	367	384	516	88	94	132	202	282–365
Personal Consumption (civilian use)	119	122	125	128	130	134	137	140	143
Exports	...	...	1	21	34	44	92	139	116
Unidentified Consumption	317	235[a]	71[a]	305[a]	213[a]	788	2,709	2,489	3,062–6,779 (2,979–6,862)[b]

[a] If the export allotment estimates were used instead of the exports given in the table, unidentified consumption for 1953 through 1956 would be (thousand tons): 225, 55, 233, and 47, respectively.

[b] The figures in parentheses are computed by subtracting (a) the smaller of the two estimates of domestic consumption and export from the larger estimate of total available supply, and (b) the larger of the two estimates of domestic consumption and export from the smaller estimate of total available supply. This range then covers both the extreme low and the extreme high possible values.

the years 1953-1956.[25] The published data given in this connection are cumulative totals for the four-year period and consist of the following:

Category	Thousand Metric Tons	Percent of Total Allotment
Central Government Ministries in Charge of Industries and Their Enterprises	4,650	39.0
Heavy industry	(4,510)	(37.9)
Light industry	(140)	(1.1)
Central Government Transportation, Postal, and Communications Ministries	2,220	18.6
Ministry of Foreign Trade for Export	320	2.7
Ministry of Commerce	1,660	13.9
Other	3,060	25.8
Total	11,910	100.0

If the annual allotments in 1953-1956 are then compared with the total volume of steel products available, a series of differences may be found (in thousand metric tons):

	Item	1953	1954	1955	1956	Cumulative Total
(1)	Production Plus Imports	2,604	2,801	3,370	4,555	13,330
(2)	Allocations, Annual	2,340	2,410	2,880	4,280	11,910
(3)	(1) − (2)	264	391	490	275	1,420
(4)	Export Allotment	10	17	93	200	320
(5)	Reported Export	---	1	21	34	56
(6)	(4) − (5)	10	16	72	166	264
(7)	Adjusted Discrepancy between Availability and Allocations (3) + (6)	274	407	562	441	1,684

174

If we add to this series the excess of export allotments over reported export based on the Japanese source, the adjusted differences would constitute the net discrepancy between the official data on allocations and our estimates of availability.[26] Can this discrepancy be explained?

A plausible explanation of the above adjusted discrepancy is that the data on allocations, inasmuch as they reflected planned allocations, did not take into account unplanned additions to inventory. The latter have been estimated earlier as (thousand metric tons):

1952	1953	1954	1955	Total 1952-55
242	323	362	462	1,389

For the years 1953-1955, the cumulative adjusted discrepancy between allocations and available supply amounted to 1,243,000 tons, while the unplanned addition to stock in the same period was 1,147,000 tons. The last figure may, of course, have approximated 1,389,000 tons if all or a part of the unplanned addition to inventory in 1952 actually took place in 1953 or later. If exports were actually closer to the export allotments, the cumulative discrepancy in 1953-1955 (item 3 in table above) would be 1,145,000 or almost identical with the estimated unplanned addition to inventory in the same three years. Thus, while uncertainties remain, the official statistics on allocations seem to bear out our estimates of available supply, offering at the same time support to the hypothesis advanced earlier on unplanned additions to inventory.

The statistics on finished-steel allocations contain 3,060,000 tons allotted to "other" purposes in 1953-1956, including allocations to (a) the provincial and municipal authorities, (b) official inventory of stockpile, and (c) other users in the central government not otherwise listed. Item (a) was not likely to be important, because all major heavy constructions and large productive enterprises were under the jurisdiction of the central government. Item (b) corresponds to our concept of planned addition to inventory and has been estimated at 208,000 tons for 1953-1956.[27] Subtracting 208,000 tons from 3,060,000 tons,

175

we obtain a difference of 2, 852, 000 tons, which may be interpreted as an approximate value of item (c), item (a) being quantitatively unimportant. What could this figure represent?

The reader is reminded in this connection of Gardner Clark's discussion on steel consumption by the Soviet munitions industry and in the construction of the "miscellaneous machine building" plants. It may not be unreasonable if we were to take item (c) as indicative of the sum of steel products used for military purposes--namely, arms production, military constructions, and investment in ordnance plants. The order of magnitude involved, according to our estimates and interpretations, would then be:

Allotment	1953-1956 (million metric tons)	
	Total	Annual Average
Total Military Uses	2. 85	. 71
Arms Production (unidentified consumption in Table 5. 10)	.56 - .82	. 14 - . 21
Military Constructions and Building of Ordnance Plants (residual)	2. 29 - 2. 03	. 57 - . 50

That is to say, about 20 to 30 percent of the finished steel absorbed by the military effort was devoted to arms production. In contrast, a far higher proportion was devoted to investment in military "fixed assets. "

Consumption, Demand, and Supply of Finished Steel

The existence of an apparently large unplanned addition to stock throughout the period under investigation, although no estimate for it has been made in Table 5. 10 from 1957 on, is a clear indication of an excess of supply over demand during the period. This "surplus" had become exceedingly large by the end of 1960 as may be seen in the very high residuals included in "unidentified consumption" in 1957-1960, which contained both the amount supplied to the arms industry and unplanned additions to stock during the last four years.

There may, of course, be some attenuating circumstances which would

176

make the actual stockpile smaller than the statistics suggest. First, the output data may include semifinished steel which had subsequently undergone further processing, thus resulting in double counting. This possibility looms large especially for 1958-1960.[28] Second, other semifinished products, which were not fabricated further, may be present in both the output statistics and the inventory figures. On the consumption side, the coefficient of steel consumption per thousand yuan of capital construction expenditure may very well include "indirect" uses in the form of semifinished products,[29] thus rendering the data on consumption and available supply mutually consistent and reconcilable. Thus the excess supply of really finished products would be less.

Nevertheless, even if we disregard the large "surplus" years (1957-1960), the accumulated stock by the end of 1956 would still reach 1,647,000 million metric tons, or more than one-third of the available supply in 1957 and about two-fifths of the year's identified consumption. This extraordinarily large accumulation of working capital would seem to be in flagrant violation of the principles of good planning. Since capital goods were scarce in Communist China and were relatively highly priced, the users may indeed have had to economize in their use, perhaps inordinately on occasion. But if the planners did not wish to be wasteful in steel consumption, why had the capacity of the machine-building and construction industries not been expanded to a greater extent than they were? To this question we can only offer some tentative answers.

First, the steel product users, in order to assure themselves of an adequate supply to safeguard their own production quotas, may have requested larger allocations than warranted by their anticipated need. Second, transport difficulties during the "Great Leap Forward" may have led to an accumulation of products awaiting shipment at the mills. Third, the unceasing drive for greater and still greater output may have been carried out without regard to prevailing demand. Fourth, the quality of the product, which doubtless suffered during the production drives, may have been such that a fair proportion of the stock would consist of defective goods which could not be used. Fifth, the steels produced did not comprise a large enough variety in sizable quantities. Finally, the capacity of the steel users could not be readily expanded because of the shortage of other resources, such as machine tools, and the limited usefulness of the available steels.

177

An examination of Table 5.11 would show that, apart from the period of
the "Great Leap," when the consumption and production estimates were both
less reliable,[30] capital construction tended to account for a relatively stable
proportion of "current consumption," i.e., available supply less addition to
stock, and during the First Five-Year Plan it varied from 80 to 90 percent.
Machine building for investment purposes in the civilian sector accounted for a
gradually diminishing share in the same period, decreasing from about 28 percent in 1953-1954 to 19 percent in 1957. The same relative decline took place
in the railway sector, while the "other" categories took up the slack. The last
item included both civilian and military constructions, as well as the building
of factories producing arms. The relative stability of the share of capital construction in the "current consumption" of steel products, as well as the seem-
ingly orderly expansion of the "other" categories under capital construction,
albeit with fluctuations, strongly suggests that the amount of finished steel that
could be usefully, and without waste, absorbed by capital construction was
limited, if not inflexible. The limits were probably to be found in the last three
of the factors mentioned above. The accumulation of excessive, if not useless,
stock would seem to be a hallmark of either managerial or technical deficiency
or, in all probability, of both.

The Role of Imports

The technological deficiency of Communist China's steel industry is felt
most keenly in the limited variety of the product mix, notwithstanding the many
new products trial tested, as mentioned in Chapter 3. As lamented by the authors
of Major Aspects:

> The needs for iron and steel products by China's machine industry
> and national defense industry cannot be satisfied; steel materials
> in particular do not meet the demands. For example, in 1956 only
> 58 percent of the steel materials for use in aircraft could be sup-
> plied, only 53 percent of the steel materials for tanks could be
> supplied, and only 69 percent of the steel materials used in auto-
> mobiles could be supplied. [31]

At first glance, this situation, however, is not fully revealed by the import statistics as long as they are viewed in the aggregate. As we can see in

178

Table 5. 11

PERCENT DISTRIBUTION OF "FINISHED STEEL" IN "CURRENT CONSUMPTION"
(in thousand metric tons)

Year	Total Available Supply	Addition to Inventory	Current Consumption
1952	1,818	292	1,526
1953	2,604	367	2,237
1954	2,801	384	2,417
1955	3,370	516	2,854
1956	4,555	88	4,467
1957	4,890	94	4,796
1958	7,950	132	7,818
1959	10,140	202	9,938
1960	13,623-17,423	282-365	13,341-17,058

Item	Percent Distribution of Current Consumption									
	1952	1953	1954	1955	1956	1957	1958	1959	1960	
Total Current Consumption	100	100	100	100	100	100	100	100	100	100
Capital Construction	71.4	84.0	91.8	84.1	91.6	79.9	62.4	72.1	75.1	58.7
Railways	20.9	11.3	12.8	13.7	13.9	7.6	9.0	9.2	12.6	9.8
Machine building	25.4	26.6	27.7	23.7	21.1	19.0	13.7-20.5	12.8-25.6	11.0-19.0	14.9-8.6
Other	25.1	46.1	51.3	46.7	56.6	53.3	39.7-32.9	50.2-37.4	51.5-43.5	34.0-40.3
Personal Consumption	7.8	5.5	5.2	4.5	2.9	2.8	1.8	1.4	1.0	0.8
Unidentified Consumption	20.8	10.5	2.9	10.7	4.8	16.4	34.6	25.0	23.0[a]	39.7[a]
Exports	...	...	...	0.7	0.8	0.9	1.2	1.4	0.9	0.7

Source: Table 5.10.

[a]Since the end-use estimates here are independent of the estimates of total available supply, it is logical to assume that the estimates of current consumption can either be paired with the right column of the end-use estimates or with the left column. Following this assumption, therefore, four separate estimates of "unidentified consumption" can be derived from the four possible pairings. The "unidentified consumption" estimates in the column for 1960 would then read as follows: 23.0, 22.3, 39.7, 40.2.

Table 5.12

THE RELATIVE IMPORTANCE OF IMPORTED "FINISHED-STEEL" PRODUCTS

Year	Percent in Total Available Supply	Percent in "Current Consumption"*
1952	27. 8	33. 2
1953	32. 6	38. 0
1954	29. 8	34. 6
1955	25. 7	30. 3
1956	13. 9	14. 2
1957	12. 9	13. 1
1958	24. 5	24. 9
1959	9. 3	9. 5
1960	6. 0–4. 7	6. 2–4. 7

*"Current Consumption" = total available supply less addition to inventory.

Notes and Sources: Derived from Tables 5. 10 and 5. 11.

Table 5.13

FINISHED-STEEL IMPORTS BY MAJOR CATEGORIES*

(in thousand metric tons)

Year	Rails and Accessories	%	Steel Shapes and Rods	%	Heavy Plates	%	Steel Tubes	%	Thin Plates	%	Other	%	Total[a]	%
1952	123.3	24.4	169.7	33.5	110.1	21.8	27.3	5.4	3.3	0.6	72.3	14.3	506.0	100
1953	146.4	17.2	200.8	23.6	181.2	21.3	31.4	3.7	40.9	4.8	251.3	29.5	852.0	100
1954	90.6	10.8	144.8	17.3	115.6	13.8	42.5	5.1	15.7	1.9	428.8	51.2	838.0	100
1955	193.7	22.7	165.8	19.4	137.3	16.1	70.6	8.3	32.6	3.8	253.0	29.7	853.0	100
1956	74.5	11.3	101.6	15.4	242.4	36.8	66.7	10.1	14.8	2.2	158.2	24.0	658.2	100
1957	32.8	6.5	39.4	7.8	137.8	27.4	52.1	10.4	91.9	18.3	149.2	29.6	503.2	100
1958	21.4	1.4	70.6	4.7	552.1	37.0	267.1	17.9	332.0	22.2	249.1	16.7	1,492.3	100
1959	49.8	6.5	25.9	3.4	232.1	30.2	189.6	24.7	85.6	11.2	184.2	24.0	767.2	100
1960	60.9	8.1	38.7	5.2	148.8	19.9	164.9	22.0	128.3	17.2	206.2	27.6	747.8	100

* Left-hand column under each category represents tonnage; right-hand column represents percentage of year's total.

[a]The totals in this table differ somewhat from the total imports given in Table 5.9 due to the possible omission of minor items in several years, especially 1957-1960.

Source: Chukyo: Tekko Suryo Chosa, op. cit., p. 11.

Figure 5.2. Percent Distribution of Finished Steel Imports

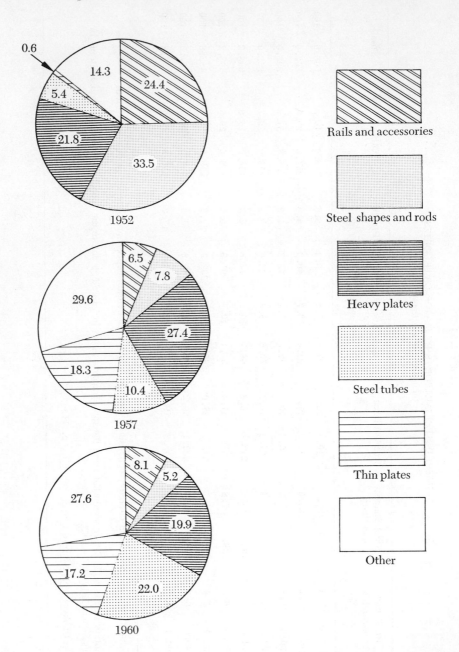

Rails and accessories

Steel shapes and rods

Heavy plates

Steel tubes

Thin plates

Other

Source: Table 5.13

Table 5.14

"FINISHED-STEEL" IMPORTS BY COUNTRIES OF ORIGIN

Quantity
(in thousand metric tons)

Country	1958	1959	1960
U.S.S.R.			
Ordinary	178	165	172
Special	---	---	2
Other	78	8	18
Total	256	173	192
Other Communist Bloc[a]			
Ordinary	145	92	90
Special	...	...	...
Other	...	...	...
Total	145	92	90
Japan and other Pacific Countries[b]			
Ordinary	101	128	38
Special	1	...	...
Other	25	...	2
Total	127	128	40
Western Europe[c]			
Ordinary	1,005	308	385
Special	13	63	18
Other	50	26	72
Total	1,068	397	475
Total Identified	1,596	790	797
Other	354	150	26
Total	1,950	940	823

Sources: Data for "other" countries are derived from Bulletin of the Association for the Study of the Soviet-Type Economies (ASTE), Johns Hopkins University, Bethesda, Maryland, June, 1961, pp. 18-20.

Quantities for "other" countries derived from Chukyo: Tekko Suryo Chosa, 1950-1960 (Communist China, Survey of Iron and Steel Production, 1950-1960), prepared by the Investigation Committee of the Overseas Iron and Steel Market Affairs, Tokyo, Oct. 1962, p. 20; also Chugoku Tekkogyo Chosa Chukan Kokoku (Interim Report of the Survey of the Iron and Steel Industry in Communist China), No. 8, Tokyo, May 1962, pp. 4-12.

(a) Including Poland, Czechoslovakia for 1958-59; for 1960, also Yugoslavia. (b) Including Japan and Hong Kong for 1958-59; for 1960, other Pacific countries were added. (c) Including West Germany, Britain, France, Italy, Holland, Norway, Sweden, Austria, Belgium, and Luxemburg.

Table 5.14, continued

Percentage

Category	1958	1959	1960
Ordinary			
U.S.S.R.	12.5	23.8	25.1
Other Communist Bloc	10.1	13.3	13.2
Japan and other Pacific countries	7.1	18.5	5.5
Western Europe	70.3	44.4	56.2
Total identified	100.0	100.0	100.0
Special			
U.S.S.R.	0.0	0.0	10.0
Other Communist Bloc	0.0	0.0	0.0
Japan and other Pacific countries	7.1	0.0	0.0
Western Europe	92.9	100.0	90.0
Total identified	100.0	100.0	100.0
Other			
U.S.S.R.	51.0	23.5	19.6
Other Communist Bloc	0.0	0.0	0.0
Japan and other Pacific countries	16.3	0.0	2.2
Western Europe	32.7	76.5	78.2
Total identified	100.0	100.0	100.0
Total			
U.S.S.R.	16.0	21.9	24.1
Other Communist Bloc	9.1	11.6	11.3
Japan and other Pacific countries	8.0	16.2	5.0
Western Europe	66.9	50.3	59.6
Total identified	100.0	100.0	100.0

Table 5.14, continued

Percentage

Country	1958	1959	1960
U.S.S.R.			
Ordinary	69.5	95.4	89.6
Special	0.0	0.0	1.0
Other	30.5	4.6	9.4
Total	100.0	100.0	100.0
Other Communist Bloc			
Ordinary	100.0	100.0	100.0
Special	0.0	0.0	0.0
Other	0.0	0.0	0.0
Total	100.0	100.0	100.0
Japan and other Pacific Countries			
Ordinary	79.5	100.0	95.0
Special	0.8	0.0	0.0
Other	19.7	0.0	5.0
Total	100.0	100.0	100.0
Western Europe			
Ordinary	94.1	77.6	81.0
Special	1.2	15.9	3.8
Other	4.7	6.5	15.2
Total	100.0	100.0	100.0
Total Identified	89.5	87.7	85.9
Ordinary			
Special	0.9	8.0	2.5
Other	9.6	4.3	11.6
Total	100.0	100.0	100.0

185

Table 5.10, the relative share of imports in both the total available supply and current consumption declined steadily in 1953-1955, then sharply in 1956. A large increase then took place in 1958, but the decline was resumed thereafter. The statistics themselves may have distorted the apparent trend beginning in 1956 because of the failure to exclude unplanned additions to inventory from "current consumption." Exaggeration of output statistics, and hence of availability, from 1958 on--a fact with which we are by now thoroughly familiar--would accentuate the distortion in the last few years. Furthermore, debt repayment and other balance of payments considerations may also have been the cause of the sharp decline in steel imports in 1960. The crux of the problem, it seems, however, lies in the possibility that continued heavy dependence on imports in some products has been overshadowed by overproduction in others. To the extent that the import items in continued short supply are needed to complement the products in relative abundance, the latter have really been produced in vain.

According to statistics of steel product imports by major categories, beginning in 1953, the volume of imported steel rails and accessories fell steadily from 146,400 tons in 1953 to 60,900 tons in 1960, the only principal exception being 1955. (See Table 5.13.) Steel shapes and rods imported also fell from 200,800 tons in 1953 to 38,700 tons in 1960, with 1958 as the only significant exception. On the other hand, imports of heavy plates showed a much more checkered course during the period, fluctuating widely from year to year. Volume ranged from 181,200 tons in 1953 to a low of 115,600 tons in 1954, and a high of 552,100 tons in 1958. Steel tubes import rose continually from 31,400 tons in 1953 to 164,900 tons in 1960, having attained a peak of 267,100 tons in 1958. The same general upward trend may be said to apply to thin sheets and cold-rolled plates. [32]

Table 5.14, which gives partial import statistics for 1958-1960 by countries of origin, also identifies imports of ordinary steel as the category suffering the largest decline in 1958-1959. Special steels, on the other hand, did not decline in 1958-1959. Again, balance of payments considerations have doubtless influenced the changes to a certain extent.

Thus, while it is always hazardous to try to summarize a complex

Table 5.15

IRON AND STEEL IMPORTS BY COUNTRIES OF ORIGIN
(in percent)

Country	1950	1955	1958	1959	1960
Japan	19	...	...	...	...
England	...	...	...	9	9
West Germany	...	...	32	12	17
Austria	...	...	...	14	...
France	...	...	12	14	12
Belgium	...	...	11	...	16
Communist Bloc					
U.S.S.R.	65	79	20	23	26
Poland	2	...	...	...	...
Czechoslovakia	...	11	...	...	...
Other	...	...	9	12	11
Total	67	98	29	35	37
Other	14	2	16	16	9
Total Identified	100	100	100	100	100

Source: Chukyo: Tekko Suryo Chosa, 1950-1960, op. cit., p. 10.

Table 5.16

PIG IRON EXPORTS TO THE U.S.S.R. AND JAPAN IN SELECTED YEARS
(in thousand metric tons)

Year	Pig Iron Exports			Percent of
	U.S.S.R.[a]	Japan[b]	Total	Output (Modern)[c]
1955	583	...	583	16
1956	468	3	471	10
1957	103	29	132	2
1958	189	---	189	2
1959	97	5	102	1
1960	166	24	190	1.5

(a) Data for U.S.S.R. from Vneshniaia torgovlia, 1957, Moscow, p. 127; 1958, p. 128; 1960, p. 153. (b) Data for Japan from Shin Chugoku Nenkan, 1962 (New China Yearbook), Tokyo, 1962, p. 293. (c) Percent computed on the basis of the output estimates of the modern sector in Table B-12, Appendix B.

situation, the burden of evidence seems to point to Communist China's continued shortage of quality and special steels and reliance on imports. Needless to say, these are essential inputs both in the defense industry and in machine manufacture. Since Communist China is also dependent on essential machine imports in the country's investment program,[33] inadequacy of the steel-finishing industry would tend to prolong the dependence of the machine industry. If the reader bears in mind that this situation has been accompanied by an apparent overdevelopment in certain sections of the steel industry as a result of a most zealous and unprecedented drive to produce steel, he cannot but wonder at the magnitude of the failure in planning.

In conclusion, one should also note that as of 1960 about 67 percent of Communist China's iron and steel imports were derived from Western suppliers. In contrast, the Communist Bloc supplied 67 percent in 1950 and 98 percent in 1955. It remains to be seen whether Communist China's industrial development will henceforth resume on the basis of expanding steel imports from the Bloc or of larger imports from the West.

Pig Iron and Iron Ore Exports in the Changed Structure of the Iron and Steel Industry of Communist China

Finally, a word should be said on the declining role of exports in the distribution of pig iron and iron ore output in the light of the growth of the domestic iron and steel industry. Whereas pig iron from Manchuria and iron ore from China proper were produced during the prewar period primarily for the export market,[34] the share of exports in the total output of these products has declined sharply under the Communist regime. In the case of pig iron, the proportion of exports in the total output of the modern mills fell to 2 percent in 1957 and 1.5 percent in 1960 in comparison with over 70 percent during the early 1930's. The bulk of the exports also went to the Soviet Union, while only relatively small quantities went to Japan. In the case of iron ore, negligible volumes have been reported.[35] Even if we allow for omissions in the export statistics, it is quite plain that the relative role of exports has diminished rapidly in both cases. In absolute terms, pig iron export has also fallen below the level attained by export from Manchuria during the prewar period. These changes are of course entirely in line with the structural change the industry has undergone.

188

6

REGIONAL DISTRIBUTION OF THE
IRON AND STEEL INDUSTRY BEFORE 1949

Up to this point, the Chinese iron and steel industry has been discussed on a national basis; regional differences have been indicated only in so far as major divergencies between developments in Manchuria and the rest of China existed. Relatively little attention has been given to a close-up view of the pattern of regional distribution and the underlying factors in location. Since both external economies and vested interests, including inertia and resistance to change, tend to have a cumulative effect as time passes, the locational pattern of plants at any time is to a large extent a result of the pattern created in earlier times. In order to understand the geographical distribution of the industry today, we must therefore go back to the beginning, from the time the industry first made its appearance. This is an effort that cannot be avoided if we bear in mind the important and far-reaching effect of the relationship of the location of steel mills to that of the machine industry and the effect both have on industrial concentration (or decentralization), the scale of industrial works, and the Chinese developmental model as a whole.

Selection of Sites for the Early Plants

Iron Ore Supply

Up to the end of World War I the modern iron smelters and steelworks were almost invariably established at places close to the ore supply. Adequate transport facilities for bringing in fuel and other raw materials and for sending shipments to the market constituted a second prerequisite. For the country as a whole, these works were all located in six provinces--Hupeh, Liaoning, Chahar, Anhwei, Shantung, and Shansi--plus the city of Shanghai. The Shanghai mill was the only one entirely dependent on ore supply from a distance and located at the market rather than the source of supply.

189

The fact that most of the early mills were located in the provinces of Hupeh and Liaoning was chiefly a result of the discovery of the first principal iron ore deposits within their borders. As shown in Appendix A, the total iron-ore reserve estimated for the entire country by 1921 was 677,899,000 metric tons, of which 387,580,000 tons were found in Liaoning and 52,660,000 tons in Hupeh, accounting for 57 percent and 7.8 percent of the total, respectively.

While the reserve in Hupeh ranked below that of Hopeh, the ferrous content of the former reached 56.6 percent on the average and was higher than that of deposits in other provinces. The high iron content minimized the task of ore dressing and beneficiation and justified to a large degree the establishment of the iron and steel works in Hupeh by lowering the cost of production. Statistics also show that the ore deposits in Hupeh were concentrated in a few places, such as Ta-yeh and Hsiang-pi-shan. At the time, out of the known total reserve of 52,660,000 metric tons in the province, that at Ta-yeh amounted to 35,000,000 metric tons or 66 percent. This was an additional favorable factor for the development of the industry in Hupeh.

In Manchuria, Liaoning has the largest iron ore reserve of any province in the country, but in contrast to those of Hupeh, most of the deposits consist of lean ores, and the comparatively thin seams were scattered over a vast area. This condition, together with the remoteness of the province from the then established economic centers, tended to discourage risk capital. Furthermore, reluctance on the part of the Manchu rulers to open up their royal Manchurian preserve to non-Manchu exploitation may also have inhibited early industrial development. Establishment of modern iron mining in Manchuria was, therefore, postponed and left to the Japanese who, depending heavily on other countries for iron ore and pig iron to supply their industries at home, and for other political and military reasons as well, were thus destined to play a pioneering role in the exploitation of the Manchurian deposits.

Discovery of adequate local deposits also prompted the establishment of the remaining iron and steel works. Thus, discovery of the deposits at Hsüan-hua, Lung-kuan, Huai-lai, and Yen-t'ung-shan in the former Chahar province (now abolished) led to the construction of the Lung-yen Iron and Steel Works. The rich reserves at I-tu, Ling-tzu, Ch'ang-shan and Huan-tai served as the

Table 6.1

IRON CONTENT OF IRON ORE DEPOSITS
IN VARIOUS PROVINCES, 1921
(in thousand metric tons)

Province[a]	Total Iron Ore Deposits	Total Iron Content	Percent of Total Reserve
Liaoning	387,580	105,205	27.1
Chahar	69,200	36,200	52.3[b]
Hupeh	52,660	29,780	56.6
Anhwei	50,000	25,125	50.3
Kiangsu	35,000	17,500	50.0
Shantung	29,920	14,138	47.3
Hopeh[b]	22,279	9,234	41.4[b]
Kiangsi	18,060	8,671	48.0
Fukien	7,500	3,650	48.7
Honan	3,400	1,640	48.2
Chekiang	2,300	1,050	45.7
Total	677,899	252,193	37.2

Source: General Statement, 1st Issue, op. cit., pp. 32-34.

[a]Arranged in diminishing order of available iron content.

[b]Iron ore deposits in Hopeh province under the Communists include the deposits of both Chahar province and Hopeh province. Thus, the iron content as percent of total reserve becomes 49.7 for Hopeh.

chief source of ore supply to the Chin-ling-chen Iron Works. The Yü-fan Co. Ltd. relied upon the iron ore deposits of Fan-ch'ang, Tang-t'u and T'ung-shan of Anhwei province.

This close correspondence between local ore supply and the location of modern smelters may also be brought out most vividly if we rank the individual provinces included in the first General Statement of the Geological Survey of China both with respect to the estimated metal content of their iron ore reserves and with respect to the productive capacity of the iron smelters. In terms of ore reserve, the relative order of importance was Liaoning, Chahar, Hupeh, Anhwei, Kiangsu, and Shantung,[1] as shown in Table 6.1. In terms of blast furnace capacity, the order would be Liaoning, Hupeh, and Chahar, followed by Shanghai (Kiangsu), Shansi, and small units elsewhere.[2] The minor discrepancy between the two series can be easily explained by other considerations, such as the availability of adequate financing and government support.

Although iron smelting and steelmaking require considerable quantities of limestone, manganese, and refractory materials, these inputs were apparently not matters of serious concern in the location of plants during the early period. The same was true with respect to the supply of water and labor.

In 1913, according to Gardner Clark, coke consumption per metric ton of pig iron averaged 1,087 kg in the United States, 1,180 kg in Russia, 1,400 kg in Britain, and 1,110 kg in Germany.[3] Coke consumption in China in as late as 1952 has been estimated at 1,000 kg. It was undoubtedly much higher during the early years. Because of the large consumption of coking coal, adequate fuel supply was a major determinant in location. In this connection, although coal deposits are ubiquitous in China, what called for serious consideration was its coking quality, mining cost, and the coking and transportation expenditures. These in turn depended, inter alia, on the quality of coal deposits and the ease with which they could be tapped--the thicker the coal seams and the closer they are to the surface, the lower the cost of production would be. Other factors were the distance between the iron mills and the coal mines, and the availability of adequate transportation facilities. The merger of the Han-yang Iron and Steel Works with iron and coal works at P'ing-hsiang and Ta-yeh into a combined enterprise of the Han-yeh-p'ing Coal and Iron Co. in 1908 was, for instance,

192

Table 6.2

LOCATIONAL RELATIONSHIP BETWEEN THE MAJOR IRON AND STEEL MILLS AND
THEIR PRINCIPAL SOURCES OF IRON ORE AND COKING COAL, 1890-1920

Province	Plant	Year Established	Location	Sources of Iron Ore and Coking Coal			
				Iron Ore		Coking Coal	
				Location	Approximate distance to mill (km)	Location	Approximate distance to mill (km)
Hupeh	Han-yang Iron and Steel Works	1890	Han-yang	Ta-yeh	130	P'ing-hsiang (Kiangsi)	650
	Ta-yeh Iron Works	1914	Ta-yeh	T'ieh-shan (Ta-yeh)	20	P'ing-hsiang	710
	Yang-tze Machine-building Co.	1919	Shen-chia-chi	Hsiang-pi-shan	local	Liu-ho-kou	680
	Hsiang-pi-shan Iron Mining Co.	1920	Hsiang-pi-shan	Hsiang-pi-shan	local	P'ing-hsiang	750
Liaoning (Manchuria)	Pen-ch'i-hu Iron Works	1910	Pen-ch'i-hu	Miao-erh-kou	28	Fu-shun Pen-ch'i	131 local
	Anshan Iron and Steel Works	1916	An-shan	Kung-ch'ang-ling An-shan	50 local	Fu-shun Pen-ch'i	118 120
Chahar	Lung-yen Iron and Steel Co.	1918	Hsüan-hua	Yen-t'ung-shan Lung-kuan	45 local	T'ai-yüan Yang-ch'üan	590 590
Anhwei	Yü-fan Co.	1919	Fan-ch'ang	Fan-ch'ang	local	Hsün-keng-shan (Huai-yüan)	370
Shantung	Chin-ling-chen Iron Works	1919	Chin-ling-chen	Chin-ling-chen	local	Po-shan Tzu-ch'uan Fen-tzu	60 20 100
Shansi	Yang-ch'üan Iron Works	1917	Yang-ch'üan	Pao-t'ou Shou-yang	20 50	Shih-chia-chuang T'ai-yüan	105 125
Shanghai (Kiangsu)	Ho-hsin Co.	1917	Shanghai	Nan-shan (Anhwei)	405	Tsao-chuang Hsün-keng-shan	770 419

Source: See Chapter 2.

aimed at making better use of the rich coal deposits at P'ing-hsiang, the largest coal producing area of Kiangsi province bordering Hupeh.[4] Coal mining development in Anhwei by the well-known Huai-nan Coal Mining Company was initiated for a similar purpose. Development of iron- and steelmaking in Shanghai was doubtless influenced by easy access to coking coal by sea.

Transportation Facilities

A rather interesting phenomenon may be noted if comparison is made between the respective distances from the mill to the principal sources of iron ore and coking coal (Table 6.2). All the early mills were without exception located nearer to their ore supply than to their sources of coking coal. This fact, however, was not necessarily a reflection of any comparative advantage based on the relative transport cost of ore versus that of coal. The main explanation lay in the proximity of the mills to their principal markets. A more striking phenomenon, however, was the fact that the works at Pen-ch'i and An-shan were much closer to their coking coal sources than the mills in Hupeh. This was a clear disadvantage for the Hupeh mills and may have partly accounted for their slower rate of development later, although lagging economic development in China proper in comparison with Manchuria was probably the more important cause.

Although coal had to be shipped over a considerable distance in several cases, the existence of railway transport could usually be counted on. As for transportation to the market, the choice of the Hankow area, a trading center in Central China, for many of the mills is easily understandable. The same applies to Shanghai where an iron works was set up by the Ho-hsin Company in the P'u-tung district within the city limits although neither iron ore nor coal deposits were found in the vicinity. The locational advantage lay in the existence of the growing commercial market in Shanghai and easy access to imported ore and coal because of the plant's position at the junction of the Yangtze River and the sea. For the same reason, most of the iron and steel plants during the early years were located along railways or rivers. Alternatively, they became important reasons why rail connections were subsequently developed. Moreover, once the iron and steel works were established, they in turn became a major

194

attraction to the location of new industries. The geographical propinquity of the early iron and steel plants to major transportation facilities may be seen from Table 6.3.

Foreign Influence

Finally, as we have already shown in Chapter 2, an outstanding feature of the early iron and steel industry was production for export. Japan was the chief importer of ore from China proper and of pig iron from Manchuria. As a means to assure herself of uninterrupted supply, in addition to political considerations, large capital investments were made by Japan. Nearly all the iron and steel mills in Manchuria were operated under joint Sino-Japanese ownership. In China proper, the Japanese secured the right of mining iron ore in Shantung and were creditors to several other works. (See Table 6.4.)

During the period from 1913 to 1924, for instance, the Han-yang Iron and Steel Works received 57,000,000 yen in twenty-two loans from Japan, [5] and was kept in operation entirely by these loans. Since the foreign investors' interest was best served by locating the mills in places where their political influence was also paramount, the coastal provinces and places along large navigable rivers became areas of first choice. This preference again coincides with the locational pattern described above.

Development Trends during the Interwar Period

Pre-1937

For reasons outlined earlier, the paper plans mapped out in 1928[6] for the construction of a large-scale steel industry were not carried out before the Sino-Japanese War (1937-1945). The only new iron works built in the decade from 1927 to 1937 was the Hung-yü Iron Works in Hsin-hsiang, Honan province,[7] which had a reported annual productive capacity of 7,500 metric tons. However, no detailed information concerning production at this plant can be found.

With one minor exception, therefore, locational changes during the period were not a result of new plant establishments. On the other hand, in terms of production rather than capacity, the relative importance of the different

Table 6.3

DISTANCE BETWEEN EARLY IRON AND STEEL PLANTS
AND MAJOR TRANSPORTATION FACILITIES*

Plant	Location	Transportation Facilities
Han-yang Iron and Steel Works	Han-yang, Hupeh	Situated at the terminal of the Canton-Hankow (Wuhan) Railway and on the bank of the Yangtze River
Ta-yeh Iron Works	Ta-yeh, Hupeh	Some 30 kilometers from the Yangtze River bank, connected by an industrial rail line
Yangtze Machine-Building Co.	Hankow, Hupeh	Situated at the terminal of the Peiping-Hankow (now Peking-Wuhan) Railway and on the bank of the Yangtze River
Hsiang-pi-shan Iron Mining Co.	Hsing-pi-shan, Hupeh	Same as the Ta-yeh Iron Works
Yü-fan Co.	Fan-ch'ang, Anhwei	Some 20 kilometers from the Ti-kang harbor of the Yangtze River, connected by an industrial railway
Chin-ling-chen Iron Works	Chin-ling-chen, Shantung	Situated at a junction of the Tsinan-Tsingtao Railway
Lung-yen Iron and Steel Co.	Hsüan-hua, Chahar	Situated at a junction of the Peiping-Suiyuan (now Peking-Pao-t'ou) Railway
Yang-ch'üan Iron Works	Yang-ch'üan, Shansi	Situated at a junction on the Chengting-T'ai-yüan Railway
Pen-ch'i-hu Iron Works	Pen-ch'i-hu, Liaoning	Situated at a junction of the former South Manchurian (now the Shenyang-Antung Railway)
An-shan Iron and Steel Works	An-shan, Liaoning	Same as the Pen-ch'i-hu Iron Works
Ho-hsin Co.	P'u-tung, Shanghai	Situated in the P'u-tung district on the bank of the Wongpoo River leading to the Yellow Sea

*Including rail lines built subsequent to the establishment of the mills.

Source: An Atlas of the People's Republic of China, Atlas Press, Shanghai, 1953, pp. 21, 24, 34, and 36.

Table 6.4

FINANCIAL BACKGROUND OF THE EARLY IRON WORKS, 1890-1920

Plant	Ownership
(1) An-shan Iron Works	Sino-Japanese
(2) Ta-yeh Iron Works	Chinese Government
(3) Han-yang Iron and Steel Works	Chinese Government
(4) Pen-ch'i-hu Iron Works	Sino-Japanese
(5) Lung-yen Iron and Steel Co., Ltd.	Government - private
(6) Yangtze Machine Building Co., Ltd.	Private
(7) Ho-hsin Co., Ltd.	Private
(8) Yang-ch'üan Iron Works	Chinese Government
(9) Hsiang-pi-shan Iron Mining Co., Ltd.	Chinese Government
(10) Yü-fan Co., Ltd.	Private (with loan from Japan)
(11) Chin-ling-chen Iron Works	Sino-Japanese

Sources: Information on ownership from General Statement, 2d issue, op. cit., pp. 124-125. For ownership of the Yangtze Machine Building Company, Ltd., the Yang-ch'üan Iron Works and the An-shan mill, see H. D. Fong, op. cit.

According to H. D. Fong, op. cit., pp. 643-644, the principal equipment and production capacity of the above plants were as follows:

	Number of Blast Furnaces	Annual Productive Capacity of Pig Iron (in thousand metric tons)
(1)	2	180
(2)	2	320
(3)	2 to 4	230
(4)	4	90
(5)	1	90
(6)	1	36
(7)	2	16
(8)	1	4.5-6.0

areas where iron mills existed was greatly altered as a result of an uneven rate of advance. The greater part of the iron smelting and steelmaking equipment of the existing firms remained idle during this period. The exception was provided by the enterprises in Manchuria, which had come under complete Japanese control beginning in 1931. Most iron and steel works in China proper, on the other hand, were faced with serious financial difficulties and production came to a standstill. Statistics show that out of the country's total pig iron capacity of 1,144,000 metric tons per year, including that of the An-shan and Pen-ch'i-hu Iron Works in Manchuria, only 37 percent was in use in 1934. The proportion of pig iron produced in the modern Manchurian mills increased from 73 percent of the total mainland output in 1925 to well over 90 percent a few years later and remained at 97 percent in 1937.

In China proper, of the seven mills for which data in 1934 are given in Table 6.5, only the Liu-ho-kou and Yang-ch'üan works were in operation. No production was reported from the three larger mills.

In contrast to the general dormancy in iron smelting, however, new interest was shown in steelmaking during this period. Open hearth furnaces were built by some machine building factories, shipyards, cement manufacturers, and arsenals, which began to produce steel on a small scale within their own organizations as an auxiliary business. According to statistics compiled by the Shen Pao (Table 6.6),[8] four arsenals, located in the provinces of Hupeh, Liaoning, Szechwan, and Honan, together with a few machine building firms and shipyards in Shanghai, were thus engaged. The establishment of these auxiliary plants, small though they were, had the short-run effect of expanding the base of the steel industry to a certain extent. On the whole, these steel furnaces were also located in the same cities where modern iron smelters were found. Moreover, since they were intended to serve certain minor internal requirements, they were not themselves designed for expansion. No significant change in the locational pattern therefore ensued.

Wartime Changes in the Locational Pattern

Several radical developments took place during the Sino-Japanese War that exercised a decisive influence on the locational pattern of the industry and

Table 6.5

CAPACITY UTILIZATION OF IRON WORKS, 1934
(thousand metric tons of pig iron)

Plant	Annual Productive Capacity	Annual Production	Production in Percent of Total Capacity
Manchuria			
An-shan Iron Works	450	322	72
Pen-ch'i-hu Iron Works	96	81*	84
China Proper			
Ta-yeh Iron Works	270	---	nil
Han-yeh-p'ing Iron and Coal Co., Ltd.	195	---	nil
Liu-ho-kou Iron Works (former Yangtze Machine Building Co. at Shen-chia-chi)	30	17	57
Lung-yen (Shih-ching-shan) Iron Works	75	---	nil
Ho-hsin (Shanghai) Iron Works	14	---	nil
Hung-yü (Hsin-hsiang) Iron Works	8	---	nil
Yang-ch'üan Iron Works	6	4	67
Total	1,144	424	37

*In 1932.

Source: General Statement, 5th issue, op. cit., pp. 184-185.

Table 6.6

REGIONAL DISTRIBUTION OF STEELMAKING PLANTS IN CHINA PROPER, 1934

Plant	Location	Number of Open Hearth Furnaces	Annual Capacity (thousand metric tons)
Principal Mill			
Han-yeh-p'ing Iron and Coal Co., Ltd.	Han-yang, Hupeh	7	90
"Auxiliary" Plants			
Han-yang Arsenal	Han-yang, Hupeh	2	5
Ho-hsin Iron and Steel Works	Shanghai	2	8
Shanghai Machine Building Factory	Shanghai	2	8
Chiang-nan Ship Building Co.	Shanghai	1	...
Ch'i-hsin Cement Co., Ltd.	T'ang-shan, Hopei	1	...
Szechwan Arsenal	Ch'eng-tu, Szechwan	1	...
Kung-hsien Arsenal	Kung-hsien, Honan	1	...
Yü-ts'ai Iron Works	T'ai-yüan, Shansi	1	4
Shen-yang Arsenal	Shen-yang, Liaoning	1	3
Total		19	118

Source: Shen-pao Yearbook, 1936, compiled by the Shanghai Shen Pao, Shanghai, 1936, pp. 710-711

prepared in many ways for the more recent changes under the Communist regime. First, relocation of plants to the free zone in Southwest China resulted in the concentration of many medium-sized[9] and small mills in the Chungking (Szechwan) area, thus laying the groundwork for its development as a principal center of the industry after 1949. Second, establishment by the Japanese of several smaller mills in North and East China helped to prepare the basis for the more recent development of a number of secondary centers as distinguished from such major concentrations or complexes as An-shan. Third, prompted by wartime demand for steel products, the many small mills in the "new" areas were frequently invested not only with steelmaking facilities, but also with rolling equipment. In a very limited fashion, they were no longer only iron smelters. The broadening move and dispersal process were accompanied by a somewhat greater degree of integration involving the several principal stages of the industry. This trend in Free China paralleled development in Manchuria under the Japanese undertaken also in the exigencies of the war. Finally, a number of small mills made their appearance in provinces hitherto untouched by the iron-making industry at all and thus may have made some far-reaching impact on future industrial development in these areas, even though the effect could not be immediately assessed and the mills were not destined to expand rapidly.

Dismantling and relocation of equipment at Han-yang, Shen-chia-chi (the Liu-ho-kou Works) and Shanghai were ordered by the Nationalist government at the beginning of the war with Japan as a part of a broader policy which also affected many other industrial establishments. The largest relocated iron and steel mill set up under this policy was at Ta-tu-k'ou near Chungking. More than twenty iron and steel works came into existence as a result of government action as well as private initiative. Of the twelve smelting and finishing plants all but two were in Szechwan, and seven were concentrated in Chungking itself. The remaining two were both located at An-ning in Yunnan.

The total iron ore reserves of Szechwan, as published in the General Statement, 7th issue, in 1945, were estimated at 22,023,000 metric tons; coal reserves were estimated at 3,833,000,000 tons. The largest iron ore deposit was located at Chi-chiang, adjacent to Chungking, and totaled 4,598,000 tons.[10] Most of the remaining iron ore deposits of the province were also found along

Table 6.7

PRINCIPAL IRON AND STEEL MILLS IN FREE CHINA, 1938-1945

Province	Plant	Location	Principal Equipment			Annual Pig-Iron Capacity (in metric tons)
			Iron Smelting	Steelmaking	Steel Rolling	
Szechwan	Ta-tu-k'ou Iron and Steel Works	Chungking	One 100-ton blast furnace Two 20-ton blast furnaces	Two 10-ton open hearth furnaces	Eight steel-rolling machines	42,000 (60,000)[a]
	Tzu-yü Iron and Steel Works	Chungking	One 30-ton blast furnace One 5-ton blast furnace	Two 2-ton Bessemers One 0.5-ton Bessemer		6,000[b] 10,500[c]
	The 24th Arsenal	Chungking		Two 2-ton Bessemers Two 3-ton electric furnaces	Three steel-rolling machines	---
	The 28th Arsenal	Chungking		Twelve crucibles		
	Chung-kuo Hsin-yeh Co., Ltd.	Chungking	One 30-ton blast furnace	One 10-ton open hearth furnace One 75-ton electric furnace One 1-ton Bessemer	Two steel-rolling machines	15,000[b] (9,000)[b]
	Yü-hsin Iron and Steel Works	Chungking		Two 1-ton electric furnaces Two 1-ton Bessemers One 5-ton Bessemer One 5-ton open hearth furnace	Three steel-rolling machines	---
	Chung-kuo Steel Co., Ltd.	Chungking		One 1.5-ton Bessemer	One steel-rolling machine	
	Wei-yüan Iron Works	Wei-yüan	One 15-ton blast furnace			6,000

[a]Survey Report on the Steel Industry of Communist China, Enterprise Edition, Vol. 2, p. 2.

[b]Kang-t'ieh, pp. 20-21.

[c]National Resources Commission Quarterly, Vol. VI, nos. 1-4, June-December, 1946, pp. 102-103.

Table 6.7 (continued)

| Province | Plant | Location | Principal Equipment | | | Annual Pig Iron Capacity (in metric tons) |
			Iron Smelting	Steelmaking	Steel Rolling	
Szechwan	Electric Iron Works	Ch'i-chiang		One 15-ton open hearth furnace Two 500-kg and one 150-kg electric furnaces	One steel-rolling machine	---
	Jen-ho (later known as Tzu-shu) Iron and Steel Works	Chiang-pei	Two 7-ton blast furnaces	One 15-ton Bessemer One 5-ton Bessemer		3,000
	Shu-chiang Metallurgy Co.	Chiang-pei	One blast furnace			3,000
	Ching-p'ing Iron Works	Chiang-pei	One blast furnace			1,500
	Hsing-lung Coal and Iron Co.	Chiang-pei	One blast furnace			1,500
	Fu-ch'ang Iron Co.	Ta-chu	One blast furnace			1,500
	Yung-ch'ang Iron Co.	Yung-ch'ang	One blast furnace			1,500
	Ch'u-chiang Metallurgy Co.	Ta-hsien	Two blast furnaces			2,400
	Tung-yüan Enterprise Co.	Ch'i-chiang	Seventeen blast furnaces			15,750
	Chung-hua Industrial Co.	Ch'i-chiang	One blast furnace			750
	Shang-ch'uan Iron Co.	Yung-ch'uan	One blast furnace			1,500

Table 6.7 (continued)

| Province | Plant | Location | Principal Equipment | | | Annual Pig Iron Capacity (in metric tons) |
			Iron Smelting	Steelmaking	Steel Rolling	
Szechwan	Yung-ho Enterprise Co.	Yung-ch'uan	One blast furnace			1,500
	Ta-ch'ang Metallurgy Co.	Ho-ch'uan	One blast furnace			1,500
	Tung-hsi Iron Works	Ch'i-chiang	One blast furnace			900
Yunnan	Yunnan Iron and Steel Works	An-ning	One 50-ton blast furnace	One 1-ton Bessemer One 2-ton Bessemer (unfinished)		15,000
	Chung-kuo Electric Steel Works	An-ning		One 1.5-ton electric furnace One 2-ton Bessemer (unfinished)	One steel-rolling machine	---
Hunan	Chung-yang Iron Works	Hsiang-t'an	Two blast furnaces			150,000
	Min-sheng Iron Works	Hsiang-t'an	One blast furnace			1,500
	Hsiang-hua Iron Works	Heng-shan	One blast furnace			1,500
	Lu-chiang Iron Works	Heng-shan	One blast furnace			600
	Yi-chung Iron Works	Ch'i-yang	One blast furnace			600
Kiangsi	Kiangsi Iron Works	Chi-an	One blast furnace			1,500
Kwangsi	P'ing-kuei Iron Works	Ho-hsien	One blast furnace			3,500

the Yangtze and the Chia-ling Rivers which converge on Chungking. This geo-graphical distribution of iron-ore deposits was probably the chief reason that nearly all iron and steel plants built during the war were concentrated in the suburbs of the wartime capital along the two rivers. Other locational factors included availability of transportation facilities and propinquity to consumption markets. Since water transport was the sole means of bulk transportation in Free China during the war, there being no railway in Szechwan at that time, it was natural that all plants were located along the two rivers in the vicinity of Chungking. As the wartime capital, Chungking was also the nerve center of military and economic administration and the largest consumption market where population growth and wartime activities had boosted the demand for iron and steel products.

Of the thirty-two separate plants in five provinces (Szechwan, Yunnan, Hunan, Kiangsi, and Kwangsi) reported by various government agencies, [11] five had some steelmaking and/or -rolling facilities in addition to blast furnaces; six others were small steel mills only. The remaining twenty-one were iron smelters only. Although the integrated plants were not all larger, the noninte-grated iron smelters were, with only two exceptions, very small iron works.

Whereas only a few cities in six provinces had iron and steel works dur-ing the early period, at the end of the war, fifteen provinces--namely, Liaoning, Hopeh, Shansi, Chahar, Shantung, Honan, Anhwei, Kiangsu, Hupeh, Hunan, Szechwan, Yunnan, Kiangsi, Kwangsi, and Kwangtung (Hainan)--could now boast of some producing iron and steel works. It is noteworthy that the remote southwestern province of Yunnan, which had for many long years been known as a desolate and backward area, had managed to build iron and steel works. In the meantime, small plants had appeared in the unoccupied parts of such provinces as Hunan and Kiangsi in Central China. [12] The Japanese had also be-gun to make some investment in iron ore mining on Hainan Island, off the shore of the southernmost province of Kwangtung. These were all significant changes in the locational pattern.

In the occupied areas, expansion of the established iron ore mining and smelting facilities at An-shan, Pen-ch'i-hu, Shih-ching-shan, etc., were accompanied by the formation of several new or reorganized plants at Shanghai,

Table 6.8

IRON AND STEEL MILLS IN JAPANESE-OCCUPIED AREAS, 1945

Region	Province	Plant	Location	Annual Productive Capacity (in thousand metric tons)		
				Pig Iron	Steel Ingot	Steel Products
Northeast China	Liaoning	An-shan Iron and Steel Works	An-shan	1,960	1,438	913
		Pen-ch'i-hu Coal and Iron Works	Pen-ch'i-hu	550	20	9
		T'ung-hua (Tung-pien-tao) Development Co.	T'ung-hua	14	23	...
		Fu-shun Iron and Steel Works	Fu-shun	---	39	10.4
		Dairen Iron and Steel Works	Dairen	---	17	10
		Shen-yang Iron and Steel Works	Shen-yang	---	86	17
		Li-shan Iron and Steel Works	Li-shan	...	...	3
		Regional total		2,524	1,623	962.4
North China	Hopeh (including Peking)	Shih-ching-shan Iron and Steel Works	Peking	240	---	---
		T'ang-shan Iron and Steel Works	T'ang-shan	144	12	25
		Tientsin Steel Works	Tientsin	30	13.8	28
		Subtotal		414	25.8	53
	Shansi	T'ai-yüan Iron and Steel Works	T'ai-yüan	70	50	45
		Yang-ch'üan Iron Works	Yang-ch'üan	19.5	...	...
		Subtotal		89.5	50	45
	Chahar*	Hsüan-hua Iron Works	Hsüan-hua	84	...	...
		Regional total		587.5	76	98
East China	Shantung	Tsingtao Iron and Steel Works	Tsingtao	150	...	...
	Anhwei	Ma-an-shan Iron and Steel Works	Ma-an-shan	6	...	...
	Kiangsu	Shanghai Iron and Steel Co., Ltd.	Shanghai	30.2	41	170
		Regional total		186.2	41	170
Central China	Honan	Chiao-tso Iron and Steel Works	Chiao-tso	...	...	...
	Hupeh	Ta-yeh Iron and Steel Works	Ta-yeh	...	15	...
		Regional total		...	15	...

*Subsequently incorporated into Hopei.

Source: See Appendix B, Table B-13.

T'ang-shan, Tientsin, Ma-an-shan, T'ai-yüan, Tsingtao, Shih-ching-shan, and Hainan Island. Here too the new mills were not simple smelters, but relatively integrated mills planned to produce finished products.

Locational Characteristics at the End of World War II

With the exception of Soviet removals of industrial equipment from Manchuria at the end of World War II, which drastically affected the iron and steel industry, little locational development of significance took place between the end of the war with Japan and the establishment of the Communist regime in 1949. Although the locational pattern of production was altered because of the surrender of Japan and the return of all economic activities to the eastern seaboard, lack of adequate statistical record precludes any detailed analysis. On the other hand, there apparently was no major change in capacity, while little information is available on the relocation of some minor plants from their wartime homes, which had been planned but was probably not carried out. An analysis of the locational pattern at the end of the war, modified by changes in Manchuria, would provide us with a bird's-eye view of the situation on the eve of the Communist period, and we might then be able to appraise more fully the subsequent changes described in the following chapter.

Two principal aspects of the locational pattern may be examined. The first is the correlation between iron smelting capacity and known iron ore deposits, and involves the long-term issue of resource development, which, other conditions being equal, might in general be expected to favor the development of iron smelting capacity where greater ore deposits are available. The second is the relationship between successive stages of iron- and steelmaking, inasmuch as, other things being equal, it would be more reasonable to achieve a higher degree of integration of the several stages at each location. In view of the later development of steelmaking and finishing in China, compared with iron smelting, there was of course an over-all imbalance in favor of pig iron production. But this condition was not necessarily true with respect to all the localities where one or more of the stages were found. The intraindustry structure at the end of World War II could not but present a serious problem to Communist planners.

207

Iron Smelting and Iron Ore Deposits

In terms of iron ore deposits, the regional ranking in decreasing order
at the end of World War II was as follows:

1. Northeast China
2. Central China
3. North China and Inner Mongolia
4. East China
5. Southwest China
6. Northwest China
7. South China

The order of ranking by provinces and territories was:

1. Liaoning
2. Hopeh
3. Hupeh
4. Fukien
5. Kwangtung
6. Kweichow
7. The Tibet and Chamdo
   Autonomous Region
8. The Sinkiang Uighur
   Autonomous Region
9. Hunan
10. Shansi
11. Szechwan
12. Anhwei
13. Honan
14. Kirin
15. Kiangsi
16. Shantung
17. Yunnan
18. Shensi
19. The Ningsia Hui
    Autonomous Region
20. Kiangsu
21. The Inner Mongolian
    Autonomous Region
22. Tsinghai
23. Chekiang
24. Kansu
25. Kwangsi
26. Heilungkiang

In terms of the annual productive capacity of pig iron before the Soviet removals,
including both the large and the small mills,[13] the order in the regional ranking
was:

1. Northeast China
2. North China and Inner Mongolia
3. East China
4. Central China
5. Southwest China
6. South China
7. Northwest China

The order of ranking by provinces and territories was:

1. Liaoning
2. Hopeh
3. Hunan
4. Shantung
5. Szechwan
6. Shansi
7. Kiangsu
8. Yunnan
9. Kirin
10. Honan
11. Anhwei
12. Kwangsi
13. Kiangsi

On the basis of the above series, the regional rank correlation coefficient equals
+0.857 while the rank correlation coefficient in terms of provinces is only +0.298.

208

At first glance, it might appear that the higher regional correlation is vitiated by the low provincial correlation between the two series. Such a conclusion can, however, be refuted for the following reasons:

First, the exact location of the iron ore deposits in a province plays a very important role in the above computation. If the ores happen to be near the border of a province and are more accessible from the adjacent province or provinces, large deposits in the province do not necessarily lead to high pig iron production there. As may be noted from the above, each region consists of at least two adjacent provinces. Thus the adjacent provinces might be contained in the same region, and their pig iron production would be included in the regional total, which could lead to a high rank correlation coefficient for the regions and a low rank correlation coefficient for the provinces.

Second, large iron ore deposits are not always easily accessible. Fukien, Kweichow, Tibet, and Sinkiang are among the obvious examples where lack of bulk transport facilities effectively ruled out the exploitation of known ore deposits. Since the ore deposits of these areas are just a portion, and possibly a small portion, of the deposits of the regions to which they belong, the regional ore- and pig iron production positions are not too much affected. This again explains why the regions have a higher rank correlation coefficient. The examples of Northwest and Southwest China illustrate this point rather clearly.

Third, one-half of the provinces and territories having iron ore deposits did not report any pig-iron production in 1945 at all. Six of these--namely, Hupeh, [14] Fukien, Kwangtung, Kweichow, the Tibet and Chamdo Autonomous Region, and the Sinkiang Uighur Autonomous Region--rank as high as third, fourth, fifth, sixth, seventh, and eighth, respectively, in the provincial ranking of iron ore deposits. In the computation of the rank correlation coefficient for provinces, all thirteen provinces have had to be treated on the same footing with respect to pig iron capacity, which would not have been the case if some capacity had been reported in some of them. This is a major factor underlying the low rank correlation coefficient for provinces.

The above considerations serve to explain the discrepancy between the regional rank correlation coefficient and the corresponding coefficient in terms of provinces and territories. They also point to the conclusion that, allowing for the inaccessibility of iron ore deposits in certain areas, there was a fair degree of general correspondence between the location of iron smelting capacity and that of iron ore at the end of World War II. This correspondence was adversely affected by the wartime relocation of pig iron capacity from Hupeh in Central China to the Southwest. Further improvement in the locational relationship between iron ore and iron smelting would depend on both reconstruction of blast furnaces in Hupeh and the development of transport facilities in areas where ores were inaccessible.

The Effects of Soviet Removals and Wartime Relocation

The preceding rank correlation was based on pig iron production capacity before Soviet removals from Manchuria. After the removals, the regional ranking in terms of pig iron was:

1. North China and Inner Mongolia
2. Northeast China
3. East China
4. Central China
5. Southwest China
6. South China
7. Northwest China

As we may notice, this is the same order as before Soviet removals with Northeast China and North China and Inner Mongolia interchanged. This causes the rank correlation coefficient to drop from +0.857 to +0.785. The provincial ranking in terms of pig iron was also changed slightly, the order being:

1. Hopeh
2. Liaoning
3. Hunan
4. Shantung
5. Szechwan
6. Shansi
7. Kiangsu
8. Yunnan
9. Honan
10. Anhwei
11. Kwangsi
12. Kirin
13. Kiangsi

The major change is the interchange of Liaoning and Hopeh as compared to the order before Soviet removals. From the point of view of the locational relationship between ore deposits and smelting capacity, restoration of the Liaoning facilities must therefore be added to the list of needed improvements which the Communist planners had to take into account.

210

The Intraindustry Structure at the End
of World War II

Turning to the question of intraindustry balance in fabrication and the possible developments that might be required to achieve greater regional balance and integration--not that such a goal would necessarily be adopted--we may first compute the capacity ratios between pig iron and steel ingot, and between ingot and finished steel, respectively.

Prior to the Soviet removals, the individual provinces may be divided into two groups:

1. Provinces which had an excess of pig iron capacity in relation to steel ingot capacity: Liaoning, Hopeh, Shansi, Shantung, Anhwei, Honan, Hunan, Kiangsi, Kwangsi, and Szechwan.

2. Provinces which had an excess of steel ingot capacity in relation to that of finished-steel products: Liaoning, Kirin, Shansi, Hupeh, and Yunnan.

The effect of Soviet destruction in Manchuria was to remove Liaoning from the first group while leaving all other data unchanged. Abstracting from export of pig iron and ingot steel, greater intraindustry balance and vertical integration within the province would require construction of blast furnaces and ingot smelting facilities as indicated in the preceding list. [15]

More steelmaking plants would increase the need for more plants for finished-steel products. This is obviously the case if the crude steelmaking plants mentioned above were established. Hopeh, Hunan, and Shantung would belong to this category.

The above survey of vertical imbalance by provinces has not given consideration to the problem of markets for finished steel. It is also a static view based on information and accomplishment before 1949. We shall return to these issues and subsequent developments presently.

211

Table 6.9

DEGREE OF VERTICAL INTEGRATION BY PROVINCES, 1945,
BEFORE (AND AFTER) SOVIET REMOVALS

Region	Annual Capacity (in thousand metric tons)			P.I./S.I.	S.I./F.S.	Provinces	Annual Capacity (in thousand metric tons)			P.I./S.I.	S.I./F.S.
	Pig Iron	Steel Ingot	Finished Steel				Pig Iron	Steel Ingot	Finished Steel		
Northeast China	2,524 (396)a	1,622 (580)	962.4 (324)	1.555 (0.683)	1.686 (1.790)	Liaoning	2,510 (393.8)	1,600 (571.8)	962.4 (324)	1.569 (0.689)	1.633 (1.765)
						Kirin	14 (2.2)	23 (8.2)	0 (0)	0.609 (0.268)	** (**)
North China and Inner Mongolia	587.5	75.8	98.0	7.751	0.773	Hopeh	498	25.8	53.0	19.302	0.487
						Shansi	89.5	50.0	45.0	1.790	1.111
East China	186.2	42	170	4.433	0.247	Shantung	150	0	0	**	--b
						Anhwei	6	0	0	**	--
						Kiangsu	30.2	42	170	0.719	0.247
Central China	167.7	15	0	11.180	**	Honan	12	0	0	**	--
						Hupeh	0	15	0	0	**
						Hunan	154.2	0	0	**	--
						Kiangsi	1.5	0	0	**	--
South China	3.0	0	0	**	--	Kwangsi	3.0	0	0	**	--
Southwest China	138.3	63	90	2.195	0.700	Szechwan	123.3	45	90	2.740	0.500
						Yunnan	15.0	18	0	0.833	**
China Total	3,606.7 (1,479.2)	1,817.8 (776.8)	1,320.4 (682)	1.984 (1.904)	1.377 (1.129)						

**No steel-ingot (S.I.) and/or no finished-steel (F.S.) production.

a Since no data are given in pig iron and steel ingot for Liaoning and Kirin after Soviet removals, the figures given above are computed proportionately from the data before Soviet removals and the total capacity of the two provinces before and after Soviet removals.

b Both S.I. and F.S. are zero.

Data in this table are taken from Tables B-5 and B-13, Appendix B.

7

LOCATIONAL DEVELOPMENT AND ITS IMPACT IN 1949–60

Locational Changes in the Modern Sector

A number of major developments under the Communist regime have exerted a considerable influence on the location of the steel industry. Some of these have also had a far-reaching effect on industrial location and economic development in general. These developments may be considered under the following headings: (1) the new locational pattern of the industry; (2) the emergence of a few major modern iron and steel complexes, supplemented by a larger number of secondary centers; (3) the relationship of the steel finishing mills to regional economic development and industrial location in general; (4) the nationwide iron and steel drive of 1958-1959 and its locational impact; and (5) changes in regional intraindustry balance. Examination of these factors will afford us further understanding of the role of the steel industry in Communist China's economic plan and in the performance of Chinese planning itself.

The Changing Regional Pattern of the Industry

One way of describing the locational changes would be to examine the shifts in the relative importance of the major economic and administrative regions in the principal stages of the industry over time. As the principal benchmark years we may select 1952, the last pre-plan year, and 1957, the last year of the First Five-Year Plan. Our observations will be based primarily on this period. The conditions in 1960 will then be examined, although conclusions in this case would have to be more tentative in view of the nature of available plant data.

Inasmuch as regional production data are lacking, we have to base our observations on the locational pattern of annual capacity. It should therefore be borne in mind that the result of our study would not necessarily correspond to the regional distribution of output. With this qualification in mind, we can see

213

in Table 7.1 that the ranking of the individual regions in pig iron production showed only minor changes between 1945 (prior to Soviet removals) and 1952, and no change at all between 1952 and 1957. The minor changes observed concern the relative positions of Central and Southwest China on the one hand and those of Northwest and South China on the other. In both cases the relative positions of the regions were interchanged between 1945 and 1952, reflecting, however, almost entirely the inclusion of only the larger modern mills in the present statistics, which are based on the plant lists in Table B-13 of Appendix B. On the other hand, the restoration of Northeast China to the first place it had occupied in 1945 before Soviet removals and from which it had fallen after the removals was far more significant. This shift was a clear index to the concentrated effort to rehabilitate the metallurgical industry of Manchuria in the first phase of Communist rule.

The absence of any change in the relative ranking of the regions between 1952 and 1957 conceals substantial differences in the regional rates of growth. The higher rates attained by Central and Southwest China during the First Five-Year Plan were a reflection of the establishment of new or restored mills in these two regions, especially at Ta-yeh in Hupeh. However, these differential growth rates were not yet sufficient to bring about any real shift in regional ranking. This was to take place only as a result of the "Great Leap Forward." It should also be noted that rehabilitation and new construction during this period had substantially boosted the iron smelting capacity of Manchuria so that the effect of postwar Soviet devastation had been wiped out by 1957.

The same general trend was exhibited in the location of the steelmaking and -finishing mills. In the case of the former, with the exception of the greater importance of Southwest China (principal base of Free China in World War II) relative to East China during 1945, there was no change in the order of ranking of the individual regions between 1945, prior to Soviet removals, and 1952. No change was observed during the same period in the case of steel finishing (Tables 7.2 and 7.3). Nor was there any change in ranking at both stages during the First Five-Year Plan. Thus, with the exception of the Southwest, the relative importance of which lost ground to Central China in ingot capacity, the locational pattern up to 1957 again reflected faithfully the Communist Chinese

Table 7.1

PERCENT OF ANNUAL PIG IRON CAPACITY BY REGIONS

Region	1945*	Region	1952	1957
Northeast	70.0	Northeast	43.2	47.6
North and Inner		North and Inner		
Mongolia	16.3	Mongolia	38.8	22.8
East	5.2	East	11.9	13.6
Central	4.6	Southwest	4.7	9.6
Southwest	3.8	Central	0.7	6.0
South	0.1	Northwest	0.7	0.4
Northwest	---	South	---	---
Total	100.0		100.0	100.0

*Before Soviet removals.

Source: Data for 1945 are derived from Table 6.9; for 1952 and 1957, from Table B-13, Appendix B. The smaller mills in Table B-5 which were included in ranking in 1945 have been excluded as they might no longer be operative during this period. Their inclusion would not, however, affect the order of the first three regions. The 1957 percent distribution is based on operating capacity.

Table 7.2

PERCENT OF ANNUAL STEEL INGOT CAPACITY BY REGIONS

Region	1945*	Region	1952	1957
Northeast	89.2	Northeast	68.5	65.0
North and Inner		North and Inner		
Mongolia	4.2	Mongolia	16.9	16.5
Southwest	3.5	East China	6.6	7.4
East China	2.3	Southwest	5.8	5.0
Central	0.8	Central	2.2	6.1
Northwest	---	Northwest	---	---
South	---	South	---	---
Total	100.0		100.0	100.0

*Before Soviet removals.

Table 7.3

PERCENT OF ANNUAL "FINISHED-STEEL" CAPACITY BY REGIONS

Region	1945*	Region	1952	1957
Northeast	72.9	Northeast	48.5	64.6
East	12.9	East	25.0	20.7
North China and Inner Mongolia	7.4	North China and Inner Mongolia	14.8	7.8
Southwest	6.8	Southwest	10.0	6.2
Central	---	Central	1.7	0.7
Northwest	---	Northwest	---	---
South	---	South	---	---
Total	100.0		100.0	100.0

*Before Soviet removals.

Table 7.4

PERCENT* OF ANNUAL CAPACITY AT 1960 YEAR END

Pig Iron		Steel Ingot		"Finished Steel"	
Central	20.6+	East	24.8+	Northeast	25.3
East	19.5+	Northeast	22.9	East	24.4
North and Inner Mongolia	18.4	North and Inner Mongolia	20.3	Central	22.0+
Northeast	17.7	Central	13.0	North and Inner Mongolia	11.9
South	10.7+	South	8.9	South	7.2
Southwest	6.8	Northwest	5.1	Southwest	5.0
Northwest	6.3	Southwest	5.0	Northwest	4.2

*The + sign indicates a significant rise in rank.

Completion of further constructions at Pao-t'ou may enhance the importance of North China and Inner Mongolia considerably.

216

policy to rehabilitate and then expand the industry on the basis of the existing centers.

Again, however, there was considerable discrepancy in some regional growth rates. During 1952-1957, Central China exhibited an especially high rate of growth in steelmaking. Northeast China demonstrated the most rapid rate of expansion in the same period in steel finishing. These instances were, however, symptomatic of expansion based on mills already in existence in 1952 or restored to production since.

In general, therefore, no major locational change in the steel industry took place before the end of the First Five-Year Plan. The long lead time[1] necessary for the construction of new centers probably precluded any different course of development at this stage. On the other hand, the same consideration would mean the fairly large locational changes which were soon to take place in 1958-1960 implied, at least to the degree that large mills were involved, deliberate decisions taken some years earlier.

As we can see from the plant list in Table B-13, Appendix B, new constructions during 1958-1960, some of which had of course been started earlier, consisted of a few major and secondary mills and a much larger number of smaller mills.[2] Where the latter were large in number, they exerted a strong influence on the locational pattern portrayed by the statistics. The smaller mills included both constructions planned as new secondary iron and steel centers and plants that had evolved from smaller and semimodern mills built during the "Great Leap Forward." Because of the general deterioration of statistical reporting during the period, possible inclusion of planned targets as completed constructions, failure to exclude entirely the nonmodern sector from the list, and possible errors in identification, including duplications which may be offset by omissions, the locational pattern based on the plant lists may not correspond to the actual situation at the end of 1960 when the "Great Leap" ended in disaster. Furthermore, in view of possible closing and suspension of construction in some cases since 1961, the locational pattern viewed as of the end of 1960 has no doubt undergone further changes. These are the principal qualifications which we have to bear in mind in evaluating the state of the regional pattern in Table 7.4 and in comparing it with the situation in 1957. However, in spite of these qualifications,

217

the trends exhibited by the sharp changes in the relative importance of several regions are sufficiently interesting to warrant special notice, even though the new order of ranking and the percent data shown in the table cannot be regarded as accurate. The major indications of these trends were: (1) increasing importance of East China as an iron- and steel smelting center; (2) rising prominence of Central China as an iron smelting and steel finishing center; (3) growing importance of the southern region; (4) emergence of the Northwest as a new area of expansion for the steel industry; and (5) the diminishing relative importance of Manchuria except in steel finishing. In particular, the major locations exemplifying these changes were Shanghai and Ma-an-shan in the East, Wu-han and Ta-yeh in Central China, and Kwangsi province in the South. Perhaps the most significant of all the changes in the locational pattern were the declining importance of Manchuria, the rising role of Central China, and the emergence of new areas in the South and the Northwest.

The Emergence of Multiple Centers

To lend further substance to the preceding paragraphs and to relate development in the steel industry to industrial location in general, we may examine our plant list more closely. Such a survey would show that, in general, one or two locations predominate in every region and that wide gaps exist between these large centers and the smaller ones. The major locations, as of 1960, were: An-shan (Northeast); T'ai-yüan and Pao-t'ou (North and Inner Mongolia); Shanghai (East); Wu-han and Ta-yeh (Central); Chungking (Southwest); Liu-chou and Canton (South); Urumchi, Ha-mi and Sian (Northwest). It would be interesting to determine next whether these or other principal centers are destined to play a key role in regional economic development, inasmuch as the situation remains highly fluid.

In this connection it appears that a plan to divide the entire country into seven regions of "mutual economic assistance" or cooperation probably came into being in July, 1957. Although the status of the plan did not seem to have become fully stabilized by 1962,[3] it is more than likely that some such regional structure has been contemplated as a part of national planning. Again, the implementation of the program must have been seriously affected by the economic

218

Table 7.5

LOCATIONAL AND INTERINDUSTRY STRUCTURE OF THE
"ECONOMIC MUTUAL ASSISTANCE REGIONS"

Region	Provinces or Areas Included	Location of Selected Major Iron Ore Reserves	Location of Iron and Steel Centers	Location of Metal Working and Machine Building Industries
Northeast (Manchuria)	Liaoning, Kirin, and Heilungkiang	Ta-ku-shan, Ying-t'ao-yüan, Kung-ch'ang-ling, etc.	An-shan	Fu-la-erh-chi, Ch'i-ch'i-ha-erh, Shen-yang, Ch'ang-ch'un, Harbin, etc.
North	Hopeh, Shansi, and Inner Mongolia	Lung-kuan, Huai-lai, Hsüan-hua, and Yang-ch'üan	T'ai-yüan, Pao-t'ou, and Shih-ching-shan	Peking and T'ai-yüan
Northwest	Shensi, Kansu, Sinkiang, Tsinghai and the Ningsia Hui Autonomous Region	Ching-t'ieh-shan, Ti-hua (Urumchi)	Chiu-ch'üan	Lan-chou, Chiu-ch'üan and Sian
East	Shantung, Kiangsu, Anhwei, Chekiang, and Fukien	Fan-ch'ang	Shanghai and Ma-an-shan	Shanghai
Central	Honan, Hupeh, Hunan, and Kiangsi	Ta-yeh, O-ch'eng, Lin-hsiang, and Ching-ling-chen	Ta-yeh and Wu-han	Wu-han and Lo-yang
South	Kwangtung (including Hainan) and Kwangsi	Hainan	Canton and Liu-chou	Canton
Southwest	Szechwan, Yunnan, Kweichow	Pa-tung and Chien-shih	Chungking and Hsi-ch'ang	Ch'eng-tu and Chungking

Source: Ti-li Chih-shih (Geographical Knowledge), Peking, no. 4, April, 1958, pp. 154-156; also see Chapter 3.

crisis which brought the "Great Leap" to an inglorious end. Yet the long-term thinking of Communist Chinese planners is well illustrated by this locational pattern (Table 7.5).

One striking fact about Table 7.5 is its close correspondence to the data we have previously developed from Table B-13 in Appendix B. A few minor discrepancies concern mostly the Northwest where only a bare start has been made thus far in developing a modern steel industry. Otherwise, our observations seem to substantiate the avowed aspirations of the regional economic plan.

Of the major centers, large iron and steel works designated for South and Northwest China are as yet not in being. Nor can their construction be expected in the near future in view of the cessation of most new investments in 1960-1962. On the other hand, An-shan, Wu-han, Shanghai, and Chungking, major metallurgical centers designated for Manchuria and Central, East and Southwest China, were already well established at the end of World War II. The first three locations can also trace their historical development to the very inception of China's modern iron and steel industry. The only newcomer among the existing and developing major iron and steel centers is Pao-t'ou in Inner Mongolia although its development had been foreshadowed by discoveries of large iron ore deposits under Japanese occupation and preliminary discussion of their exploitation under the Nationalists. Thus, except for some subtle shifts of emphasis and direction, the regional pattern of the major props of the steel industry has also demonstrated a close correspondence to past development and plans, implying that the changes in the locational pattern under the Communist regime involve mostly the more recent secondary and smaller works.

Some Locational Aspects of Input Availability

Communist China's First Five-Year Plan calls for the location of new industrial enterprises in the vicinity of raw materials, fuel supply, and consumer markets. New enterprises should also be set up with a view to defense requirements. The principal considerations in this connection are apparently decentralization and avoidance of overconcentration, as well as the selection of militarily less vulnerable and exposed locations. However, Chinese planners have been extraordinarily reticent on the manner in which conflicts among these locational criteria should be resolved. We are compelled therefore to deduce from actual developments whatever general rules of planning there might appear to be.

Let us first consider the availability of inputs from the point of view of several of the major centers.

The locational advantage of An-shan in this respect has already been firmly established historically. Large iron ore deposits are available at Ta-ku-shan, Ying-t'ao-yüan, Kung-ch'ang-ling, and other mines. Clay, mica, and silicon are also found in large quantities in the area. Supply of manganese and refractory materials are available at Ta-shih-ch'iao, also near An-shan. The renowned coal mines at Pen-ch'i, Fu-shun, and Fou-hsin are all "around the corner."

The new Wu-han iron and steel complex was designed to make use of the iron ore deposits of Ta-yeh, O-ch'eng, and Lin-hsiang in Hupeh province. Some large coal mines are located within several hundred miles at P'ing-hsiang (Kiangsi province), Tzu-hsing and Hsiang-t'an (Hunan). The Huai-nan Coal Mine in Anhwei is also within easy reach. The Wu-han area enjoys excellent water and land transportation facilities since it is situated on the bank of the Yangtze River and is the terminal of the Peking-Wu-han and Canton-Wu-han railways.

In the case of Pao-t'ou, discovery of rich iron ore deposits at the Pai-yün-o-po Mountain in the vicinity has been a determining factor in the development of this metallurgical center. Deposits at Lung-yen and in the northern part of Shansi province are also easily accessible. The coal mines at Ta-ch'ing-shan are capable of supplying large quantities of coking coal. Limestone and refractory materials are also found in abundance. The area is expected to have cheap hydroelectricity once the water resources of the Yellow River are developed. Similar to Wu-han, Pao-t'ou is now the terminal of two railways, the Peking-Pao-t'ou and the Pao-t'ou-Lan-chou lines, which cut through the vast regions of North and Northwest China.

Discovery of large iron ore reserves has been reported in recent years along the upper reaches of the Yangtze River in the eastern part of Szechwan province. The reports refer to the rich iron content and easy access of the

221

deposits. In the western part of Kweichow province discovery of coal deposits in excess of 18 billion metric tons has been reported.[4] These are supporting reasons for the further expansion of the Chungking plants.

Similar results from recent geological surveys in Northwest China have also been forthcoming. Large iron ore deposits are said to exist at Ching-t'ieh-shan in the Chiu-ch'üan district of Kansu province. In the P'ing-lo basin along the Ho-hsi corridor, Communist geological workers have reported the discovery of some large coal fields. These underground resources may have led to the selection of Chiu-ch'üan as a potential new steel base in Northwest China.

This quick sketch presents a favorable aspect of the locational pattern. It shows that so far as the major steel industry centers are concerned, their location has been strongly influenced by the presence of large iron ore deposits on the spot or in adjacent areas. There is still another side to the picture, however, that is, the general relationship between the location of iron ore deposits and that of iron smelters.

In this respect, curious though it may seem, it is far from being clear that new iron smelters have in general been established in iron rich areas. On the one hand, the number of provinces or autonomous regions without blast furnaces declined from seventeen in 1952 to sixteen in 1957 and two in 1960. This was unmistakably a result of the broadening of the industrial base and the advent of the smaller mills in many areas during the steel drive in 1958-1960. Correlated with the 1945 ore distribution in the individual provinces, the rank correlation coefficient between ore deposits and blast furnace capacity progressed from +0.298 in 1945 (before Soviet removals) to +0.470 in 1952 and +0.501 in 1957. It fell again to +0.471 in 1960. On the other hand, on a regional basis, while the rank correlation coefficient had stood at +0.857 at the end of World War II, it fell to +0.786 in 1952 and 1957, and then to +0.643 in 1960. Admittedly, lack of up-to-date ore deposit estimates by provinces and regions precludes a more precise analysis. But there is little evidence that such information, if available, would necessarily give us a better correlation. On the contrary, the decline of the regional, as well as provincial, rank correlation coefficient in 1957-1960 may simply mean that development of iron smelting during this period was essentially haphazard and unplanned. The general performance of locational planning displayed in the steel industry may therefore be much weaker than the corresponding planning of the major centers. But since this broad-gauged development has been rather limited in most locations, what would be undesirable from the point of view of relative resource availability in the long run has thus far caused little material harm.[5]

The "Backyard Furnace" Drive and Location

It is likely that the most exemplary case of poor locational planning, or its complete absence, is the "backyard furnace" drive of 1958. Reports on this period have mentioned the construction of some 2 million small native blast furnaces in the course of this massive campaign.[6] While many of these constructions consisted of replacements, the scale of the operation was nevertheless monumental. On the basis of a large number of press reports, the regional distribution of 370,600 native and "semimodern" furnaces, i.e., a sample of less than 18 percent of the total, was[7]

Region	Thousand Furnaces
East	94.9
Northwest	88.4
Central	74.3
North and Inner Mongolia	61.5
Southwest	36.2
South	14.0
Northeast	1.3
Total	370.6

The largest number reported for a single province in this sample was 80,000 for Sinkiang, followed by Shantung, 38,000; Kiangsu, 31,000; Inner Mongolia, 30,700; Hopeh, 28,800; Kiangsi, 25,000; etc. No rationale or order is at all apparent in this distribution either with respect to the relative degree of development of the modern sector of the steel industry in the region or province or with respect to its rank in ore deposits.

223

Location and Intraindustry Balance

Regional Intraindustry Balance

Turning to the state of intraindustry balance, let us inquire (1) whether the relation between the successive stages of smelting and fabrication is in better balance on a regional basis than on a national basis and (2) whether improvement in regional intraindustry balance has taken place through the years. Regional production data are not available, and the capacity data alone must be used. Inasmuch as the 1957 and later capacity statistics given in our plant list in Appendix B refer to operating capacity, to facilitate comparison with the earlier years, the ratios employed in the tables below have been adjusted to a designed capacity basis. Lastly, we shall continue to assume that the normal pig iron-to-ingot and ingot-to-product ratios in the present stage of development of Communist China's steel industry are 1.1-1.2 and 1.3-1.4, respectively. Comparison with these "normal" levels will determine whether there is excess capacity at any of the three stages of processing while comparison with preceding years will indicate "improvement," "deterioration," "no change," and "overcorrection," the last term to indicate a shift of the imbalance from one stage to an earlier or subsequent stage.

From Table 7.7, which summarizes the detailed data in Table 7.6, we can see that while there was a shortage of ingot capacity with respect to pig iron in all regions (except Manchuria as a result of Soviet removals) in 1945, by 1952 there had developed an excess of ingot over pig iron capacity in three of the seven regions. East China continued to show an excess of iron smelting capacity while North China had an excess of iron smelting capacity in relation to ingots and an excess of ingot capacity in relation to final products. East China and the Southwest also had an excess of steel fabrication facilities in relation to ingot capacity. The same situation prevailed at the end of the First Five-Year Plan in 1957 except that Southwest China had by now developed the same pyramidal structure as North China. As a matter of fact, as of 1957 not a single region exhibited intraindustry balance between any two of the three stages.

If attention is focused on change, it can also be seen that during 1945-1952 improvements and deteriorations (or overcorrections) were nearly balanced

Table 7.6

CHANGES IN INTRAINDUSTRY STRUCTURE, 1945, 1952, 1957, AND 1960

Region	1945	1952	1957		1960	
			Operating Ratio	Adjusted[1,2] Ratio	Operating Ratio	Adjusted[3,4] Ratio
The Ratio of Pig Iron to Steel Ingot						
Northeast	1.56 (0.68)*	0.60	0.91	0.67	0.81	0.59
North and Inner Mongolia	7.75	1.70-2.17	1.71	1.27	0.95	0.70
Northwest	—	xx	xx	xx	1.82	1.33
East	4.43	1.72	2.23-2.27	1.65-1.68	0.82[a]	0.60[e]
Central	11.18	0.31	1.21	0.89	1.67	1.23
South	—	—	—	—	1.26[b]	0.93[f]
Southwest	2.20	0.72-0.76	2.37	1.75	1.44	1.06
All China	1.98 (1.90)*	0.86-0.95	1.23-1.24	0.91-0.92	1.05	0.77
The Ratio of Steel Ingot to "Finished Steel"						
Northeast	1.69 (1.79)*	2.83	1.76	2.17	2.08	2.57
North and Inner Mongolia	0.77	2.29	3.70	4.57	3.93	4.85
Northwest	—	—	—	—	2.79	3.44
East	0.25	0.53	0.63	0.77	2.33[c]	2.87[g]
Central	xx	2.48	17.25-16.24	21.29-20.04	1.35	1.66
South	—	—	—	—	2.82[d]	3.49[h]
Southwest	0.70	1.16	1.41	1.74	2.27	2.80
All China	1.38 (1.13)*	2.00	1.75-1.75	2.16-2.16	2.29	2.83

Source: Chapter 3, Table 3.13 and Appendix B, Table B-13.

Note: If the province of Fukien were included in South China instead of East China as in the above regional division, the figures marked "a" through "h" in the columns for 1960 operating ratio and adjusted ratio would become: (a) 0.82, (b) 1.21, (c) 2.26, (d) 2.79, (e) 0.60, (f) 0.89, (g) 2.79, and (h) 3.65. These minor changes would not, however, have any effect on Tables 7.7 and 7.8 or on the remarks in the text.

*Post-Soviet removals.

— Both the denominator and numerator are nil.

xx Either the denominator or numerator is nil.

[1] Adjusted ratio, pig iron - steel ingot, 1957: operating ratio x (0.91/1.23).

[2] Adjusted ratio, steel ingot - finished steel, 1957: operating ratio x (0.77/1.05).

[3] Adjusted ratio, pig iron - steel ingot, 1960: operating ratio x (2.16/1.75).

[4] Adjusted ratio, steel ingot - finished steel, 1960: operating ratio x (2.83/2.29).

Table 7.7

STATE OF INTRAINDUSTRY IMBALANCE BY REGIONS

Region	Pig Iron				Steel Ingot				Finished Steel			
	1945*	1952	1957	1960	1945*	1952	1957	1960	1945*	1952	1957	1960
Northeast					E↕	E↕	E↕	E↕				
North and Inner Mongolia	E↑	E↑	E↑			E↑	E↑	E↑	E↓			
Northwest		E↑	E↑	E↑				E↑				
East	E↑	E↑	E↑			E↕		E↕	E↓	E↓	E↓	
Central	E↑			E↑		E↕	E↑	E↕				
South	E↑							E↑				
Southwest	E↑		E↑			E↓	E↑	E↑	E↓	E↓		
All China	E↑					E↕	E↕	E↕	E↓			

*Post-Soviet removals.

E = Excess

↑ = in relation to the following stage

↓ = in relation to the preceding stage

Table 7. 8

CHANGE IN REGIONAL INTRAINDUSTRY BALANCE

Region	1945-1952		1952-1957		1945-1957		1957-1960	
	P.I. / S.I.	S.I. / F.S.	P.I. / S.I.	S.I. / F.S.	P.I. / S.I.	S.I. / F.S.	P.I. / S.I.	S.I. / F.S.
Northeast China	–	–	+	+	– o	–	–	–
North and Inner Mongolia	+	C	+	–	C	C	C	–
Northwest China	xx	---	xx	---	xx	---	xx	xx
East China	+	+	+ o	+	+	+	C	C
Central China	C	+	+	–	C	+	C	+
South China	---	---	---	---	---	---	xx	xx
Southwest China	C	+	C	C	+	C	C	–
All China	C	C	– o	–	C	C	–	–

P.I. = Pig iron

S.I. = Steel ingot

F.S. = "Finished steel"

+ = Improved

– = Worse

C = Overcorrection

o = Almost unchanged

xx = No valid comparison

regionally. On the other hand, there was some general improvement in Manchuria and East China in 1952-1957 although improvements tended to be more than off-set by deteriorations (or overcorrections) in general. If comparison is made between 1945 and 1957, only in the case of East China are the results slightly better.

The above observations lead us to the inevitable conclusion that from 1945 up to 1957 locational planning had not brought about a general improvement in intraindustry balance on a regional basis. Although more improvements were observed during the First Five-Year Plan, the performance was not consistent. No distinctive trend of regularity of change can be detected. The outcome, there-fore, must be the continuation of interregional trade, or, alternatively, the emergence of unused capacity. The first alternative would in turn exert greater pressure on available transport. Existing evidence does not suggest that the Chinese planners had resolved this dilemma in practice or had even arrived at a rational solution.

The above verdict would be strengthened if we were to consider the data in 1960 in spite of their lesser reliability. As one can see from Table 7.7, there was an almost universal excess of ingot capacity in both directions, the only exceptions being Central and Northwest China where there was a very slight excess of pig iron capacity. The excess ingot capacity in relation to pig iron in the Southwest was also not too significant. On the other hand, there was no ex-ception to the excess of ingot capacity in relation to that of steel finishing. Table 7.8 further points out that only one region showed partial improvement between 1957 and 1960, the majority experiencing either deterioration or over-correction. Thus the result of the "Great Leap" was predominantly disappointing from the point of view of structural improvement by regions and the implicit aim of relative self-sufficiency within every region.

Steel Finishing Mills, Machine Manufacturing, and Industrial Location

Finally, on the basis of the data we now possess, it is possible to relate the major steel finishing mills to their principal markets as represented by the major machine manufacturing plants, and vice versa, and to deduce from the pattern of distribution certain general principles of location which seem to hold. For every zone, the four largest steel finishing plants as of 1960 on the basis of Table B-13 are taken as the principal mills of the zone in question. If fewer than four mills exist in any zone, all of them would be included. On the other hand, four cities with the largest number of machine building factories, based on a separate locational study,[8] are selected as the principal machine building centers within the zone. Within the zone, the largest steel finishing center and the largest machine building center are regarded as serving as the primary source of steel and market of each other, respectively. For the remaining three finishing mills, every one is "paired" with the nearest machine building center within the same zone, which may be any one of the four in question. The same is done with respect to the remaining three machine building centers other than the largest; every one of the three is "paired" with the nearest of the four steel finishing centers within the same zone. Distance is assumed to be the principal determinant of whether a machine building center is the primary market of a steel finishing center, and a particular steel town is the primary source of supply of a machine building center. Distance is measured in terms of rail transportation in most cases. The results are summarized below in Figures 7.1 and 7.2. The arrows indicate the "pairing" of a steel finishing center with its primary market and of a machine manufacturing center with its principal source of steel supply. Further, both the steel and the machine building centers are divided into "old" and "new" centers. The "old" steel centers are those which were in operation in 1952. The "old" machine building centers are those that were the eight principal machine building centers in 1947 on the basis of availability of machine tools, plus the city of An-shan selected on the basis of data from the Pauley Report.[9]

The following categories of market-source of supply relationships may be established from the preceding figures:

1. Seven new steel centers have established machine industry centers as their primary markets.

New machine industry centers	Established machine industry centers as primary markets
Peking	Peking
Tsinan	Tientsin

Nanking	Nanking
T'ung-kuan-shan	Nanking
Ta-yeh	Wu-han
Han-yang	Wu-han
Canton	Canton

2. Nine new machine industry centers derive their principal steel supply from established steel finishing centers.

New machine industry centers	Established steel finishing centers as primary source of steel supply
Harbin	Mukden
Lü-ta	An-shan
Ch'ang-ch'un	Mukden
T'ang-shan	T'ang-shan
Foochow	Shanghai
Wu-hsi	Shanghai
Tsingtao	Shanghai
Ch'ang-sha	Wu-han
Lo-yang	Wu-han

3. (a) Seven new steel finishing centers and seven new machine industry centers serve as the nearest sources of supply and nearest markets for each other respectively. Local iron smelters are available at the steel finishing centers, indicating thereby the existence of exploitable iron ore supply locally.

New machine industry centers	New steel finishing centers
T'ai-yüan	Han-tan
Nan-ch'ang	Chi-an
Nan-ning	Nan-ning
Sian	Sian
Urumchi	Urumchi
K'un-ming	K'un-ming
Kuei-yang	Kuei-yang

(b) One new machine industry center and one new steel finishing center bear the same relationship as 3 (a), but no known local iron smelter is available at the steel center.

New machine industry centers	New steel finishing centers as primary source of supply which are also new machine industry centers
Ch'eng-tu	Ch'eng-tu

4. Three new machine industry centers derive their principal steel supply from new steel finishing centers which are at the same time new machine industry centers themselves.

New machine industry centers	New steel finishing centers as primary source of supply which are also new machine industry centers
Liu-chou	Nan-ning
Lan-chou	Sian
Hsi-ning	Sian

5. One new machine industry center derives its steel supply from a new steel center which has an established machine industry center as its nearest primary market.

New machine industry center	New steel center as primary source of supply
Chiang-men	Canton

One can probably argue that categories (1) and (3-b) are new steel centers established with a distinct "market orientation,"[10] and that the remaining twenty cases represent new machine industry centers established with a distinct or probably orientation toward the source of steel supply. While many more factors are as important as, or even more important than, the relative strength of the pull from the market and from the source of major inputs, the above analysis seems to bear out the hypothesis that apart from the existence of established economic centers as markets, in a regimented economy, the location of the principal inputs may exert a much stronger pull than would be the case in an economy not subject to central planning. Perhaps the explanation lies in the fact that the location of new markets is much more flexible in a planned economy where even population movements can be directed almost at will.

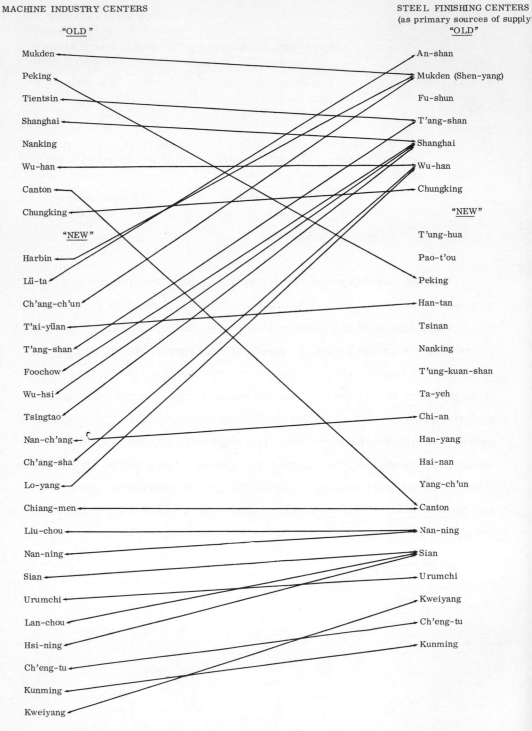

MACHINE INDUSTRY CENTERS

STEEL FINISHING CENTERS
(as primary sources of supply)

"OLD"

"OLD"

Mukden

An-shan

Peking

Mukden (Shen-yang)

Tientsin

Fu-shun

Shanghai

T'ang-shan

Nanking

Shanghai

Wu-han

Wu-han

Canton

Chungking

Chungking

"NEW"

"NEW"

T'ung-hua

Harbin

Pao-t'ou

Lü-ta

Peking

Ch'ang-ch'un

Han-tan

T'ai-yüan

Tsinan

T'ang-shan

Nanking

Foochow

T'ung-kuan-shan

Wu-hsi

Ta-yeh

Tsingtao

Chi-an

Nan-ch'ang

Han-yang

Ch'ang-sha

Hai-nan

Lo-yang

Yang-ch'un

Chiang-men

Canton

Liu-chou

Nan-ning

Nan-ning

Sian

Sian

Urumchi

Urumchi

Kweiyang

Lan-chou

Ch'eng-tu

Hsi-ning

Kunming

Ch'eng-tu

Kunming

Kweiyang

Figure 7.2. Principal Steel Finishing Centers and Their Probable Primary Markets

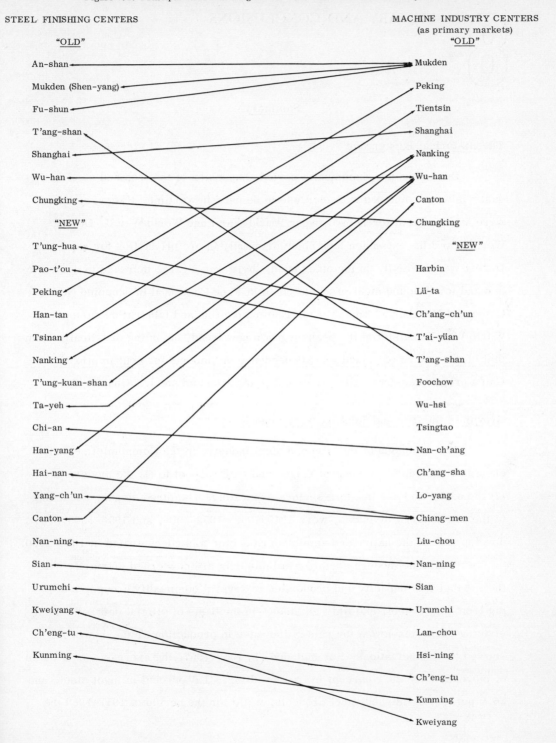

STEEL FINISHING CENTERS

"OLD"

An-shan
Mukden (Shen-yang)
Fu-shun
T'ang-shan
Shanghai
Wu-han
Chungking

"NEW"

T'ung-hua
Pao-t'ou
Peking
Han-tan
Tsinan
Nanking
T'ung-kuan-shan
Ta-yeh
Chi-an
Han-yang
Hai-nan
Yang-ch'un
Canton
Nan-ning
Sian
Urumchi
Kweiyang
Ch'eng-tu
Kunming

MACHINE INDUSTRY CENTERS
(as primary markets)
"OLD"

Mukden
Peking
Tientsin
Shanghai
Nanking
Wu-han
Canton
Chungking

"NEW"

Harbin
Lü-ta
Ch'ang-ch'un
T'ai-yüan
T'ang-shan
Foochow
Wu-hsi
Tsingtao
Nan-ch'ang
Ch'ang-sha
Lo-yang
Chiang-men
Liu-chou
Nan-ning
Sian
Urumchi
Lan-chou
Hsi-ning
Ch'eng-tu
Kunming
Kweiyang

8 SUMMARY AND CONCLUSIONS

Summary

The Historical Background

During the pre-Communist period, expansion of the iron and steel industry always coincided with increase in demand in wartime. However, there were significant differences between World War I and World War II. During World War I the expansion took place primarily in ore production for exports. During World War II, on the other hand, there was a large increase in domestic demand for iron and steel products, both in Free China and in occupied North China and Manchuria. The shift to greater smelting and fabrication during World War II registered the beginning of a new trend, deviating drastically from that of the interwar period when dependence on imports for consumption in China proper was especially prominent in pig iron and steel. (Chapter 2)

Growth of the Iron and Steel Industry since 1949

The expansion of the iron and steel industry in the Communist period should be considered in several stages and with respect to (1) the modern and (2) the native and semimodern sectors separately. The three stages, according to the conventional divisions, were 1949-1952, 1953-1957, and 1958-1960. The development of the native and semimodern sector was concentrated in 1958-1960.

Within the modern sector, available data are concerned primarily with the expansion of capacity and production in several commodity groups, i. e., pig iron, ingot steel, and finished steel. On the basis of official data, the most striking phenomenon was the rate of increase in production which, however, showed large fluctuations. For instance, in 1952-1957, the average annual rates of increase were 25. 3 percent in iron smelting, 31. 7 percent in ingot steel, and 26. 6 percent in finished-steel products, while for the period of 1957-1960 the corresponding annual rates of increase average 27 percent in pig iron, 30.9 percent in ingot steel, and 44.3 to 57.4 percent in finished steel. As for the 1949-1952 period, the average annual rates of expansion of production were even higher: 97.7 percent in pig iron, 104.4 percent in ingot steel, and 110.4 percent in finished steel. The increase in production was partly due to an increase in capacity and partly due to an increase in the efficiency of utilization of existing capacity.

The rate of growth of capacity was widely different from that of production. There were several reasons behind this phenomenon. First, the statistics were inaccurate and unreliable. Semifinished steel may have been included in the output of steel products while the capacity of "finished-steel" production in 1957-1960 may have been exaggerated as well. Second, so far as the improvement of equipment utilization was concerned, there were three principal factors: (1) technological innovation; (2) the emulation campaigns and worker competition; and (3) changes in the size of the plants. The emulation campaigns had two functions: (a) training and the transmission of knowledge and (b) quantitative increase in output. Often these two functions conflicted with each other. There was a tendency toward the larger plant, which tended to be more efficient, although the trend was not a distinct one in 1958-1960.

In spite of the expansion of capacity, the original level attained prior to Soviet removals was not reached until 1956-1958. Thus one might speak of two phases of development: a recovery period from 1949 to 1957 and a period of uncertain expansion beginning in 1958.

Developments within the modern sector reflected the contents of the First Five-Year Plan, which focused its attention on the recovery and expansion of the established centers such as An-shan, Pen-ch'i, Shanghai, Shih-ching-shan, and T'ai-yüan. The new or regenerated centers at Pao-t'ou and Wu-han did not appear until the Second Five-Year Plan.

During 1949-1952, investment in capital construction in the metallurgical industry amounted to 329.3 million yuan or 11.6 percent of total capital construction in industry. The amount increased substantially during 1953-1957 to 13 percent of the planned capital construction expenditure. Ferrous metallurgy and machine production together accounted for about one-quarter of industrial investment during the First Five-Year Plan period. The increment in

235

fixed assets for production in the iron and steel industry during 1953-1955 was larger than that in metal processing of which machine building was a part. (Chapter 3)

Failure of the Native Iron and Steel Drive

There are no reliable and complete statistics of the effective expansion of capacity in the native sector during 1958, but there is no doubt that the effort was massive. It was followed in 1959 and 1960 by a process of consolidation and upgrading, in the course of which many of the "native" iron and steel furnaces were either abandoned or replaced by furnaces of improved design. The purposes of the native and semimodern sector of the iron and steel industry were to increase the scale and speed of industrial development, to offer the large modern mills more sources of supply of raw materials, thus contributing to the stability of the industry's output, and to provide the large modern mills with the opportunity of experimentation and training without an adverse effect on output.

The immediate causes of the failure of this experiment were overestimate of the technical possibilities of the labor-intensive methods in iron- and steelmaking, underestimate of the cost, and an undue emphasis on breaking quantitative records at the expense of quality. (Chapter 3)

High material cost and low quality of product gave rise to a negative contribution from the native iron smelting sector to the GNP during the period of the "Great Leap Forward." Even when the improved semimodern steel sector in 1959-1960 is taken into consideration, the net contribution of the entire mass movement in iron and steel to the GNP remained negative in 1958 and was minimal during 1959-1960. These estimates are believed to be still conservative. (Chapter 4)

Intraindustry Balance

One problem of the new steel industry was the failure to achieve intraindustry balance. By 1960 there was too much ingot capacity relative to the other stages on a national basis. On the other hand, although the imbalance was less serious in production, this was largely a result of the inadequate supply of quality steel to be converted into suitable finished products that were in demand

and of possible double counting in finished products output. The continued large import of finished quality steel products and the absence of large steel ingot exports both seem to point to the shortage of quality steel and its products. (Chapter 3)

A comparison between the production of iron ore and its consumption in producing pig iron shows a deficiency during 1958, which was probably extended to 1959-1960. There was also a deficiency in the supply of up-to-grade native iron for producing steel in the native and semimodern sector. Thus, native steel production would require iron supplied by the modern blast furnaces. Since the output of the native and semimodern steel sector was questionable, this meant that the small nonmodern mills, far from being able to supplement the modern sector and relieve it of certain tasks in production, acted as a detractor instead. (Chapter 5)

On a regional basis, as of 1957, there was not a single region that showed intraindustry balance between any two of the three principal stages studied, i.e., iron smelting, steelmaking, and steel finishing. No general improvement in this respect could be observed during 1945-1957. By 1960 there had developed a virtually universal excess of ingot capacity regionally. (Chapter 7)

The Steel Industry and the National Product

The relative importance of the iron and steel industry in the economy of Communist China may be seen in a comparison of the contribution of the industry to the GNP (approximated by the gross domestic product) with the GNP itself, or with the contribution of the industrial sector (including mining, manufacturing, and construction) to the GNP. In 1952, gross value-added in the iron and steel industry was 1.7 percent of the GNP and 13.8 percent of the corresponding value in all industry. The corresponding percentages were 4.9 and 22.4, respectively, in 1957; in 1960 the percentages were 10 and 26.7, respectively. In terms of value-added, the rate of growth of the iron and steel industry in 1952-1960 exceeded that of industry as a whole and was much higher than that of the GNP. However, there is some question as to whether valuation at constant prices is meaningful if excessive supplies which cannot be used, possibly because of deficient quality, are produced.

237

The annual wage rate in the iron and steel industry of Communist China increased at a much lower rate than that of value-added per worker. In 1952-1956 wages accounted for 6 to 10 percent of the gross value-added. The corresponding proportion in the Soviet Union during the First Five-Year Plan was 53 percent. In the United States, wages accounted for about 65 percent of the gross value-added in the steel industry during 1946-1961. The high proportion of profit and taxes which accrued to the Communist government was a source of the large investment funds absorbed by the iron and steel industry itself. (Chapter 4)

Distribution of Output and Product Quality

During 1953-1957, 80 to 90 percent of the steel products consumed (including possibly semifinished steel) was absorbed by capital construction, including military constructions. Only 3 to 6 percent represented personal consumption, and less than 1 percent was exported. One of the striking characteristics of the consumption pattern was the large unplanned addition to inventory. Military consumption other than military constructions amounted to 140,000 to 210,000 tons a year during 1953-1956. Another half million tons were probably absorbed by military constructions. (Chapter 5)

An adverse factor in the domestic steel supply is the limited variety and low quality of products. An increasing variety of products in quantity production and the maintenance of high quality of the output are, of course, not easily achieved, while efforts to achieve these goals constitute the cause of the usual growth pains of a developing industry. But in the Chinese case, the "conservatism" among the managers is said to be a major obstacle. Much of this "conservatism" may have been plain common sense and prudence while a part of it may be a reflection of the fear of failure--failure to produce the new products to the satisfaction of the plan with respect to quantity, quality, and cost, and failure to fulfill the output quotas of the established products due to the disruptive influence of experimentation and diversion of effort. (Chapter 3)

External Trade

Ore export under the Communist regime has become negligible. In 1960, pig iron export was less than 2 percent of the output of the modern sector; most of the iron exported went to the Soviet Union. These were greatly at variance with the situation in the interwar period. On the other hand, dependence on imports for quality and special steels continues although, in the aggregate, the proportion of imports in current consumption had declined from 38 percent in 1953 to 13 percent in 1957 and 5-6 percent in 1960. During 1958-1960, 65 to 75 percent of the identified imports of finished steels were supplied by Western Europe and Japan, contrary to what one might otherwise expect. Steel tubes and heavy and thin plates were among the major import categories. (Chapter 5)

The Locational Pattern

The pre-Communist locational pattern of the steel industry showed concentration in a few areas, with Manchuria dominating the scene. Wartime developments had the effect of bringing the industry to previously undeveloped regions in North and Southwest China. The several stages of smelting and fabrication showed a generally pyramidal structure, which was distorted by the postwar devastation of Manchuria under Soviet occupation. At the time Manchuria was evacuated by the Soviets, there was an acute shortage of iron smelting and steel finishing capacity in Manchuria relative to that of steelmaking. In contrast, on a national basis, ingot capacity was relatively short. (Chapter 2)

Before the establishment of the Nationalist government in China, the early iron and steel mills were confined to six provinces and the city of Shanghai. Location was determined largely by the availability of ore supply in adjacent areas--with Shanghai furnishing an important exception--and by the influence of foreign investors and creditors.

The interwar period witnessed no addition of new mills so that the locational pattern was affected by differential regional growth rates of established mills. By 1937 Manchuria, then under the control of the Japanese sponsored Manchoukuo, was responsible for 97 percent of China's pig iron output.

During World War II, several important developments affected the location of the steel industry. These were: (1) the relocation of certain mills to Southwest China; (2) establishment of new mills in North and East China by Japan; (3) the addition of steel rolling and finishing facilities, especially but not exclusively in Manchuria; and (4) the establishment of new mills in areas without the steel industry before. At the end of World War II, fifteen provinces had one or more producing mills some of which were admittedly very small ones. There was also a fairly high regional rank correlation between iron smelting capacity and the availability of iron ore.

Between 1945 and 1952 there were only minor changes in the ranking of the major regions of mainland China in the steel industry. Manchuria was again restored to the first place from which it had fallen following Soviet postwar removals. There was also little change during 1952-1957. This relative stability of regional distribution was a reflection of the official policy to base its expansion during the First Five-Year Plan on the existing steel centers. However, during this period, higher growth rates were exhibited by Southwest and Central China in iron smelting. The rates of capacity expansion were also greater in Central China in steelmaking and in Manchuria in steel finishing.

During 1958-1960 in the Second Five-Year Plan the significant locational changes were: (1) the increasing importance of Shanghai and Ma-an-shan as iron smelting and steel finishing centers; (2) the growth of Wu-han and Ta-yeh; (3) the emergence of new centers in Kwangsi and the Northwest; and (4) the declining importance of Manchuria in the steel industry in the light of the preceding developments. During the same period, plans to establish several economic "mutual assistance" regions with designated principal steel and metal working centers also emerged although the large steel mills planned for South and Northwest China were, and still are, not yet realized.

With the exception of the major mills, development in iron smelting in 1958-1960 had apparently little relationship to the regional distribution of ore deposits. This applied even more plainly to the backyard furnace movement in 1958. (Chapter 7)

The Steel Mills and Industrial Location in General

Available data indicate that there has been a predominant orientation of new steel finishing mills toward sources of inputs, and a weaker market orientation. The machine making industries constituting the principal markets of finished steel have been created on the whole in areas close to the steel supply. (Chapter 7)

240

Observations on Communist China's Economic Planning

From our study of the steel industry certain observations of wider applicability may be made. They reflect on the performance of Communist China's economic planning as a whole and raise some serious questions both about the usefulness of official Chinese statistics as a mirror of the true state of the Communist Chinese economy and about the validity of the Chinese experience in 1952-1960 (including the First Five-Year Plan and the "Great Leap Forward" while excluding the subsequent crisis years) as a model of self-sustained growth in an orderly and successful "bootstrap operation." The following points may be listed:

1. Measurement of the industry's output at constant prices tends to exaggerate the growth rate when poor quality of the products and interindustry imbalance result in the accumulation of useless inventory. (As an indicator of the status of Communist China's economic development in relation to other countries, Figure 8.1 nevertheless gives us a general view.)

2. Intraindustry imbalance between successive stages of the industry may result in excess capacity at certain stages, thereby causing waste of investment funds needed elsewhere.

3. Technological backwardness and undue emphasis on quantity, the latter often a victim of the mechanical approach employed in measuring industrial development, appear to be two major factors underlying the poor quality of the output and the intra- and interindustry imbalance.

4. There are definite limits to the degree to which labor can be substituted for capital, as may be seen in the fiasco of the native iron and steel drive. But these limits may have been discounted as a result of the ideological convictions of Communist China's economic planners in the invincibility of the mass movement in its many manifestations.

5. Dependence upon imports in the case of strategic items in an industry cannot be obviated as long as technological backwardness persists; nor is it possible to free the country from such dependence rapidly.

6. Locational planning has not been a strong point in the economic planning of Communist China. Many of the accomplishments in the steel industry achieved so far have been made on the basis of pre-Communist foundations.

In spite of the major effort made by Communist China which has resulted in an overexpanded and unbalanced steel industry, as of 1957, the industry's capacity was only about the level reached before the despoliation of Manchuria by Soviet troops at the end of World War II. Since expansion in 1958-1960 has to be heavily discounted because of the subsequent economic crisis and the necessary adjustments afterwards, and since the overemphasis on steel appears to have been encouraged by the Soviet example, the role of Soviet policy and its influence on the economic development of Communist China may be seen in a most revealing light.

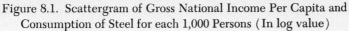

Figure 8.1. Scattergram of Gross National Income Per Capita and
Consumption of Steel for each 1,000 Persons (In log value)

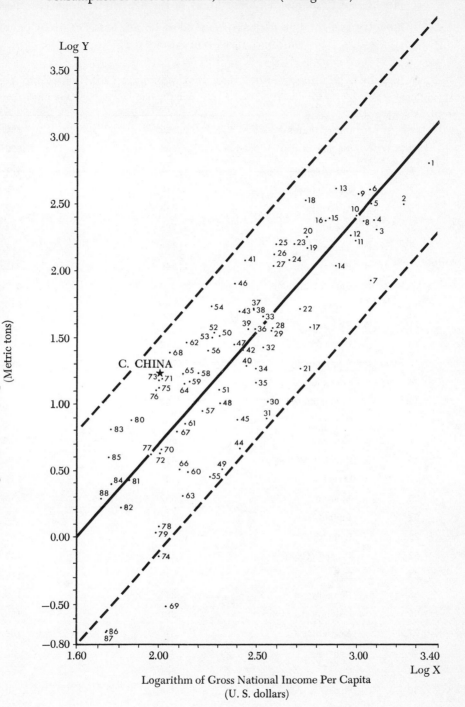

243

ORIGINAL DATA FOR FIGURE 8.1
(1961)

Code Number in Chart	Country	Gross National Income per Capita (U.S. dollars)	Consumption of Steel for Each 1,000 Persons (U.S. dollars)
1	United States	2,343	622.0
2	Canada	1,667	322.0
3	New Zealand	1,249	208.0
4	Switzerland	1,229	229.0
5	Australia	1,215	333.0
6	Sweden	1,165	402.0
7	Iceland	1,146	85.6
8	France	1,046	235.0
9	United Kingdom	998	367.0
10	Norway	969	249.0
11	Finland	941	166.0
12	Denmark	913	183.0
13	W. Germany	762	410.0
14	Venezuela	762	109.0
15	Netherlands	708	235.0
16	U.S.S.R.	682	225.0
17	Uruguay	569	36.0
18	Czechoslovakia	543	336.0
19	Israel	540	149.0
20	Austria	532	182.0
21	Puerto Rico	511	17.7
22	Ireland	509	53.0
23	Poland (1954)	468	159.0
24	Italy	442	118.0
25	Hungary	387	163.1
26	Union of S. Africa	381	138.0
27	Argentina	374	108.0
28	Cyprus	374	36.0
29	Cuba	361	35.0
30	Surinam (1950)	356	10.7
31	Panama	350	7.4

ORIGINAL DATA FOR FIGURE 8.1 (continued)

Code Number in Chart	Country	Gross National Income per Capita (U.S. dollars)	Consumption of Steel for Each 1,000 Persons (U.S. dollars)
32	Colombia	330	27.0
33	Rumania	320	45.0
34	Br. Guiana (1951)	311	17.9
35	Costa Rica	307	14.2
36	Malaya	298	36.0
37	Yugoslavia	297	51.0
38	Hong Kong (1954)	292	51.0
39	Bulgaria	285	36.0
40	Turkey	276	19.0
41	Lebanon	269	118.0
42	Brazil	262	25.0
43	Spain	254	50.0
44	Nicaragua	254	4.6
45	El Salvador	244	7.6
46	Japan	240	82.0
47	Greece	239	27.0
48	Dominican Republic	205	10.0
49	Ecuador	204	3.3
50	Portugal	201	32.0
51	Philippines	201	12.7
52	Iraq	195	33.0
53	Mexico	187	31.0
54	Chile	180	54.0
55	Guatemala	179	2.8
56	Algeria	176	26.0
57	Saudi Arabia	166	9.0
58	Morocco	159	19.0
59	Peru	140	14.0
60	Honduras	137	3.0
61	Ghana	135	7.0
62	Federation of Rhodesia and Nyasaland	134	28.0

ORIGINAL DATA FOR FIGURE 8.1 (continued)

Code Number in Chart	Country	Gross National Income per Capita (U.S. dollars)	Consumption of Steel for Each 1,000 Persons (U.S. dollars)
63	Vietnam	133	2.1
64	Egypt	133	13.9
65	Tunisia	131	17.0
66	Indonesia	127	3.3
67	Ceylon	122	6.1
68	Syria	111	24.0
69	Paraguay	108	0.3
70	Liberia	103	4.6
71	Taiwan	102	15.0
72	Thailand	100	4.3
73	Iran	100	14.7
74	Sudan	100	0.7
75	Belgian Congo	98	13.0
76	Jordan	96	12.6
77	Libya	90	4.2
78	S. Korea	80	1.2
79	Haiti	75	1.1
80	India	72	7.4
81	Nigeria	70	1.1
82	Bolivia	66	1.7
83	French W. Africa	58	6.6
84	French Equatorial Africa	58	2.4
85	Pakistan	56	3.9
86	Afghanistan	54	0.2
87	Ethiopia	54	0.2
88	Burma	52	1.9
	Communist China	98	17.6

Source: Norton Ginsburg, Atlas of Economic Development, 1961, University of Chicago Press, pp. 18 and 94.

Figures for Communist China derived from Table B-12 and Yuan-li Wu, et al., The Economic Potential of Communist China, 1962-67, pp. 28 and 355.

I. Geographical Distribution of Iron and Steel Mills

Finished Steel	Ingot Steel	Pig Iron	Operating Capacity (1960) in Metric Tons
■	●	◆	1,000,000 and above¹
◧	◑	◈	500,000 to under 1,000,000
◧	◑	◈	100,000 to under 500,000
◰	◔	◈	50,000 to under 100,000
□	○	◇	Under 50,000

II. Geographical Distribution of Major Iron Ore Deposits

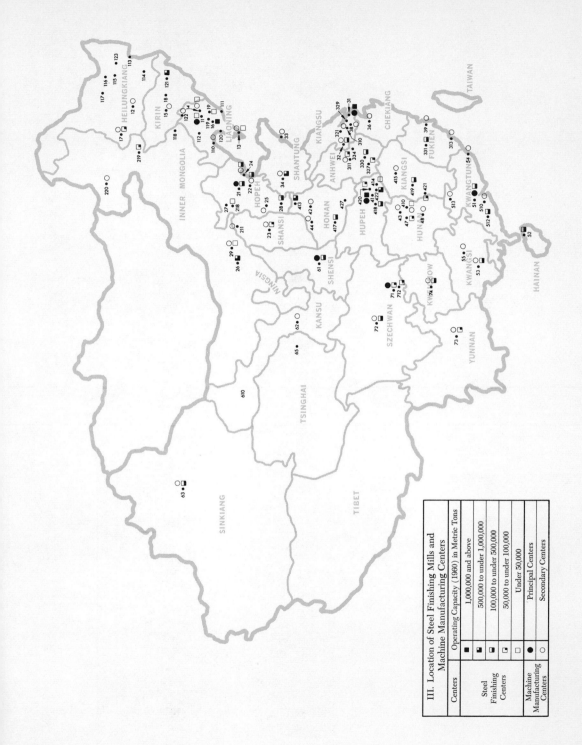

III. Location of Steel Finishing Mills and
Machine Manufacturing Centers

Centers	Operating Capacity (1960) in Metric Tons		
Steel Finishing Centers	1,000,000 and above	■	
	500,000 to under 1,000,000	▣	
	100,000 to under 500,000	◪	
	50,000 to under 100,000	◩	
	Under 50,000	□	
Machine Manufacturing Centers	Principal Centers	●	
	Secondary Centers	○	

Appendix A

ESTIMATES OF MAINLAND CHINA'S IRON ORE RESERVES

Estimates Based on Pre-Communist Data, Total Reserves

The principal estimates of the pre-Communist period were all based on findings of the Geological Survey of China. Seven separate reports under the title General Statement on the Mining Industry were made by the Survey between 1921 and 1945. With the exception of the sixth report (1941) which dealt with Southwest China, the successive issues presented estimates of increasing geographical coverage, as well as continual revisions. The seventh report, published in 1945, contains a complete statement of the last known data before the end of the war with Japan. During the few years between the end of the war and the seizure of power by the Communists in 1949, some further revisions were made by the National Resources Commission of China. Based on these revisions, as well as data from Japanese sources and other estimates which were apparently made later than the 1945 General Statement, one can piece together a revised total of 5.4 billion tons.[1] The last figure compares with the 2.1 billion tons given in the 1945 General Statement. Some of the successive estimates are listed immediately below:

ESTIMATES OF IRON ORE RESERVE BASED ON PRE-COMMUNIST DATA

Source	Year of Publication	Nature of Reserve Estimate	Million Metric Tons
Iron Ore Resources of the World, International Geological Congress, Stockholm, 1910, Summary Table 1-7	1911	"Actual" "Potential"	100 ...
General Statement			
1st issue, pp. 32-34	1921	Not specified (estimated average iron content, 37.2%)	678
2d issue, p. 123	1926	"Surveyed and exploitable" "Not verified"	396 556 952
3d issue, pp. 293-294	1929		737
4th issue, pp. 119-120	1932	Not specified	1,000

251

Source	Year of Publication	Nature of Reserve Estimate	Million Metric Tons
5th issue, pp. 175–177	1935	China proper "Deposits reliably estimated"	274
		"Deposits only roughly estimated"	49
		Manchuria Not specified	883
			1,206
7th issue, pp. 88–89	1945	"Verified and probable"	1,985
		"Deposits only roughly estimated"	166
		(Estimated iron content 45%)	2,151
United Nations, <u>World Iron Ore Reserves and Their Utilization</u>, p. 66.	1951	"Probable"	1,800
		"Potential" (including "probable") (Estimated iron content 45%)	2,700
United Nations, Economic Commission for Asia and the Far East, <u>Coal and Iron Ore Reserves of Asia and the Far East</u>, p. 20; data corresponding to those in <u>Kang-t'ieh</u> (Iron and Steel), Nanking, 1948. The same estimates are also used in United Nations, <u>Survey of World Iron Ore Resources, Occurrence, Appraisal and Use</u>, 1955, p. 32.	1951	Not specified	4,168
Yuan-li Wu, <u>An Economic Survey of Communist China</u>, p. 26. (See text for original sources.)	1956	Verified, indicated and inferred	5,433

Region	Province									
East China	Shantung	107,264	15,340	1,000	14,340	14,340	13,700	29,000	29,920	29,920
	Anhwei	19,204	19,204	...	19,204	19,864	19,818	50,000	50,000	50,000
	Kiangsu	5,700	5,700	300	5,400	5,437	2,000	35,000	35,000	35,000
	Chekiang	3,224	3,224	1,000	2,224	2,024	7,154	2,300	2,300	2,300
	Fukien	92,562	92,562	18,000	74,562	22,422	...	7,500	7,500	7,500
	Total	227,954	136,030	20,300	115,730	66,087	42,672	123,800	124,720	124,720
Central China	Honan	4,541[b]	17,897	15,000	2,897	2,740	1,019	4,400	3,400	3,400
	Hupeh	193,174	143,174	...	143,174	39,640	46,640	56,862	52,600	52,660
	Hunan	31,753	31,753	2,000	29,753	26,550	...	...	...	...
	Kiangsi	15,466	15,466	...	15,466	15,179	18,454[c]	18,060	18,060	18,060
	Total	244,934	208,290	17,000	191,290	84,109	66,113	79,322	74,060	74,120
South China	Kwangtung	257,155	52,155	45,000	7,155	12,066	4,000	...	...	...
	Kwangsi	2,067	2,067	1,500	567	...	...	...	...	...
	Total	259,222	54,222	46,500	7,722	12,066	4,000	...	...	...
Southwest China	Szechwan	22,023	22,023	...	22,023	22,023	1,000	...	...	...
	Kweichow	117,600	40,553	8,000	32,553	32,553	...	...	...	...
	Yunnan	12,156	12,156	5,000	7,156	7,156	...	...	...	...
	The Tibet and Chamdo Autonomous Region	...	...	...	...	...	...	...	...	...
	Total	39,849	39,909	3,600	36,309	...	...	...	...	...
Native Mines	(regional distribution unspecified)	191,638	114,641	16,600	98,041	95,130	...	...	273,161	273,161
	GRAND TOTAL	5,432,934	2,150,511	165,900	1,984,611	1,206,438	1,000,194	737,027	951,000	677,899

Sources: General Statement on the Mining Industry, Geological Survey of China, 1st issue, 1921, pp. 32-34; 2d issue, 1926, p. 123; 3d issue, 1929, pp. 293-294; 4th issue, 1932, pp. 119-120; 5th issue, 1935, pp. 175-177; and 7th issue, 1945, pp. 88-89. Figures for 1948 are taken from Yuan-li Wu, An Economic Survey of Communist China, op. cit., p. 26, where all the original sources are given.

[a] Including some deposits located in Honan, Shansi, and Kansu.

[b] May refer to verified reserves only.

[c] Including some small deposits located in a few other provinces.

Table A-1

PRE-COMMUNIST DATA ON IRON ORE RESERVES IN MAINLAND CHINA

(in thousand metric tons)

Region	Province	Date of Major Source								
		1921	1926	1929	1932	1935	1945 Verified and Probable Deposits	1945 Estimated or Possible Deposits	1945 Total	1948
Northeast China	Liaoning	387,580	387,580	387,580	752,000	782,182	1,385,050	5,000	1,390,050	...
	Kirin	...	...	...	...	...	10,700	5,000	15,700	...
	Heilungkiang	...	...	...	...	...	...	500	500	...
	Total	387,580	387,580	387,580	752,000	782,182	1,395,750	10,500	1,406,250	3,575,070
North China and Inner Mongolia	Hopeh	91,479	91,479	146,325	135,409	145,164	141,205	2,000	143,205	617,467
	Shansi	...	...	...	...	...	19,240	3,000	22,240	80,000
	Inner Mongolian Autonomous Region	...	...	...	...	20,700[a]	700	5,000	5,700	117,000
	Total	91,479	91,479	146,325	135,409	165,864	161,145	10,000	171,145	814,467
Northwest China	Shensi	...	...	...	...	...	4,847	6,000	10,847	10,847
	Kansu	...	...	...	...	...	2,196	300	2,496	2,496
	Tsinghai (Chinghai)	...	...	...	...	...	...	5,000	5,000	50,000
	Sinkiang Uighur Autonomous Region	...	...	...	...	...	2,811	31,200	34,011	48,737
	Ningsia Hui Autonomous Region	...	...	...	...	...	5,079	2,500	7,579	7,579
	Total	...	...	...	...	...	14,933	45,000	59,933	119,659

Estimates Based on Pre-Communist Data, by Provinces and Regions

Since information on ore reserves during the Communist period is usually devoid of data on regional distribution, a summary of the pre-Communist regional estimates is given in Table A-1. However, because of changes in provincial boundaries since 1949 and the common practice under the Communist regime of referring to _regional_ development, the original data have been adjusted where possible to conform more closely to current geographical boundaries so that subsequent comparisons with any information that may become available can be legitimately made. The principal boundary changes under the Communist regime up to this writing (1962) are as follows:

1. The provincial demarcations of seven former provinces and territories--Jehol, Chahar, Suiyuan, Ningsia, Sinkiang, Tibet and Sikang have been abolished. In their place, four autonomous regions have been created-- namely, the Inner Mongolian Autonomous Region, the Sinkiang Uighur Autonomous Region, the Tibet and Chamdo Autonomous Region, and the Ningsia Hui Autonomous Region.

2. The province of Jehol was abolished in 1955; its former territory was partitioned among the Inner Mongolian Autonomous Region, Liaoning province, and Hopeh province. Chahar was abolished in 1952 and divided between the Inner Mongolian Autonomous Region and Hopeh. However, all areas of the two abolished provinces in which iron ore reserves were formerly known to exist were annexed by Hopeh. Hence, reserve estimates listed under Hopeh in Table A-1 include those of Jehol and Chahar.

3. The term "Inner Mongolian Autonomous Region" was first given in 1947 to a part of Inner Mongolia when Communist forces entered the area. In 1949, its territorial limit was expanded to include the Che-li-mu Meng (Jerim League) of Liaopei, a province of Manchuria created by the Nationalist Government at the close of World War II and abolished by the Communists in 1949, and the Chao-wu-ta Meng (Jaoda League) of Jehol province. In 1950, the three counties of To-lun, Pao-ch'ang, and Hua-te were ceded from Chahar province to the Inner Mongolian Autonomous Region. In 1954, the province of Suiyuan was abolished and incorporated in its entirety into the autonomous region. The region now also embraces six districts belonging to the former Jehol province, namely, the Ch'ih-feng, Wu-tan and Ning-ch'eng counties; the Ao-han (Aokhan), K'o-la-ch'in (Kharchin) and Weng-niu-t'e _ch'i_ (Banners); as well as two districts formerly belonging to Kansu which have been renamed as the Pa-yen-nao-erh Meng (Bayan Nor League). However, so far as iron ore deposits are concerned, only those found in the former Suiyuan province are located in the region.

4. The Sinkiang Uighur Autonomous Region is identical with the former Sinkiang province while the Ningsia Hui Autonomous Region is identical with the former Ningsia province in territorial boundary. The Tibet and Chamdo Autonomous Region consists of the whole territory of Tibet and a part of Sikang-- the other part having been annexed by Szechwan. All iron ore reserves originally found in Tibet and Sikang are now listed under the autonomous region.

Estimates Based on Communist Data since 1949

Under the Communist regime, a number of global estimates have appeared so far. Upon scrutiny, however, the figures may be classified into two categories. The first category of extremely high estimates, especially when comparison is made with the last revised estimate based on pre-Communist data, seem to be very rough estimates of potentially available resources. The second category consists of estimates which are much more reasonable by comparison and which are not improbable on the basis of the last known pre-Communist data if new discoveries are made.

However, even in the case of the second group of estimates, some question may be raised as to the concept of "reserve" used. The last estimate (5.4 billion tons) based on pre-Communist data cited in the first section of this Appendix represents the aggregate of all "measured, indicated, and inferred" reserves. The same is true of the 2.1 billion tons in the 1945 General Statement. On the other hand, the 8 billion tons given in Ten Great Years[2] are said to consist of deposits that had been surveyed up to the end of 1958 and could be depended upon in making plans of capital construction. If the statement were a considered one, as it appears to be, the estimate would seem to be one of "verified" or "measured" reserves. Compared with the estimate of 5.4 billion tons, which represents a broader concept, the increase would be 2.6 billion tons. The actual increase within the category of "measured" reserves would be substantially larger. While such promising new discoveries should not be ruled out as impossible or even improbable on the strength of active geological surveying during 1953-1957, one would feel more firmly persuaded if there were substantial evidence and supporting data that pinpoint the new finds. Such evidence has been lacking so far, however. The actual verified reserves may therefore be less than 8 billion tons. [3]

The two groups of estimates may now be listed below:

I. Estimates Believed to Be of Potential Resources

Probable Year of Reference	Million Metric Tons	Source
1954	10,000	China Yearbook (Japanese), Tokyo, 1955, pp. 16-18.
1956-57	10,000	Nan Liu, Chung-kuo ti Tzu-yüan, (Resources of China), Hong Kong, 1957, p. 38.
1956	13,000	China Yearbook, 1957, Tokyo, 1957, p. 257.
1957-58	12,000	Ti-li Chih-shih (Geographical Knowledge), 1958, no. 4, p. 156.
1958-59	20,800	Hui-huang ti Shih-nien (The Glorious Ten Years), Peking, 1959, p. 216.
1958-59	100,000	Quoted by K. P. Wang, in Mineral Trade Notes, 1960, vol. 50, no. 3, p. 23.

II. Estimates Possibly of Verified or Measured Reserves,
but Possibly Also of Wider Conceptual Framework

Probable Year of Reference	Million Metric Tons	Source
1952	6,778	Economic Weekly, no. 15, Shanghai, April 1953, p. 2.
1952	6,800	China Yearbook, 1955, Tokyo, 1955, pp. 16-18.
1958	8,000	Ten Great Years, Chinese edition, Peking, 1959, p. 12. Also quoted in K. P. Wang, op. cit., 1960.

Some Estimates of the World's Iron Ore Reserves, 1910-1960

For purposes of comparison, three of the principal estimates of the world's iron ore reserves are presented below. The data for China are those listed in the original estimates. The three sets were published by the International Geological Congress in 1911 and the United Nations in 1950 and 1955, respectively.

1. Reserves given in the International Geological Congress' 1911 publication, Iron Ore Reserves of the World (Vol. 1, "Summary of the Reports," pp. LXXVI, 1-7):

1910
(in million metric tons)

Continent	Country	Actual	Potential	Total	Iron Content, %
Europe	Germany	3,608[a]	...	3,608	35
	France	3,300	...	3,300	34.5
	Britain	1,300	37,700	39,000	35
	Sweden	1,158	178	1,336	64
	Russia (Europe)	865	1,056	1,921	44.8
	Spain	711	...	711	49
	Norway	367	1,545	1,912	34
	Luxemburg	270	...	270	33
	Austria	251	323	574	36
	Greece	100	...	100	45
	Czechoslovakia	...	...	...	...

Continent	Country	Actual	Potential	Total	Iron Content, %
Europe	Poland	...	...	...	...
	Other European countries[b]	102	227	329	...
	Total[c]	12,032	41,029	53,061	
America	United States	4,258	75,105	79,363	54
	Canada	3,635	...	3,635	54
	Brazil	...	5,710	5,710	...
	Cuba	1,903	1,007	2,910	45
	Mexico	55	...	55	55
	Venezuela	...	...	...	...
	Other American countries[d]	4	...	4	...
	Total	9,855	81,822	91,677	
Asia	India	100	400	500	65
	Indochina	...	...	...	...
	Indonesia	...	...	...	...
Japan	Japan	56	...	56	...
	Philippines	1	...	1	...
	Korea	4	...	4	50
	China	100	...	100	...
	Russia (Asia)	...	27	27	...
	Other Asian countries[e]	...	30	30	...
	Total	261	457	718	
Oceania	Australia	72	69	141	55-65
	New Caledonia	...	...	...	...
	New Zealand	64	...	64	50
	Total	136	69	205	

Continent	Country	Actual	Potential	Total	Iron Content, %
Africa	Algeria	125	...	125	60
	Congo	...	...	...	...
	French West Africa (Mauritania)	...	...	...	...
	Morocco[f]	...	...	...	...
	Sierra Leone	...	...	...	...
	South-west Africa	...	...	...	...
	Southern Rhodesia	...	...	...	...
	Union of South Africa	...	...	...	...
	Other African countries[g]	...	...	...	...
	Total	125	...	125	...
	World Total	22,409	123,377	145,786	

[a] Including Lorraine.

[b] Including Portugal, Italy, Switzerland, Hungary, Bulgaria, Albania, Finland, Holland, Belgium, Rumania, and Yugoslavia.

[c] Including European Russia.

[d] Including Argentina, Bolivia, Chile, Colombia, The Dominican Republic, and Peru.

[e] Including Persia (1910), Hong Kong, Turkey, Israel, Pakistan, Iran, Ceylon, and Burma.

[f] Morocco includes French and Spanish Morocco.

[g] Other African countries include Egypt, Liberia, Togoland, Tunisia (1950) and Guinea.

2. United Nations, <u>World Iron Ore Resources and Their Utilization</u>
(Appendix Table A, pp. 66-68), 1950:

Continent	Country	1950 (in million metric tons)		
		Probable	Potential and Probable[a]	Iron Content, %
Europe	Germany	800	2,800	32
	France	6,700	10,500	38
	Britain	2,400	3,400	28
	Sweden	2,200	2,500	64
	Russia (Europe)	3,133	7,124	45
	Spain	800	1,800	45
	Norway	170	2,170	48
	Luxemburg	200	300	28
	Austria	...	242	35
	Greece	50	130	46
	Czechoslovakia	50	200	35
	Poland	59	175	35
	Other European countries[b]	265	929	...
	Total	16,827	32,270	
America	United States	3,800	70,800	45
	Canada	1,937	4,355	48
	Brazil	6,300	19,650	65
	Cuba	3,000	15,000	40
	Mexico	315	315	61
	Venezuela	360	960	60
	Other American countries[d]	113	394	...
	Total	15,825	111,474	

Continent	Country	Probable	Potential and Probable	Iron Content, %
Asia	India	9,347	20,320	60
	Indochina	10	56	60
	Indonesia	100	1,500	49
	Japan	...	62	61
	Philippines	1,016	1,016	47
	Korea	70	370	35
	China	1,800	2,700	45
	Russia (Asia)	1,371	3,738	45
	Other Asian countries[e]	24	93	...
	Total	13,738	29,855	
Oceania	Australia	203	330	62
	New Caledonia	...	20	...
	New Zealand	10	15	53
	Total	213	365	
Africa	Algeria	88	88	50
	Congo	100	100	50
	French West Africa (Mauritania)	2,000	2,030	50
	Morocco[f]	36	75	55
	Sierra Leone	100	100	58
	South-west Africa	...	569	...
	Southern Rhodesia	2,240	105,564	51
	Union of South Africa	2,712	10,828	47
	Other African countries[g]	39	73	...
	Total	7,315	119,427	
	World Total	53,918	293,391	

259

[a]As indicated in the original United Nations publication, potential reserves published in 1950 should include probable reserves. They are therefore identical with total reserves.

[b]Including Portugal, Italy, Switzerland, Hungary, Bulgaria, Albania, Finland, Holland, Belgium, Rumania, and Yugoslavia.

[c]Including European Russia.

[d]Including Argentina, Bolivia, Chile, Colombia, the Dominican Republic, and Peru.

[e]Including Persia (1910), Hong Kong, Turkey, Israel, Pakistan, Iran, Ceylon, and Burma.

[f]Morocco includes French and Spanish Morocco.

[g]Other African countries include Egypt, Liberia, Togoland, Tunisia and Guinea.

3. United Nations, <u>Survey of World Iron Ore Resources, Occurrence, Appraisal and Use</u>, (pp. 24, 27, 29, 31, and 34), 1955:

<u>1955</u>
(in million metric tons)

Continent	Country	Measured, Indicated, and Inferred	Potential	Total	Iron Content (average), %
Europe	Germany	1,510	...	1,510	32
	France	6,560	...	6,560	35
	Britain	3,760	...	3,760	30
	Sweden	2,400	...	2,400	62
	Russia (Europe)	3,220	...	3,220	...
	Spain	990	...	990	45
	Norway	260	...	260	35
	Luxemburg	200	...	200	30
	Austria	110	...	110	35

Continent	Country	Measured, Indicated, and Inferred	Potential	Total	Iron Content (average), %
Europe	Greece	70	...	70	50
	Czechoslovakia	90	...	90	40
	Poland	140	...	140	30
	Other European countries[a]	390	...	390	...
	Total	19,700		19,700	
America	United States	5,542[b]	65,721[b]	71,263[b]	22-63
	Canada	3,371	1,110	4,481	48
	Brazil	16,250	36,360	52,610	51
	Cuba	...	3,000	3,000	40
	Mexico	500	...	500	60
	Venezuela	2,200	520	2,720	65
	Other American countries[c]	1,263	1,380	2,643	65
	Total	29,126	108,091	137,217	
Asia	India	21,000	330	21,330	30-69
	Indochina	48	...	48	50-68
	Indonesia	12	1,309	1,321	40-65
	Japan	64	...	64	36-56
	Philippines	30	1,300	1,330	45-65
	Korea	424	2,000	2,424	30-53
	China	4,180[d]	20	4,200	25-65
	Russia (Asia)	...	...	...	...
	Other Asian countries[e]	155	...	155	...
	Total	25,913	4,959	30,872	

Continent	Country	Measured, Indicated, and Inferred	Potential	Total	Iron Content (average), %
Oceania	Australia	521	...	521	...
	New Caledonia	...	...	...	...
	New Zealand	506	...	506	...
	Total	1,027	...	1,027	
Africa	Algeria	300	...	300	50
	Congo	...	...	...	...
	French West Africa (Mauritania)	200	...	200	...
	Morocco[f]	70	...	70	45–60
	Sierra Leone	200	...	200	...
	Southwest Africa	...	...	...	...
	Southern Rhodesia	...	...	...	...
	Union of South Africa	2,600	...	2,600	...
	Other African countries[g]	825	...	825	...
	Total	4,195	...	4,195	...
	World Total	79,961	113,050	193,011	

[a]Including Portugal, Italy, Switzerland, Hungary, Bulgaria, Albania, Finland, Holland, Belgium, Rumania, and Yugoslavia.

[b]Including Alaska and Puerto Rico. Figures in long tons are converted into metric tons, taken from Martha S. Carr and Carl E. Dutton, Iron Ore Resources of the United States, Geological Survey Bulletin 1082-c, p. 87, Washington, D.C., 1959.

[c]Including Argentina, Bolivia, Chile, Colombia, The Dominican Republic, and Peru.

[d]Including Taiwan.

[e]Including Persia (1910), Hong Kong, Turkey, Israel, Pakistan, Iran, Ceylon, and Burma

[f]Morocco includes French and Spanish Morocco.

[g]Other African countries include Egypt, Liberia, Togoland, Tunisia (1950), and Guinea.

For additional data, reference may be made to such publications as Charles Will Wright, The Iron and Steel Industries of Europe, U.S. Bureau of Mines, Economic Paper 19, Washington, D.C., 1939; Martha S. Carr and Carl E. Dutton, Iron Ore Resources of the United States, Including Alaska and Puerto Rico, Geological Survey Bulletin 1082-c, Washington, D.C., 1959; and Bruce C. Netschert and Hans H. Landsberg, The Future Supply of the Major Metals, Resources of the Future, Inc., Washington, D.C., 1961.

Appendix B

CAPACITY AND OUTPUT OF THE IRON AND STEEL

INDUSTRY (EXCLUDING IRON ORE MINING):

1936, 1943, 1945–48, AND 1949–60

Any careful empirical study must begin with an examination of the alleged facts. When facts and fancy are intermingled or when reports are incomplete and distorted, even the most rudimentary fact finding can become an undertaking of major proportions. But time consuming and tedious though the task may be, it has to be done.

The present Appendix consists of a survey of available statistics on the actual production and annual capacity of the iron and steel industry of mainland China. Where such statistics are not complete or immediately available, or where available information is suspect, estimates or adjustments are made. The capacity estimates which, in the absence of information on dates, are assumed to be year-end estimates, will afford us a basis for which statistics of production that constitute the focus of most reports can be evaluated. Table B-1 summarizes all capacity and production data primarily in the modern sector as tentatively estimated for use in this volume.

Our detailed survey proceeds from year to year, covering the period 1949-1960 in addition to several pre-Communist years, of which 1936, 1943, and 1945 have been selected as benchmarks. The year 1936 represents the last prewar year; 1943 is described in official as well as unofficial reports as the pre-Communist peak year; 1945 marks the low point reached after the devastation of, and removal of industrial installations from, Manchuria by Soviet troops.

The Pre-Communist Period

1936

Capacity. According to the Japan-Manchoukuo Year Book of 1941,[1] the capacity of the Showa Steel Works at An-shan, largest in Manchuria as well as in all of China, totaled in 1936: pig iron, 650,000 metric tons; steel ingot, 500,000 tons; steel products, 305,000 tons. The pig iron capacity, however, would be 800,000 tons if the Pen-ch'i mill were included. At the same time, the daily capacity of blast furnaces in China proper, including the mills at Han-yang, Ta-yeh, Shen-chia-chi (the Yangtse Machine Building Co.), T'ai-yüan, Chiao-tso, Shih-ching-shan, and Yang-ch'üan amounted to 2,080 tons, or an annual capacity of 624,000 tons on the basis of 300 days of operation a year. The total capacity of modern mills for the entire country would therefore amount to approximately 1,424,000 tons of pig iron. The total ingot capacity can be obtained by aggregating the 500,000 tons of Manchuria and the 50,000 tons of annual output figure reported for China proper in the Geological Survey of China's

SUMMARY TABLE OF ANNUAL CAPACITY AND PRODUCTION, MODERN SECTOR
(in thousand metric tons)

Year	Capacity		Production
	Rated	Operating	

Pig Iron

Year	Rated	Operating	Production
1936	1424	...	670 (810)[a]
1943	2626	...	1883 (1970)[a]
1945[b]	3607 1479	...	...
1949	1119-1276	1180	246
1950	1119-1276	1243	978[c]
1951	1368-1514	1895-1915	1448[c]
1952	1380-1514	2064-2084	1900
1953	2040-2161	3126-3146	2175
1954	2304-2414	3570-3590	2962
1955	2557-2666	3966-3986	3630
1956	3184-3373	4879-4910	4777
1957	4561-4866	8307-8333	5860
1958	7089-7556	12912-12968	9530
1959	13729-14605	25008	9500
1960	21931-23330	39948	12700

Ingot Steel

Year	Rated	Operating	Production
1936	550	...	414
1943	1477	...	923
1945[b]	1510-1802 760	... ...	...
1949	637-639	...	158
1950	1346-1347	...	606

Table B-1 (continued)

| Year | Capacity | | Production |
	Rated	Operating	
	Ingot Steel		
1951	1428	...	896
1952	1599	1918	1349
1953	1703	2139	1774
1954	1778	2345	2225
1955	1778	2783	2853
1956	3510	4207	4465
1957	5344	6748	5350
1958	11532	14561	8000
1959	18499	23357	8630
1960	30135	38049	12000
	"Finished-Steel Products"[d]		
1936	305	...	167
1943	897	...	486–688
1945[b]	1268–1320 692	...	...
1949	681	...	141
1950	750	...	464
1951	750	...	808
1952	800	817–837	1312
1953	900	1404–1424	1754
1954	960	1460–1480	1965
1955	960	1473–1493	2505
1956	964–991	1526–1546	3921
1957	2440–2476	3861–3863[e]	4260
1958	3682–3736	5826–5828[e]	6000
1959	5809–5893	9192–9194[e]	9200
1960	10503–10652	16618[e]	12800–16600

Table B-1 (continued)

[a]May include some "native" iron.

[b]First figure for 1945 includes Manchuria before Soviet removals; the second is for after Soviet removals.

[c]May include some "native" iron.

[d]May include "semifinished" intermediate products from 1949 on. See Chapter 3.

[e]Data for 1957 through 1960 are believed to include the capacity of semi-finished products.

Table B-2

ANNUAL CAPACITY OF MODERN MILLS, MANCHURIA
(in thousand metric tons)

Item	August 15, 1945	Post-Soviet Occupation	Removal and Loss
Pig Iron	2,524	396	2,128
Steel Ingot	1,330-1,622[a]	580	750-1,042
Steel Products	910-962[a]	324	586-638

[a]The more recent Japanese Survey Report puts the capacity data at this time as 1,622,000 tons of ingot and 962,400 tons of finished products.

General Statement on the Mining Industry.[2] Since rolled products were hardly produced at all in the rest of China, the capacity data for Manchuria may also be looked upon as applicable to the country as a whole.

Production. According to the Communist Chinese State Statistical Bureau, production in 1936 amounted to: pig iron, 809,996 metric tons (including 140,000 tons of native iron) or an output of 670,000 tons from the modern mills only; steel ingot, 414,315 tons; steel products, 167,000 tons.[3]

The pig iron figure cited above for modern smelters compares with 654,600 tons obtained by aggregating 633,000 tons for Manchuria, a figure originally published in the Japan-Manchoukuo Year Book quoted above, and 21,600 tons for China proper.[4] Since these earlier data excluded the production of the smaller Tung-pien-tao (T'ung-hua) plant in Manchuria, an underestimate was present and the new Communist figure may be more accurate.

In the case of steel ingot, the figure presented by the State Statistical Bureau is identical with what one might obtain by aggregating 364,315 tons for Manchuria and 50,000 tons for China proper. The Manchuria figure is given in the Pauley report[5]; the figure for China proper is found in the General Statement[6] of the Geological Survey cited above. It appears therefore that the same sources have been adopted by the State Statistical Bureau.

The official Communist figure for steel products may be compared with that of 135,306 tons given in the Japan-Manchoukuo Year Book.[7] The difference between the two figures, or 31,694 tons, may be accounted for by the production by smaller plants in Manchuria. There is also the possibility that some output was available in the rest of China although, if this was the case, it would be of negligible proportions.

1943

Capacity. There is no general information on available capacity in 1943. However, considering the conditions during the latter part of the war, it is possible that the 1943 capacity of installed equipment would be somewhat lower than that of August, 1945, but the difference is not likely to be significant. This conclusion seems to be borne out by the data on individual plants given in Table B-13.

Production. The official Communist production data for 1943 are:

Item	Metric Tons
Pig Iron	1,801,000
Steel Ingot	922,738
Steel Products	686,000

These figures are given in Major Aspects,[8] and the first two are in agreement with the corresponding figures given in Ten Great Years;[9] the data also appear in other western sources quoting earlier official data, such as a work by D. E. T. Luard and T. J. Hughes.[10] In an article entitled "Rich Mineral Resources Spur Communist China's Bid for Industrial Power,"[11] K. P. Wang reports Chinese production of 2 million tons of pig iron, 1 million tons of ingot, and 700,000 tons of steel products, which appear to be rounded from the same figures.

In the case of pig iron, the Manchurian output has been given by the Pauley Report alternatively as 1,710,267 tons[12] and 1,727,000 tons. [13] If the total of 1,801,000 tons is accepted, the difference of 74 - 91 thousand tons between this Communist figure and the Pauley data should be attributed to China proper, as well as other plants in Manchuria excluded from the Pauley survey. But although only 20,000 tons were reportedly produced by the modern mills in 1943 in China proper, [14] it would not be reasonable to assume that the remaining 54 - 71 thousand tons could account for the output of the smaller mills in Manchuria, as well as the native iron produced in China proper. According to Kang-t'ieh, [15] the volume of native iron produced in China proper in 1940, 1941, and 1942 totaled 88, 90, and 84 thousand tons respectively, while total pig iron output amounted to 213, 259, and 449 thousand tons, respectively. Recorded production from several North China mills alone was 86,000 tons; it was 70,000 tons for Free China. [16] One would deduce that the 1943 output could not possibly be less than 243 thousand tons (156,000 for modern mills plus 87,000 tons of native iron, the mean value for 1940-1942). If these figures are used for China proper in 1943 in conjunction with 1,727,000 for Manchuria, the total for the entire country would amount to at least 1,970,000 tons (1,883,000 tons from modern mills plus 87,000 tons of native iron). Since an actual output of 2,131,-000 tons (including 84,000 tons of native iron) was reported for 1942 on the same basis, [17] the real pre-Communist peak-year output was probably attained in 1942 and was higher than that reported by the State Statistical Bureau.

In the case of steel ingot, the Bureau's figure of 922,738 tons is slightly higher than that of 853,047 tons obtained by aggregating 844 thousand tons for Manchuria[18] and 9,047 tons for China proper. [19] The difference can be attributed to the probably broader coverage of the Bureau, possibly in Manchuria and Japanese-occupied areas in North and East China, and the larger figure will therefore be accepted for our purpose.

As for steel products, the figure of 688,000 tons cited by the State Statistical Bureau is about 200,000 tons higher than the 485,693 tons of finished products reported by the Pauley mission, but is about 40,000 - 80,000 tons below the figure of semifinished steel contained in the same report (726,000-774,000 tons) and attributed to the No. 1 and No. 2 blooming mills at An-shan. On the other hand, if the reported production of finished-steel products is aggregated from the plant inspection reports contained in the Pauley Report, the total would amount to 427,000 tons. Since these reports do not include some of the smaller plants, the somewhat different figure of 485,693 tons given above would also be quite understandable.

There are two possible interpretations of the 200,000-ton discrepancy between the Pauley Report and the later official Communist report. First, one might assume that it represents primarily the production of finished products in China proper. Second, one might also assume that the Communist figure for steel products refers to the output of semifinished steel only, but that only a part of the Manchurian production is included. Inasmuch as the capacity of finished products in China proper in 1945--only two years later--was in excess of 300,000 tons, one might favor the first interpretation that the production in 1943 was in the neighborhood of 200,000 tons. On the other hand, ingot production at the time was much smaller and production of finished steel in Free China was reported at only 7,700 tons by the National Resources Commission. One may

Table B-3

ANNUAL CAPACITY, 1945
(in thousand metric tons)

Area and Source	Pig Iron	Steel Ingot	Steel Products
China Proper			
Survey Report	833. 7[a]	179. 6	358
Other plants not listed in the Survey Report	249. 0	---	---
	1, 082. 7		
Manchuria As of August 15, 1945 (Pauley Commission Estimate)	2, 524	1, 330-1, 622	910-962
Post-Soviet Removals (Pauley Commission Estimate)	396	580	324
Total As of August 15, 1945	3, 606. 7	1, 509. 6-1, 801. 6	1, 268-1, 320
Post-Soviet Removals	1, 478. 7	759. 6	682

[a]The following China proper plants listed in Table B-4 are included in the Survey Report on the Steel Industry of Communist China, Supplementary Edition, Chart 2.

Table B-4

ANNUAL CAPACITY, 1945
(in thousand metric tons)

Plant Location	Pig Iron	Steel Ingot	Steel Products
Shih-ching-shan	240[a]	---	---
T'ang-shan	144[b]	12	25
Tientsin	30	13.8	28
Hsüan-hua	84	---	---
T'ai-yüan	70	50	45
Yang-ch'üan	19.5	---	---
Tsing-tao	150	---	---
Shanghai	30.2	48.8 (42)	170
Ma-an-shan	6	---	---
Ta-yeh	---	15	---
Chungking (Ta-tu-k'ou)	60	30 (45)	90
Kunming	---	18	---
Total	833.7[c]	179.6 (195.8)	358

[a]Including 30,000 metric tons not in operation.

[b]Including 24,000 metric tons not in operation.

[c]Including 54,000 metric tons not in operation.

Table B-5

ANNUAL CAPACITY OF PIG IRON, 1945
(in metric tons)

Province	Locality	Plant[a]	Daily Capacity	Annual Capacity
Honan	Chiao-tso	Chiao-tso Iron Works	40	12,000
Szechwan	Chiang-pei	Tzu-yü Iron Works	20 (35)[b]	6,000-10,500[b]
		Jen-ho (later known as Tzu-shu) Iron and Steel Co.	10	3,000
		Shu-chiang Metallurgy Co.	10	3,000
		Ching-p'ing Iron Works	5	1,500
		Hsing-lung Coal and Iron Co.	5	1,500
	Wei-yüan	Wei-yüan Iron Works	20	6,000
	Pa-hsien	China Enterprise Co.	50 (30)[b]	15,000-9,000[b]
	Ta-chu	Fu-ch'ang Iron Co.	5	1,500
	Yung-ch'ang	Yung-ch'ang Iron Co.	5	1,500
	Ta-hsien	Ch'ü-chiang Metallurgy Co.	8	2,400
	Ch'i-chiang	Tung-yüan Enterprise Co.	52.5	15,750
		Chung-hua Industrial Co.	2.5	750
	Yün-ch'uan	Shang-ch'uan Iron Co.	5	1,500
		Yun-ho Enterprise Co.	5	1,500
	Ho-ch'uan	Ta-ch'ang Metallurgy Co.	5	1,500
	Ch'i-chiang	Tung-hsi Iron Works	3	900
Yunnan	An-ning	Yunnan Iron Works	50	15,000
Hunan	Hsiang-t'an	Chung-yang Iron Works	500	150,000
		Min-sheng Iron Works	5	1,500
	Heng-shan	Hsiang-hua Iron Works	5	1,500
		Lu-chiang Iron Works	2	600
	Ch'i-yang	Yi-chung Iron Works	2	600
Kiangsi	Chi-an	Kiangsi Iron Works	5	1,500
Kwangsi	Ho-hsien	P'ing-kuei Iron Works	10	3,000
Total			830	249,000-247,500

[a]The plants in this table are the other smaller plants not included in the Survey Report.

[b]Data for the China Enterprise Company, Pa-hsien, are from the National Resources Commission, The Quarterly Journal, vol. VI, nos. 1-4, June-December, 1946, pp. 102-103.

therefore question whether production of finished products could be as high as 200,000 tons. This therefore remains a moot point.

<u>1945-1948</u>

Capacity, 1945. In determining the capacity of China's iron and steel industry at the end of World War II, the principal problem is to account for the large-scale removals perpetrated by the Soviet Union during its occupation of Manchuria in 1945. The figures in Table B-2, based on the Pauley Report, [20] present the capacity data for Manchuria both as of August 15, 1945, when Japan surrendered to the Allied Forces, and after the withdrawal of Soviet occupation forces.

In addition to the data on Manchuria in Table B-2, which are on the conservative side, the capacity for the rest of China at about the same time can be obtained by aggregating such information as is available on all the plants in China proper. For Manchuria a separate estimate can also be made in this manner although the Pauley Report estimate is probably more reliable. Full details of the basis of these estimates are given below. The aggregate estimates are given in Tables B-3, B-4, and B-5.

Production, 1945-1948. In view of the cessation of the war in August, 1945, and the disruption of production both in Manchuria because of Soviet occupation and in China proper because of the relocation of plants and personnel, it is believed that production of all iron and steel products declined sharply during the latter part of 1945 and that further drops occurred afterwards. Production statistics became extremely fragmentary during this period, but although the lack of adequate information prevents us from asserting unequivocally that the simple explanation lay in the lack of production to report, we are inclined to believe that such was in fact the case.

In the case of pig iron, the 1948 <u>Statistical Yearbook</u>[21] reported a total output of 31,000 tons only. Production in the following year was reported as 36,000 tons by the <u>Chinese Yearbook</u>,[22] which also noted that the output of Manchuria was not fully covered. These estimates are indicative of the low level to which production had fallen, as well as the general unreliability of data and incomplete coverage during this period.

In the case of ingot- and finished-steel products no production data appear to be available for this period. Actual production, if any, would undoubtedly be negligible.

The Communist Period

<u>1949-1957</u>

Capacity. There is no direct information on available capacity in 1949 when the Communists took over the greater part of the Chinese mainland. However, military operations in Manchuria and the generally chaotic economic conditions in the country between 1945 and 1949 were definitely not conducive to plant rehabilitation, and one would be justified in assuming that the total rated capacity of iron- and steelmaking in 1949 was somewhat smaller than the estimates for the latter part of 1945. The effective operating capacity was definitely even less.

Table B-6

IRON- AND STEELMAKING CAPACITY YEAREND, 1953
(in thousand metric tons)

Region	Pig Iron		Steel Ingot		Finished-steel Products	
	Rated	Operating	Rated	Operating	Rated	Operating
Manchuria	1,159	1,926	1,129	1,305	488	897
China Proper	881-1,002	1,200-1,220	574	834	412	507-527
Total	2,040-2,161	3,126-3,146	1,703	2,139	900	1,404-1,424
	2,289-2,410[a]					

Source: See data in Table B-13.

[a]The higher range here includes small iron works established in Free China during World War II that were in existence in 1945 and might still have been partly in operation in 1953; see Table B-13.

Fortunately, the later Japanese Survey Report[23] offers us a comprehensive list of modern iron and/or steel mills for the country as a whole in 1953.

The total annual rated capacity and the estimated operating capacity under normal conditions, divided between Manchuria and China proper, are given in Table B-6.

For the remaining years under consideration, the various estimates are made in the following manner:

Rated capacity

1949-1955, reconstructed on the basis of data pertaining to changes in the individual plants as reported in the Survey Report and listed in Table B-7.

1952-1956, also estimated on the basis of cubic meters of blast furnace volume available for pig iron and square meters of effective area in open hearth furnaces. These estimates are used as a check of the reliability of the preceding estimates for the years in which both sets of estimates are available.

1957, may be estimated on the basis of the average rate of growth in 1952-56 for pig iron and steel ingot, or, perhaps more reasonably, from the operating capacities of the year.

1956-1957, for steel products, the 1956 estimate is made on the basis of the average rate in 1952-1955; the 1957 estimate is derived from operating capacity.

Operating capacity

The data for 1953 are given in the Survey Report. For the remaining years, the same ratio between rated and operating capacities in 1953 is used through 1955 for all three categories, and through 1956 for pig iron.

1952-1956, also estimated from the aggregation of individual plants as reported for pig iron in the Survey Report.

1956, for steel products, estimated from rated capacity; for ingot steel, estimated from open hearth capacity.

1957, obtained through the aggregation of data on individual plants as listed in Table B-13. Alternative estimates can also be found for pig iron and ingot steel on the basis of rated capacity.

This brief summary may now be elaborated.

1. Pig Iron

a. 1949-1955. Information on all the individual plants listed in the Japanese Survey Report is utilized in order to determine capacity changes through 1955. The individual plant estimates are then added together to arrive at the over-all annual estimates. The results are shown in Table B-7.

Table B-7

RATED CAPACITY OF BLAST FURNACES

(in thousand metric tons)

Year	(1)	(2)*
1949	1,119-1,276	1,368-1,525
1950	1,119-1,276	1,368-1,525
1951	1,368-1,514	1,617-1,763
1952	1,380-1,514	1,629-1,763
1953	2,040-2,161	2,289-2,410
1954	2,304-2,414	2,553-2,663
1955	2,557-2,666	2,806-2,915

*Includes the small iron works mentioned in Table B-5.

b. 1952-1956. The effective volume of available blast furnaces in 1952-1956 is given in Major Aspects. If we identify the volume in 1953 with the rated capacity given above, a series of estimates can be made for the remaining years. Similarly, estimates can also be made on the basis of operating capacity in 1953. It is not clear whether the data on effective volume include the plants at T'ang-shan, Tientsin, and Tsingtao which were shut down in 1953; the rated capacity used here includes these three mills while the operating capacity estimate does not. [24] In spite of this discrepancy a comparison may be made between the estimates based on the effective volume of blast furnaces with those obtained from the aggregation of data on individual mills. The difference in rated capacity between the estimates based on the effective volume of blast furnaces and those obtained from the aggregation of data on individual mills are all less than 5 percent of the estimates based on the effective volume of blast furnaces. In other words, the rated capacities from 1952-1955 estimated in this manner are very close to the figure obtained from aggregation.

Since no other basis exists for a more reliable estimate of the year-end rated capacity in 1957, the latter may first be roughly estimated by assuming that it rose from the 1956 level at the same average rate obtained between 1952 and 1956, or 23.6 percent. The estimate thus arrived at is 3,935,800 - 4,124,700 tons. The operating capacity derived from aggregation of individual plants is 8,307,000 - 8,333,000 tons. A lower estimate, 7,063,000 - 7,169,000 tons, however, can be derived by applying the 1953 ratio of operating to rated capacities to the 1957 rated capacity estimated above. On the other hand, applying the same ratio as before to the operating capacity of 8,307,000 - 8,333,000 tons obtained by aggregation, we can also arrive at another estimate of rated capacity equal to 4,561,000 - 4,866,000 tons.

276

2. Steel Ingot

a. 1949-1955. Rated annual ingot capacity during this period may be estimated by aggregating the year-to-year estimates of individual plants given in the Survey Report. The estimates are:

Year	Metric tons
1949	637,500-638,700
1950	1,345,900-1,347,100
1951	1,428,300
1952	1,598,700
1953	1,703,500
1954	1,778,500
1955	1,778,500

b. 1952-1956. The estimates of annual capacity are divided into three categories: open hearth capacity, converter capacity, and electric furnace capacity. The core of the estimate consists of open hearth steel. The procedure resembles that used in the case of pig iron.

Open hearth capacity, measured in terms of square meters of effective area, is given in Major Aspects,[25] while the annual capacity in tons in 1953 is available in the Survey Report. The mills are assumed to be in operation for 300 days a year. On the basis of the same coefficient of utilization in 1953, estimates can be derived for 1952-1956 as in Table B-9.

According to the Survey Report, converter operating capacity and electric furnace operating capacity in 1953 were 15.6 percent and 14.4 percent, respectively, of the corresponding open hearth capacity. As an approximation, the same proportions can be used for the remaining years. The annual estimates of total operating capacity are therefore equivalent to 130 percent of the corresponding open hearth operating capacity. Since the number of converters may have increased at a faster rate, the totals may be somewhat understated.

In terms of rated capacity in 1953, converters and electric furnaces amounted to about 3.1 percent and 24.5 percent, respectively, of open hearth capacity. Approximate estimates for these categories can therefore also be made for the remaining years by holding these proportions constant.

c. 1957. As an approximation, rated ingot capacity in this year may first be derived from the 1956 figure under the assumption that it increased at the average rate realized between 1952 and 1956 and was therefore 23.1 percent larger, or 4,326,000 tons. Since, however, the operating capacity is estimated at 6,748,000 tons by aggregation of individual plants, the rated capacity would be 5,344,000 tons if the same ratio between rated and operating capacity in 1953 is used.

3. Finished-steel Products

　　　　a. 1949-1955. Full details are available in the Japanese Survey Report on the designed productive capacity of finished steel products, excluding such semifinished forms as blooms and billets. Totals can be obtained by aggregating the statistics given for individual plants. The results are:

Annual Rated Capacity in Metric Tons	
1949	681,400
1950	749,632
1951	749,632
1952	799,632
1953	899,632
1954	959,632
1955	959,632

　　　　b. 1956-1957. (1) Rated capacity data for this period are not available from official sources. Preliminary estimates, however, can be made. For 1956, the average annual growth rate of 1952-1955 is applied to the 1955 figure. For 1957, the estimate is made by applying the same ratio between rated and operating capacities in 1953 to the operating capacity of 1957.

　　　　(2) Operating capacity data for 1956 are derived from the rated capacity estimate and the ratio between rated and operating capacities in 1953. For 1957, the operating capacity is estimated through aggregation.

　　　　Production.

　　　　A number of production estimates for this period have been made available by official sources, along with some unofficial estimates. Some of the official publications, quoting apparently from the same primary source(s), have offered identical figures while others have not. The same is true of some of the secondary sources. Table B-12 presents most of the principal data with source and other notations which are self-explanatory. The figures bearing asterisks are used in the present study.

1958-1960

　　　　Capacity.

　　　　Productive capacity during this period, together with that of 1957, can be obtained by means of aggregation on the basis of information on individual plants, a summary of which is presented in Table B-11.

Table B-8

ESTIMATES OF BLAST FURNACE CAPACITY BASED ON EFFECTIVE VOLUME

Year	Estimates by Aggregation		Effective Volume		Estimated Capacity (in thousand metric tons)		Divergence from Estimates by Aggregation	
	A. Rated	B. Operating	Cubic meters	Index	A.´ Rated	B.´ Operating	$\frac{A-A´}{A´}$	$\frac{B-B´}{B´}$
1952	1,380-1,514	2,064-2,084	5,179	66.9	1,365-1,446	2,091-2,104	(1.1-4.7)%	-(0.9-1)%
1953	2,040-2,161	3,126-3,146	7,739	100.0	2,040-2,161	3,126-3,146	0	0
1954	2,304-2,414	3,570-3,590	8,987	116.1	2,368-2,509	3,629-3,652	-(2.7-3.8)%	-(1.6-2.2)%
1955	2,557-2,666	3,966-3,986	9,996	129.2	2,636-2,792	4,038-4,064	-(3.0-4.5)%	-(1.7-1.9)%
1956	...	...	12,077	156.1	3,184-3,373	4,879-4,910	...	...

Data for effective volume from Major Aspects, op. cit., p. 21.

Estimated capacity data for 1953 from aggregation (see Table B-13) multiplied by the index of effective volume.

Table B-9

ESTIMATES OF OPEN HEARTH CAPACITY BY FURNACE AREA

Year	Effective Area (square meters)	Index	Annual Capacity (metric tons)	
			Operating	Rated
1952	726.1	90	1,480,500	1,201,000
1953	808.9	100	1,645,000	1,334,400
1954	886.2	110	1,809,500	1,467,800
1955	1,024.3	127	2,089,200	1,694,700
1956	1,668.6	206	3,388,700	2,748,900

Table B-10

ANNUAL CAPACITY

(in thousand metric tons)

	Open Hearth		Converter		Electric Furnace		Total	
	Rated	Operating	Rated	Operating	Rated	Operating	Rated	Operating
1952	1,201.0	1,480.5	37.4	231.0	294.2	213.2	1,533.6	1,924.7
1953	1,334.4	1,645.0	41.4	257.0	326.9	236.8	1,703.5	2,138.8
1954	1,467.8	1,809.5	45.5	282.3	259.6	260.6	1,874.4	2,352.4
1955	1,694.7	2,089.2	52.5	325.9	415.2	300.8	2,164.1	2,715.9
1956	2,748.9	3,388.7	85.2	528.6	673.5	488.0	3,510.4	4,405.3

The rated capacities as estimated in this table do not differ by more than 6 percent from the corresponding estimates obtained through aggregation of the individual plants. In the exceptional case of 1955 the rated capacity is 18 percent higher than that found by aggregation. This discrepancy may be due to the fact that the figures in the Japanese Survey Report, which was published in 1955, are incomplete and do not include new capacity installed toward the end of the year.

281

Table B-11

ANNUAL OPERATING CAPACITY
(in metric tons)

Year	Pig Iron	Steel Ingot	"Steel Products"
1957	8,333,000	6,748,000	3,863,000
1958	12,968,000	14,561,000	5,828,000
1959	25,008,000	23,357,000	9,194,000
1960	39,948,000	38,049,000	16,618,000

The above data are regarded as operating capacities. This is based on the fact that in the case of pig iron, the operating capacity of 1957 (7,063,000 tons)--estimated by applying the ratio between rated and operating capacities in 1953 to the rated capacity of 1957, which in turn is estimated by using the average rate of growth in 1952-1956 , is not too far apart from the operating capacity (8,333,000 tons) obtained from aggregation of the estimates of individual plants. The same reason ing is then applied to the figures of steel ingot and finished-steel products for 1957 and 1958-1960, inasmuch as these estimates are derived from the same sources as pig iron and identity of the concepts employed may be legitimately assumed.

Where different estimates are given for the same plants in different sources, one global estimate is obtained by adding all the highest individual plant estimates available. An alternative total is then obtained by summing all the lowest plant-estimates. For pig iron, in 1945 and 1949-1955 we have another possible sequence of a somewhat higher range which includes small iron works, established in Free China during World War II, that were in existence in 1945 and might still be available through 1949-1955.

Inspection of the series in comparison with estimates for the earlier years shows a marked discontinuity between 1957 and 1958 and between 1958 and 1959. This is partly caused by the large-scale establishment of many very small native-style furnaces in 1958 for iron- and steelmaking, followed by a general movement to convert the more efficient ones into modified small modern furnaces in 1959. A number of medium-sized mills of modern design were also built during this period. With the exception of pig iron production capacity in 1958, which does not include all the small backyard furnaces, all other estimates are probably somewhat on the high side because of the difficulty in determining whether individual reports of planned constructions have actually been completed and whether actual and alleged design capacities are the same. The 1958-1960 data should therefore be regarded as highly tentative.

Production.

Official statistics of pig iron and steel ingot production are available for the years 1958 and 1959. These are divided into production from the native and semimodern furnaces and production from the modern mills. Similar estimates are available for steel products in 1958. For 1959 output of steel products the estimated operating capacity is used.

Production statistics in 1960 are of a very tentative nature. Official data that have been published so far deal with the planned output of pig iron and the over-all production of steel only. Full details and the sources used are given in Table B-12, where figures with asterisks are those tentatively adopted for use in the present study.

Table B-12

PRODUCTION STATISTICS OF PIG IRON, INGOT STEEL,
AND "FINISHED-STEEL PRODUCTS"
(in metric tons)

Year		Pig Iron			Ingot Steel	"Finished-steel Products"
		Total	Modern Blast Furnaces	Native Iron		
1949	(1)	251,991	...	...	158,378	141,104
	(2)	...	246,000	...	158,000	140,000
		252,000*	246,000*	6,000*	158,000*	141,000*
1950	(1)	977,794*	...	...	605,796*	463,921*
1951	(1)	1,447,940*	...	...	895,982*	807,798*
1952	(1)	1,928,585	...	...	1,348,509	1,311,987
	(2)	1,929,000	...	...	1,349,000	...
	(3)	1,929,000	1,900,000	29,000	1,349,000	1,110,000
	(4)	1,929,000*	1,900,000*	29,000*	1,349,000*	1,312,000*
1953	(1)	2,234,098	...	...	1,773,954	1,754,161
	(2)	2,234,000	2,175,000	59,000	1,774,000	...
	(3)	...	2,196,350	...	1,880,780	1,333,000
	(4)	2,234,000*	2,175,000*	59,000*	1,774,000*	1,754,000*
1954	(1)	3,113,703	...	...	2,224,595	1,965,337
	(2)	3,114,000	2,962,000	152,000	2,230,000	1,176,000
	(3)	3,114,000*	2,962,000*	152,000*	2,225,000*	1,965,000*
1955	(1)	3,872,421	...	...	2,853,105	2,504,817
	(2)	3,872,000	3,630,000	?42,000	2,853,000	2,505,000
	(3)	3,872,000*	3,630,000*	242,000*	2,853,000*	2,505,000*
1956	(1)	4,826,249	...	...	4,465,422	3,920,975
	(2)	...	4,777,000	...	4,465,000	3,921,000
	(3)	4,826,000*	4,777,000*	49,000*	4,465,000*	3,921,000*
1957	(1)	5,936,000	...	...	5,350,000	...
	(2)	5,940,000	...	...	5,350,000	4,260,000
	(3)	...	5,860,000	...	5,240,000	...
	(4)	5,936,000*	5,860,000*	76,000*	5,350,000*	4,260,000*

Table B-12 (Continued)

| Year | Pig Iron | | | Ingot Steel | | | "Finished-steel Products" |
	Total	Modern	Native	Total	Modern	Native	Total
1958 (1)	13,690,000*	9,530,000*	4,160,000*	11,080,000*	8,000,000*	3,080,000*	6,000,000*
(2)	...	9,500,000	...	8,000,000	...	...	...
1959 (1)	20,500,000*	9,500,000*	11,000,000*	13,350,000*	8,630,000*	4,720,000*	9,200,000*
1960 (1)	27,500,000*(a)	12,700,000*(d)	14,800,000*(d)	18,450,000*(b)	12,000,000*(e)	6,450,000*(a)	12,800,000* – 16,600,000*(c)

*Denotes figures that are tentatively accepted for the purposes of this study; numbers in parentheses refer to specific sources in Notes (below).

1949

     (1) <u>Major Aspects</u>, <u>op. cit.</u>, pp. 10 and 14.

     (2) <u>Ten Great Years</u>, <u>op. cit.</u>, p. 95, and <u>Jen-min shou-ts'e</u> (People's Handbook), 1959, Vol. 2, p. 409; also quoted by K. P. Wang, <u>op. cit.</u>, <u>Mineral Trade Notes</u>, <u>Special Supplement</u>, No. 59, p. 10: and Hughes and Luard, <u>op. cit.</u>, p. 211. An estimate based on earlier data put the figures at 206,000 tons of pig iron, 87,000 tons of rolled steel (72,000 tons from Manchuria and 15,000 tons from China proper). The small China proper figure probably reflects incomplete coverage. See Yuan-li Wu, <u>Economic Survey of Communist China</u>, <u>op. cit.</u>, p. 292.

1950

     (1) <u>Major Aspects</u>, <u>op. cit.</u>, p. 14.

1951

     (1) <u>Ibid.</u>, p. 15. Also <u>Ten Great Years</u>, p. 95, for the pig iron and ingot steel data.

1952

     (1) <u>Major Aspects</u>, <u>op. cit.</u>, p. 14.

     (2) <u>Ten Great Years</u>, <u>op. cit.</u>, p. 95.

     (3) C. M. Li, <u>The Economic Development of Communist China</u>, p. 44, derived from official data. Practically the same figures are used in K. P. Wang's article in <u>Mineral Trade Notes</u>, <u>op. cit.</u>, p. 10.

     (4) The lower figure for rolled products probably does not include the output of some small local plants.

1953

     (1) <u>Major Aspects</u>, <u>op. cit.</u>, p. 14, and <u>Ten Great Years</u>, <u>op. cit.</u>, p. 95. The same ingot figure is also cited by Hughes and Luard, <u>op. cit.</u>

     (2) C. M. Li, <u>op. cit.</u>, p. 44. The same modern blast furnace pig iron figure is used by Hughes and Luard.

     (3) <u>Survey Report</u>, Charts 10, 11, and 12. Discrepancies with (1) and (2) probably due to differences in coverage and reporting errors.

     (4) The higher figure for rolled products is chosen to insure complete coverage.

1954

     (1) <u>Major Aspects</u>, <u>op. cit.</u>, p. 26, and <u>Ten Great Years</u>, <u>op. cit.</u>, p. 95.

     (2) C. M. Li, <u>op. cit.</u>, p. 44. The same ingot and pig-iron figures are also cited by Hughes and Luard.

     (3) See note (3) under 1949.

1955

     (1) <u>Major Aspects</u>, <u>op. cit.</u>, p. 26, and <u>Ten Great Years</u>, <u>op. cit.</u>, p. 95.

(2) C. M. Li, op. cit., p. 44.

(3) Excluding the small local plants, the output of rolled products would probably be 2,220,000 tons.

1956

(1) Major Aspects, op. cit., p. 26, and Ten Great Years, op. cit., p. 95.

(2) The same data are cited by C. M. Li, Hughes and Luard and the Chukoku Nenkan (China Yearbook), 1958, p. 189.

(3) The native iron figure is computed as a residual. Excluding the small local plants, the output of rolled products would be about 3,420,000 tons.

1957

(1) Ten Great Years, p. 95.

(2) K. P. Wang, op. cit.

(3) Hughes and Luard, op. cit., p. 211.

(4) Native iron computed as a residual.

1958

(1) Ten Great Years, op. cit., p. 95; NCNA, Peking, April 14, 1959; People's Handbook, op. cit., vol. 2, p. 409.

(2) K. P. Wang, op. cit., "Rich Mineral Resources Spur Communist China's Bid for Industrial Power," in Mineral Trade Notes, Special Supplement, no. 59, March, 1960, p. 5.

1959

(1) Survey of China Mainland Press, no. 2186, February, 1960, p. 2.

1960 (1)

(a) Planned target, Far Eastern Economic Review Yearbook, 1961, p. 64.

(b) Survey of China Mainland Press, no. 2504, May 26, 1961, p. 19.

(c) The lower figure for finished-steel products in 1960 is estimated on the basis of a 39 percent increase over the 1959 level. This is the same rate of increase registered in ingot production from modern mills. The higher estimate is derived from the rate of operation in 1959 (nearly 100 percent of 9,194 thousand tons) in terms of a higher capacity estimate (16,618 thousand tons).

(d) Estimated at the ratio of 1959 between modern mill production and the total output or 46.34%.

(e) "Modern" steel estimated at 65% of total output on the basis of 1959 data.

Appendix C

A TENTATIVE RE-ESTIMATE OF FINISHED STEEL
PRODUCTION

Throughout the discussion in Chapters 3, 4, and 5, we pointed to the apparently excessive output of "finished-steel products" reported in official Communist publications on the basis of its high ratio to (1) steel ingot output and (2) the estimated annual operating capacity of steel finishing and fabrication, as well as the distribution of the reported output by use. We have suggested that the explanation may lie in the inclusion of semifinished intermediate products in the official statistics.

A bold attempt is made in this Appendix to estimate the real output of finished-steel products if the hypothesis that there is in fact a large component of semifinished products is accepted and if it is then eliminated from the reported output of "finished steel." The adjustment is carried out under the assumption that the ratio between "finished" and "semifinished" products in the total output is the same as the corresponding capacity ratio. Furthermore, the annual capacity of semifinished products is estimated to be at least equal to that of the bloom mills at An-shan. The latter's rated capacity was 500,000 tons a year in 1949 through 1955, according to the Survey Report, and rose to 1,250,000 in 1956. The capacity ratios between semifinished and finished steels in the years 1950 through 1956 were as follows:

Category	Rated Capacity (in thousand metric tons)						
	1950	1951	1952	1953	1954	1955	1956
Semifinished steel	500	500	500	500	500	500	1,250
Finished steel	750	750	800	900	960	960	991
	Ratio						
Semifinished steel	.67	.67	.63	.56	.52	.52	1.26
Finished steel	1	1	1	1	1	1	1

As an approximation, the production statistics of "finished-steel products" in Table B-1 are divided by 1.67 for 1949-1951, 1.63 for 1952, 1.56 for 1953, 1.52 for 1954-1955, and 2.26 for 1956 and the subsequent years. The results of this adjustment are given in Table C-1.

288

Table C-1

ADJUSTMENT OF "FINISHED-STEEL" PRODUCTION
(in thousand metric tons)

Year	"Finished-Steel" Production	Adjusted Finished-Steel Production
1949	141	84
1950	464	278
1951	808	484
1952	1,312	805
1953	1,754	1,124
1954	1,965	1,293
1955	2,505	1,648
1956	3,921	1,735
1957	4,260	1,884
1958	6,000	2,655
1959	9,200	4,071
1960	12,800-16,600	5,664-7,345

If the adjusted finished-steel production estimates are now compared with the reported production of ingot steel in the modern sector, the result would be a dramatic reversal of the situation described in Chapter 3. The production ratio becomes distinctly unfavorable to finished products, especially during 1956-1959 when ingot production was expanded at great speed. On the other hand, the ratio is far more plausible if it is compared with that of the U.S.S.R. given in Table 3.13. The Communist Chinese steel industry, being far less advanced than that of the Soviet Union, produces far more ingot steel in relation to finished products.

Table C-2

OUTPUT RATIO OF INGOT STEEL TO ADJUSTED
FINISHED-STEEL PRODUCTS
(in thousand metric tons)

Year	Ingot Steel Output	Adjusted Finished-Steel Output	Output Ratio
1952	1,349	805	1.67
1953	1,774	1,124	1.58
1954	2,225	1,293	1.72
1955	2,853	1,648	1.73
1956	4,465	1,735	2.57
1957	5,350	1,884	2.84
1958	8,000	2,655	3.01
1959	8,630	4,071	2.12
1960	12,000	7,345	1.63

Furthermore, it should be noted that the above adjusted output estimates are now much closer to the capacity estimates given in Chapter 3.

Another effect of the adjustment is the reduction of the growth rate of finished steel in 1952-1957 from 26.6 percent per annum to 18.5 percent, which, though substantially higher than the Soviet rate of 9.4 percent in 1927-1932, is much less than that of 24.8 percent in 1932-1937.

Admittedly, the foregoing adjustment is an extremely crude one and we therefore are not presenting the result as the estimate to be accepted in preference to all other available data. Nevertheless, there seems to be a good case for us to consider rather seriously that the adjusted figures may be far closer to the truth than the official statistics as an estimate of the output of end products from the point of view of the iron and steel industry.

CHANGES IN PRODUCTION TECHNIQUE

Ronald Hsia

University of Hong Kong

Changes in production technique in China's steel industry have been focussed in the past decade on increasing the productivity of capital equipment. To the extent that the productivity of the existing capital equipment can be increased by changes in production technique; such changes are capital-saving and should be of interest to students of economics. In fact, the key to the rapid growth of Communist China's steel industry lies in changes in production technique which have been responsible not only for tapping the potentialities of the western-type equipment, but also for improving to some extent the indigenous production methods.

In the following, only the major changes in production technique in the iron smelting and steel refining sectors of the steel industry are examined. Whenever data permit, the effects of new production techniques on output and/or input will be pointed out, even though such effects are only known with reference to individual plants or localities. Changes in production technique as noted here include also modifications of equipment which have been brought about by changes in the methods of production.

Organization of Metallurgical Research

Before examining specific changes in production technique, let us take a cursory look at the organized research in ferrous metallurgy, which was directly or indirectly responsible for most of the technological changes in the steel industry.

In its anxiety to industrialize China, the Communist regime has emphasized the need for technical research. Accordingly, in all the iron and steel enterprises (except the very small producing units), plant laboratories have been set up to engage in research and experiment. These laboratories are reasonably well equipped and are assigned the best available metallurgical engineers and technicians to carry on research and development projects. They serve as the center for solving problems concerning production techniques of the individual enterprise, for introducing new technology and new products, and for improving output quality. They are thus highly important in terms of practical developments actually adopted.

In addition, national institutions have been organized to carry on research of importance to the iron and steel industry. They include the Iron and Steel Research Institute of the Ministry of Metallurgical Industry, the Metal

Research Institute, the Metallurgical Clay Research Institute, and the Metallurgical Chemistry Research Institute, all under the Chinese Academy of Sciences. These national research organizations engage experienced engineers and technicians from the iron- and steel-production units, as well as academicians, in order to keep their work within the realm of Chinese reality. The technical competence of these research organizations was also enhanced by the initial participation of Soviet experts and experts from East European countries. Their presence was particularly helpful in the introduction of Soviet techniques and technology.

Large and Medium Blast Furnaces

While changes in production technique examined in this section bear reference primarily to the large and medium furnaces, they are not completely inapplicable to small furnaces, particularly in view of the latter's continued enlargement and modernization. Changes in production technique in the operation of small furnaces are examined separately because of the special technical problems confronting them, at least at the present stage.

Increase in Smelting Intensity

The method of raising smelting intensity (the amount in tonnage of coke consumed per cubic meter of useful furnace volume in 24 hours) while at the same time reducing the coke ratio (the amount in tonnage of coke input per ton of pig-iron output) represents a notable change in blast-furnace operation in mainland China.

This accomplishment has invalidated previous beliefs that smelting intensity cannot be raised much beyond 1.0 and that any increase in the smelting intensity is necessarily accompanied by an increase in the coke ratio. Such beliefs were attributable to the unpleasant experiences of 1953 and 1954, when nearly all the blast furnaces throughout the country were plagued by "lumping of slag" as a result of raising the smelting intensity beyond 1.2. From that point on, the practice was to keep the smelting intensity within the boundary of 1.1 for large blast furnaces and 1.2 for smaller ones.

During the spectacular steel drive of 1958, the Pen-ch'i Iron and Steel Company with a better grasp of the proper relation between the ability of the gas to permeate the mix and the volume of air blast forced through the furnace, took the lead in raising the smelting intensity of blast furnaces. At the First Pen-ch'i Iron and Steel Plant, for instance, the smelting intensity of blast furnaces was raised continuously from 1.013 in 1937 to 1.550 in April-May, 1959. Concomitantly the average coefficient of blast furnaces (derived by dividing the daily output in tons by the volume of useful capacity of the furnace in cubic meters) increased from 1.392 in the first quarter of 1958 to 2.436 in May, 1959.[1]

The nationwide adoption of this production technique in 1959 resulted in raising the productivity of the nation's large and medium blast furnaces and in lowering their coke consumption relative to the output level. From January to November, 1959, the national average of the utilization coefficient of blast furnaces with a useful volume of over 100 cubic meters increased 30 percent, and the national average of their coke ratios decreased by about 100 kilograms.[2]

Use of Self-fluxing Sinter

The use of self-fluxing sinter has been an important change in production technique for raising blast furnace productivity. The basicity ratio (CaO/SiO_2) of sinter produced in mainland China prior to 1955 was below 0.5. Toward the end of the First Five-Year Plan, it was raised to 1.0. This was accomplished chiefly by crushing the stone more finely and by adding manganese oxide in the sinter. The experience of An-shan shows that when the charge consists of 60-percent sinter, the increase of basicity from 0.6 to 1.0 resulted in (1) a reduction of limestone consumption by 60-70 kilograms per ton of pig iron output; (2) a 4-5 percent reduction in coke ratio; and (3) a 5-7 percent increase in the utilization coefficient of the blast furnace.[3] An additional advantage was that the "lumping of slag" was practically eliminated.

The use of high basicity sinter was by no means confined to An-shan and Pen-ch'i; it reflected a nationwide trend. Together with general increases in the basicity ratio of sintered ores, the percentage of sinter in the furnace feed increased on a national average from 27.8 in 1955 to 29.7 in 1956 and 38.0 in 1957.[4]

A further development was to change high-basicity sinter to ball-shape. This change, while maintaining the basicity ratio at above 1.2, has the following additional advantages: (1) assuring more complete utilization in the burning process; (2) lending itself more readily to the agglomeration of powdery ore; and (3) minimizing the loss of basicity during long-distance shipment.

Improvement in Charging Technique

The technique of charging the mix into the furnace has been changed by increasing the amount of the charge, and by distributing the burden more evenly throughout the furnace. This improved charging technique was disseminated to all the iron producing enterprises in 1954. By adopting this method, the T'ai-yüan Iron and Steel Company raised the quarterly average utilization coefficient of its No. 2 blast furnace from 0.890 in the first quarter of 1954 to 1.158 in the second quarter of the same year. In terms of iron output, the increase amounted to approximately 23 percent. The application of this charging technique in An-shan brought forth an output increase of 34 percent, a decrease in coke ratio from 1.04 to 0.799, an increase in the carbon dioxide content of the blast furnace gas from 8.3 to 10.8 percent, and a decrease in the frequency of "dump" failures from 0.7 to 0.3 times in 24 hours.[5]

Use of Controlled Moisture in the Blast

The technique of adding a certain amount of steam in the blast to stabilize its moisture as a means of increasing volume and controlling temperature was first investigated at the No. 7 blast furnace of An-shan in 1954. By adding 20-25 grams of steam to each cubic meter of blast whose temperature was preheated to 760-810° C, the productivity of the furnace was raised by 5 percent.[6] By the first half of 1955, this technique had been extended to ten blast furnaces in the country (six at An-shan, two at Shih-ching-shan and two at Pen-ch'i), all of which reported favorable effects on furnace productivity and coke consumption.

Increase in Blast Temperature

Raising the temperature to which the blast is preheated and at which the furnace operates is a precondition for increasing the smelting intensity. It is, therefore, an essential measure for lowering the coke ratio and for raising the productivity of the blast furnace. Although the optimum temperature varies with individual furnaces, generally speaking the temperature of all the furnaces with a useful volume of 300 cubic meters or more reached 850° C or above by the end of 1958, with the record temperature of 1,080° C attained by the Shih-ching-shan Iron and Steel Company. [7] When the temperature of the No. 2 blast furnace at Shih-ching-shan was increased from 680° C to 720° C, its productivity went up by 2.5 percent whereas its coke ratio dropped by 2.17 percent. Changes in blast temperature and the corresponding changes in coke ratio at the An-shan Iron and Steel Company for the period 1953-1958 are shown in Table D-1.

It is interesting to note in Table D-1 the apparent negative correlation between the two series. When the blast temperature dropped from 671° C in 1953 to 653° C in 1954, the coke ratio increased from 0.918 to 0.920. From 1954 onward, however, the blast temperature showed continual increase and the coke ratio continual decrease. From the standpoint of raising blast furnace output and economizing coke consumption, the continual increase in blast temperature and the concomitant decrease in coke ratio have been entirely desirable. However, the lowering of the coke ratio has, on the other hand, reduced the amount of heat in the gas generated by the iron-smelting process, and thus affected the fuel supply of the air preheating installations and the open hearth. This problem needs to be solved in order to maintain fuel balance in iron and steel combines.

Use of High Top Pressure

This production technique was introduced in 1956. By the latter part of 1959, there were five blast furnaces in the country employing this technique. The relatively slow adoption of the technique can be attributed to the fact that the use of high top pressures requires special top construction and additional investment. Nevertheless, the steel industry is determined to extend its application, inasmuch as the additional investment is accompanied by a low incremental capital-output ratio.

The experiences of the An-shan, Pen-ch'i, and Wu-han Iron and Steel Companies show that as a rule the use of high top pressures intensifies the smelting process, lowers the coke ratio, reduces the wastage of blast furnace gas, and enlarges the volume of air blast forced through the furnace. The specific effect of employing high top pressure on furnace productivity can be detected from Table D-2 which gives top pressures of an unidentified blast furnace at An-shan in June and November, 1958, along with its other technical data.

It can be seen from the table that while the effect of top pressure on coke ratio may have been counteracted by the reduction in blast temperature, its effects on smelting intensity and productivity are unobscured. With every increase in top pressure by 0.1 kilograms, productivity improves by 3 percent. Regarding the effect of increasing top pressure on the volume of air blast, the experience of the No. 2 blast furnace at Pen-ch'i's No. 2 Iron Smelting Plant shows that when the top pressure was raised to 0.7 atmosphere, the volume of air blast can be increased by 200-250 cubic meters per minute. [8]

Table D-1

BLAST TEMPERATURE AND COKE RATIO AT AN-SHAN, 1953-1958

Year	Blast Temperature (^{O}C)	Coke Ratio (metric ton)
1953	671	0.918
1954	653	0.920
1955	763	0.851
1956	857	0.737
1957	860	0.711
1958	900+	0.655

Source: Kang-t'ieh, no. 18, 1959, p. 801.

Table D-2

AN-SHAN BLAST FURNACE DATA, JUNE AND NOVEMBER, 1958

Item	June	November
Utilization coefficient (ton/m^3/24 hours)	1.672	1.859
Smelting Intensity (ton/m^3/24 hours)	1.142	1.351
Coke Ratio (ton/ton output)	0.672	0.705
Sinter in Burden (percent)	100	100
Top Pressure (kg./cm^2)	0.40	0.80
Blast Temperature (^{O}C)	821	806

Source: Ibid.

Small Blast Furnaces

The importance of small blast furnaces (with a volume of 100 cubic meters or less) to mainland China cannot be overestimated. In 1959, their combined capacity amounted to nearly two-thirds of the nation's total blast furnace capacity, and they contributed in that year 51 percent of the over-all pig-iron output.[9] Furthermore, the relatively lower productivity of the small furnaces[10] leaves more room for increasing output through changes in production technique. Their productivity can be improved by reducing either the amount of input per unit of output, or the length of time the mix remains in the furnace. In changing the methods of operating small blast furnaces, equal emphasis was laid on the improvement of output quality.

Use of Lime Instead of Limestone

This change was directed at improving output quality, raising productivity, and lowering the coke ratio. The use of lime as fluxing material was expected to prevent the absorption of heat that occurred when limestone was used in the roasting process. It was also expected to lower the carbon dioxide content of the gas, thus increasing the indirect reducibility of the mix. Since small blast furnaces as a rule use high sulphur content "native coke," improvement in output quality was expected from a low coke ratio which minimized the high sulphur coke penalty, as well as from the elimination of sulphur contained in the limestone.

The use of lime to replace limestone as a flux is a measure particularly effective for smaller furnaces because of the low iron content of their ore input. The experience of the T'ang-shan Iron Plant shows that the use of lime instead of limestone in its blast furnace of 13 cubic-meter capacity resulted in a 67-percent increase in productivity and a 37-percent decrease in coke ratio. Similarly when the No. 2 "red flag" small blast furnace of the Ma-an-shan Iron and Steel Company employed this technique, its productivity went up 36 percent and its coke ratio was lowered by 25 percent.[11]

Sizing of Ore and Coke

The benefits of limiting and to some extent standardizing the size of raw materials have been demonstrated by the Li-min Iron Plant. By reducing the size of coke from 25-60 millimeters to 5-20 millimeters and restricting the ore size to the range of 5-12 millimeters the 7-cubic-meter blast furnace at Li-min achieved a higher permeability within the mix and a greater stability in the temperature at which the furnace was operating. When this production technique was applied simultaneously with the methods of enlarging the volume of air blast and increasing the furnace temperature, the utilization coefficient of some small furnaces went up above 4 and their coke ratio was lowered to the level of 0.3.[12]

Use of Air Preheater of the Multitubular Type

This technique was introduced into small blast furnace operation by the People's Iron Plant in Yü-hsien, Hunan Province, and made it possible to preheat the blast to 600-800° C, thus intensifying the smelting process and increasing the productivity of the small blast furnace. Meanwhile, coke consumption per unit of output showed decreases. The purpose in using a multitubular type of air preheater was to maintain a reasonable degree of uniformity in temperature throughout the device keeping the difference within 150° C. [13] Since the gas generated in the iron smelting process is used as the fuel for the preheater, additional operating expenses involved in the use of the multitubes are limited. Furthermore, such preheaters are inexpensive to build. Therefore, this technique was widely adopted among the small blast-furnace operators in the country.

Open Hearth

In spite of its somewhat declining _relative_ importance in more recent years if allowance is made for the side-blown converters in some of the small mills, open hearth remains the dominant steelmaking process in mainland China. Its productivity on the average slightly more than doubled between 1952 and January, 1960; this increase was partially due to changes in operating techniques toward enlarging the tonnage capacity of the furnace and raising the melting intensity. The more important changes along these lines will be examined in this section.

Charging the Furnace in Excess of Its Rated Capacity

This production technique was introduced as early as 1950. With such a practice, the capacity of the tilting open hearth furnace at An-shan was raised from 180 to 200 tons. However, successful application of this technique calls for modifications in the structure of the furnace. Therefore, the extent to which this technique can be effectively applied depends preponderantly upon the degree to which the interior of the furnace can be redesigned at a given time in order to take in a bigger charge properly.

This explains why the An-shan tilting furnace mentioned above was able further to raise its charging capacity to 300 tons in 1958, and the reason for the steady increase in the charging capacity of the 10-ton open hearth furnace at the No. 3 Shanghai Steel Plant from 14.14 tons in 1954 to 19.09 tons in 1956 and to 45 tons in 1958. [14] It also explains, on the other hand, why the frequency of repairs for some open hearth furnaces increased after the adoption of the "overcharging" method of production.

Redesigning the interior of the furnace in order to accommodate a bigger charge involves essentially deepening the bath, heightening the roof, and trifurcating the tapping apparatus. It was in the latter direction that the open hearth operators in mainland China made their greatest contribution. A major limiting factor to increasing the charge is the capacity of the casting cranes. To eliminate this bottleneck, the Soviet experience was to bifurcate the spout and tap steel into two ladles. While this practice has been widely followed in the open hearth shops in China, the T'ai-yüan Iron and Steel Company in March, 1958, succeeded in developing a three-ladel steel-tapping method by trifurcating the spout. With this innovation, the T'ai-yüan No. 3 open hearth furnace with an original rated capacity of 49 tons increased its charging capacity to 130 tons, resulting in a 47.5 percent increase in its productivity and a 4.5 percent decrease in per ton production costs. [15]

The adoption of this method has the further advantage of lowering the investment-output ratio. Preliminary estimates show that with the introduction

297

of two- and three-ladle steel tapping, investment outlays on plant construction and casting cranes on the basis of per-unit output can be reduced by 15-20 percent.[16]

Reducing the Heat Time

In spite of the continual increase in the size of the charge, open-hearth furnaces in the country have generally been able to cut down the time required for melting each charge. At the No. 3 Shanghai Steel Plant, for instance, whereas the average size of the charge was raised from 14.1 tons in 1954 to 41.0 tons in 1958, the average heat time for each cast was lowered from 5 hours 30 minutes to 5 hours and 6 minutes. Similarly, at the No. 1 Steel Plant of An-shan, the average heat time was reduced from 10 hours 34 minutes in 1950 to 8 hours 42 minutes in 1958. This 17.7 percent cut in the heat time was accompanied by a 38.8 percent increase in the average output per heat.[17]

The shortening of the heat time has been effected essentially through increasing the heating load and improving the heating method. With the increase in the size of the charge, the heating load of the furnace must increase in order to provide the amount of heat required for the bigger charge. The increase in the heating load, at the same time, raises the temperature of the furnace, cuts down the heat time, and consequently pushes up the productivity of the furnace. The relationship between the heating load of its open hearth furnaces was 1.05×10^6 kilocalories per square meter per hour in 1958, or twice that of the furnaces in other steel centers. Concomitantly, their average utilization coefficient reached 14.3 tons per square meter of hearth in 24 hours.[18]

An improvement in the method of heating the open hearth furnace is by injecting outside air through compressed air jets in the gas port. This new measure, as the experience of An-shan shows, can cut down the heat time for each cast by 20-30 minutes and increase productivity by 4.0 - 4.5 percent.[19] This method has been widely adopted in the country. Another improvement in the heating method in order to reduce the heat time is by adding a small amount of tar in the furnace ends to impart luminosity to the flame. This production technique can also cut down the heat time by 20-30 minutes.

A third improvement toward cutting down the heat time is the change to hot charge. Prior to 1954, the method of hot charge with the use of mixers was employed only at An-shan and T'ai-yüan. In 1954, the Chungking Iron and Steel Company experimented with hot charge by using melting furnaces. By 1956, this method of hot charge was introduced in open hearth shops in Tientsin, Shanghai, and Ta-yeh. The effectiveness of this method in reducing the heat time can be illustrated by the experience of the No. 3 Plant of the Shanghai Iron and Steel Company. In July, 1956, before the introduction of this production technique, the average heat time was 5 hours 24 minutes. But after the application of this new technique, the heat time was shortened to 4 hours 2 minutes, or by 18.5 percent. Similarly with the use of this method, the heat time per cast at the No. 1 Plant of Shanghai was reduced by one hour.[20] By 1959 all the open hearth furnaces in mainland China adopted this hot charge method with the use of melting furnaces.

Use of Magnalium Roof Bricks

The relevancy of the use of magnalium roof bricks to the productivity of the open-hearth furnace lies in (1) prolonging life of the roof and therefore lengthening the period of furnace operation; and (2) facilitating the increase in the heating load of the furnace. In 1955, the Refractory Plant of the An-shan Iron and Steel Company succeeded in manufacturing chrome-magnesite bricks. Such new basic bricks were subsequently used in the roofs of all open hearth furnaces at An-shan with the result of lengthening roof life two and a half times.

Further extension of this practice was restricted by scarce domestic supply of chrome and the inadequate imports to meet the needs of the fast growing steel industry. Accordingly research was undertaken jointly by the Metal Research Institute of the Academy of Sciences, the Iron and Steel Research Institute of the Ministry of Metallurgical Industry, and the laboratories at the An-shan and Chungking Iron and Steel Companies, in order to find a substitute for the scarce chrome. This joint research and experiment resulted in the successful manufacture of the superior magnalium bricks from the richly-endowed alumina and magnesite. Its use in An-shan lengthened roof life to 520 heats or 14 percent longer than the roof made of chrome-magnesite bricks.[21]

Electric Furnace

Production of electric furnace steel kept pace with the over-all steel production. In 1952, electric furnace output amounted to 10.6 percent of the total, and in 1959 it remained in the neighborhood of 10 percent. In comparison with the open hearth process, electric furnaces showed a greater increase in productivity. The average coefficient of electric-furnace transformers was 7.4 tons per 1,000 KVA in 1952 and 21.5 tons in 1959.[22] Such a substantial increase in productivity can be attributed, at least in part, to changes in production technique, notably the increase in the amount of the charge, and the use of a joint production process with oxygen converters.

Increasing the Charge

Over 80 percent of mainland China's electric furnaces have changed their practice from charging through the doors to charging through the top. This change was in many instances coupled with the installation of charging machines. While it has speeded up the charging process, this new practice has also facilitated certain changes in furnace structure to take in a bigger charge, such as raising the position of the door and reducing the thickness of the side bricks. Other changes in furnace structure include deepening and widening of the bath and heightening of the walls. The experience of the Dairen Steel Plant shows that by increasing the diameter of the bath from 2,140 to 2,460 millimeters and its depth from 350 to 780 millimeters, the tonnage capacity can be raised from 5 to 15, thus tripling the rated capacity of the furnace.[23]

Increase in the amount of the charge did not entail any increase in the melting time per unit of the charge. On the contrary, the latter at the same time decreased, as can be seen from Table D-3. Shortening of per unit charge melting time was made possible through tapping more fully the potentiality of the furnace transformer. Consequently, the consumption of electricity per ton of steel output was substantially reduced. In Pen-ch'i, for instance, while the melting time for each ton of the charge was lowered from 16 minutes in 1957 to 10 minutes in the last quarter of 1958, the electricity consumption per ton of steel output was reduced from 742 to 492 KWH. [24]

Oxygen Converter-Electric Furnace Joint Process

The process of charging liquid steel coming out of oxygen top-blown converters directly into electric furnaces was developed by the Pen-ch'i Steel Plant. The chief advantage of such a joint process involving both types of furnace lies in a drastic reduction or a complete elimination of the time required for melting and oxidizing in the electric furnace. As this time requirement normally amounts to half the operation time of an electric furnace using the cold charge process, its elimination, as the experience of Pen-ch'i reveals, has shortened the blowing time from 3-1/2 – 4 hours to 2 – 2-1/2 hours. [25] Correspondingly, the utilization rate of electric furnaces was raised to the extent of increasing their daily output by about 50 percent. The utilization coefficient of electric furnaces fed by converter steel exceeded 35 tons per 1,000 KVA in 1958, as compared with the over-all average of 22.64 tons. [26]

With this method, the consumption of electricity per unit of output can be halved and the life of electrodes lengthened. [27] In addition, it can help to alleviate the shortage of steel scraps, which has been accentuated by the introduction of continuous steel casting.

The joint production technique, however, requires a high degree of synchronization in operating the two types of furnaces, in order to ensure that the charge for the electric furnace is always ready when needed. If the electric furnace has to wait for its feed, the linings start to cool off. This cooling and reheating will not only prolong the heat time and reduce the daily output, but also shorten the life of the furnace and lower the quality of its product. Therefore, in a joint workshop the total productivity of converters must be appropriately larger than that of electric furnaces.

Basic Side-Blown Converters

Conversion of pig iron into steel by converters had become increasingly important in mainland China even before 1958. The share of converter steel in the over-all steel output rose from 7.18 percent in 1952 to 14.9 percent in 1957. The steel drive of 1958 made more pronounced the advantages of melting steel by converters, such as the economy in investment outlays, the short construction period, the use of domestic material, and the dispensibility of scraps as an input. In addition, after some changes in production technique to be discussed below, they were said to be suitable for treating low quality iron (with a sulphur content of above 0.3 percent) produced by some small native furnaces.

Although the theory of steelmaking in side-blown converters has been widely known, mainland China was the first country to adopt it on a mass production basis. Experiments in the use of basic side-blown converters began at the T'ang-shan Steel Plant in August 1951. By January 1952, this process was adopted for regular production. Such converters are lined with tarred dolomite refractories. They do not require high-pressure blowing machines. In fact, the converters, the blowers, the ancillary pit-side teeming equipment, as

Table D-3

INDICES OF QUANTITY OF CHARGE AND MELTING TIME FOR DC-5M
ELECTRIC FURNACES AT THE DAIREN STEEL PLANT, 1956-1959
(1955 = 100)

Year	Quantity of Each Charge	Melting Time per Ton of Charge
1956	121.0	76.5
1957	131.0	65.5
1958	154.5	46.3
1959*	191.0	34.0

*For the first quarter only

Source: Kang-t'ieh, op. cit., no. 18, 1959, p. 823.

well as refractories are all made domestically. This consideration plus their suitability for refining high sulphur iron, points to a continuing growth of basic side-blown converters.

The Keep-slag Process

This technique was developed to cope with the problem of refining iron with high phosphorous and high sulphur contents. The method is to retain one-half or two-thirds of the slag of the requisite quality, composition, and characteristics in the converter, prior to the addition of hot metal, and then add a small amount of lime and ferro-oxide afterwards. This technique is intended to utilize fully the slag to reduce high phosphorous and sulphur contents of input iron, to economize the consumption of lime, and to raise the melting temperature. With this technique, 56-80 percent of the phosphorous content and 30-40 percent of the sulphur content can be removed.[28]

Raising Iron-input Temperature

Raising the temperature of iron input is an effective means of attaining a high melting temperature in the converter, which tends to shorten the heat time, reduce the blowing losses as well as raw material consumption, and improve the output quality. By 1959, most of China's converter shops had adopted the method of raising the temperature of iron input in the basic melting furnace before charging it to the converter.

Three major improvements have been made toward increasing the temperature of the melting furnace. First, the size of charging boxes was cut down in order to effect a more even distribution of the charge in the melting furnace. This simple change in the T'ang-shan Steel Plant was able to raise the temperature of molten iron from the melting furnace by 50° C. Second, the air intake of the melting furnace was preheated to $200-300^{\circ}$ C. Experiments at the Hsin-hsing Steel Plant reveal that when the air temperature reached 150° C and 300° C, the temperature of molten iron rose by 50° C and 100° C, respectively.[29] Finally, the number of airholes on the melting furnace was increased from one or two rows to three rows, so as to intensify the burning of carbon oxide in the furnace. Such a change has been effected in almost all the converter shops in the country.

With an assured supply of high temperature and low sulphur molten iron[30] from the melting furnaces, the basic side-blown converters can turn out steel with a sulphur content of 0.055 percent, thus meeting the quality requirement of the Ministry of Metallurgical Industry.[31] This achievement has a far-reaching significance: it ensures the place of the "small, modern mass-production units" in the development pattern of China's steel industry, if the latter can be otherwise efficiently run.

NOTES

Chapter 1

1. See Edmund K. Faltermayer's report in <u>The Wall Street Journal</u>, Western Edition, March 4, 1963, in which Khrushchev was quoted as saying, "There was a time when the power of a state was determined by the quantity of metal it produced. In its time this criterion was correct. But now, when other materials have been created which compete with metal, this criterion is no longer adequate. " In this he was supported by P. N. Demichev of Moscow who remarked to the same meeting, "In the U.S.A. industrial production as a whole grew 2. 8 times between 1929 and 1961, including a 3. 7-fold rise in (production of) machinery and related products. But the production of steel increased only 1. 6 times. This is explained largely by the changing structure of the machinery industry, the decreasing use of metal in machinery products, the rapid growth of progressive forms and methods of metalworking (casting under pressure, stamping, etc.), the widespread introduction of high-alloy steels, aluminum, plastics. "

2. Another condition favorable to economic growth would result if the rapid expansion of, say, the steel industry would somehow increase the rate of savings.

3. <u>Wo-kuo Kang-t'ieh, Tien-li, Mei-t'an, Chi-hsieh, Fang-chih, Tsao-chih Kung-yeh ti Chin-hsi</u> (Major Aspects of the Chinese Economy through 1956, hereafter referred to as <u>Major Aspects</u>), Peking, July, 1958, p. 48.

Mention should be made here that the transliteration of all Chinese names used in this text follows the Wade-Giles system, with the exception of certain place names which have become so well known that the traditional spelling has been preserved to avoid confusion.

Chapter 2

1. <u>Baron Richthofen's Letters, 1870-1872</u>, 2d ed. , printed by the <u>North China Herald</u>, Shanghai, pp. 43 and 54.

2. Executive Committee of the International Geological Congress, <u>The Iron Ore Resources of the World</u>, Stockholm, 1910. See especially "Summary, " pp. LXXIV 1-7.

3. Different figures for a number of European countries are available in other sources. See, for instance, Charles Will Wright, <u>The Iron and Steel Industries of Europe</u>, Economic paper 19 of the U.S. Bureau of Mines, Washington, D. C. , 1939.

4. See Appendix A.

5. United Nations, <u>Survey of World Iron Ore Resources, Occurrence,</u> <u>Appraisal and Use</u>, 1955, pp. 31 and 34.

6. United Nations, Economic Commission for Asia and the Far East, <u>Coal and Iron Ore Resources of Asia and the Far East</u>, Nanking, 1948, pp. 47-51.

7. <u>Ibid</u>.

8. The other two are Hankow and Wu-ch'ang.

9. <u>Major Aspects</u>, <u>op. cit</u>. , pp. 2-3.

10. <u>Ibid</u>. However, according to H. D. Fong, <u>Chung-kuo Ching-chi Yen-</u> <u>chiu</u> (Studies on the Chinese Economy), The Commerical Press, Shanghai, 1938, all the furnaces were for iron smelting only.

11. See H. D. Fong, <u>op. cit</u>. , pp. 635-646.

12. <u>General Statement on the Mining Industry</u>, 2d issue, pp. 124-125, 128-129, and 133. See also <u>Survey Report on the Steel Industry of Communist China</u>, Cabinet Research Office, Tokyo, 1955.

13. See note 12.

14. The production statistics are from <u>General Statement</u>, 2d issue. See also note 12.

15. T'an Hsi-hung, <u>Shih-nien-lai chih Chung-kuo Ching-chi</u> (Ten Years of the Chinese Economy), p. G-2.

16. Cf. the pig-iron-capacity data in Appendix B, for 1936.

17. Alternatively, one might say that the downswings of ore output in China proper coincided with periods of general cyclical decline elsewhere in the world, while similar coincidence in the case of Manchuria's iron-ore production was modified by the underlying secular trend of expansion, so that the downturns were rendered far more moderate.

18. Beginning in 1932, there was a small net import of ore into Manchuria although this may have been a reflection of importation from the rest of China, not recorded as such previously.

19. Edwin W. Pauley, <u>Report on Japanese Assets in Manchuria to the</u> <u>President of the United States</u>, 1946, pp. 60-64. See also Appendix B.

20. See Appendix B.

21. **Russian Destruction of Our Industries in the Northeastern Provinces**, compiled by the Chinese Association for the United Nations, Taiwan, 1952, p. 3.

22. T'an Hsi-hung, op. cit., p. G-3.

Chapter 3

1. The aid would, however, have to be paid for later.

2. Ching Lin, "Kuan-yü Kang-t'ieh Kung-yeh ho Chi-ch'i-chih-tsao Kung-yeh ti Pi-li Kuan-hsi" (On the Proportion between Iron and Steel and Machine Manufacturing), Chi-hua Ching-chi (Planned Economy), no. 9, Peking, September, 1957.

The Soviet data cited were:

Period	Percent Increase of Finished-Steel Output	Percent Increase of Machine Production	Ratio
1928-32	129	399	1:3.09
1932-37	293	283	1:0.97
1937-40	101	176	1:1.74
1940-50	159	215	1:1.35
1950-55	169	221	1:1.31
1955-60	152	180	1:1.18

3. **Major Aspects**, op. cit., p. 11; also reported as 313 million yuan in Chao I-wen, Hsin-chung-kuo ti Kung-yeh (New China's Industry), pp. 39-41, Peking, 1957. The data refer to "capital construction" which consists of the bulk of domestic investment excluding work in progress, inventories, and stockpiles, but including ancillary expenses.

4. Investment in capital construction in industry both within and outside the State plan was 25.03 billion yuan under the First Five-Year Plan; total investment in capital construction for all purposes was 55 billion yuan.

5. These refer principally, if not exclusively, to the An-shan Iron and Steel Company and the Iron and Steel Bureau.

6. Ching Lin, op. cit., p. 13. According to Major Aspects, op. cit., p. 185, realized investment in the machine-building industry in 1953-56 was 2.08 billion yuan or 11.7 percent of 17.8 billion invested in all industry (presumably investment within the State plan only).

7. In the First Five-Year Plan, the norm consisted of 10 million yuan for iron and steel enterprises, according to Chao I-wen, op. cit., p. 223. Later, according to Li Fu-ch'un's report on the 1960 economic plan, the norm for iron and steel combines was fixed at 20 million yuan. See Union Research Institute, Shih-nien-lai ti Chung-kung Kung-yeh Kai-k'uang (Ten Years of Communist Chinese Industry), Hong Kong, 1960, p. 257.

8. Chao I-wen, op. cit., p. 39, and Major Aspects, op. cit., p. 18.

9. Chang Chien-yüan, "Wo-kuo Kang-t'ieh Kung-yeh ti Fa-chan ho Sheng-ch'an P'ei-chih" (The Development and Location of China's Iron and Steel Industry), Ti-li Chih-shih (Geographical Knowledge), no. 4, p. 154, Peking, 1958. The provinces included in the several regions are as follows: Northeast Liaoning, Kirin, and Heilungkiang; North - Hopeh and Shansi, although Inner Mongolia is sometimes bracketed together with North China in line with recent practice on the Chinese mainland; Northwest - Shensi, Kansu, Sinkiang, Tsinghai, and the Ningsia Hui Autonomous Region; East - Shantung, Kiangsu, Chekiang, Anhwei, and Fukien; Central - Honan, Hupeh, Hunan, and Kiangsi; South - Kwangtung (including Hainan) and Kwangsi; Southwest - Szechwan, Yunnan, and Kweichow. This division corresponds closely to the provincial divisions when the Greater Administrative Regions were still in existence prior to 1955. It also corresponds to the more recent practice with the possible exception of Fukien province which had no iron and steel production until about 1959 or 1960. For further discussion on this point see note 3, Chapter 7.

10. People's Daily, Peking, September 23 and 26, 1959.

11. As pointed out earlier, planned expenditure in 1953-1957 totaled 2.93 billion yuan while the cumulative total in 1953-1956 was 2.06 billion yuan. At the same time, the annual average in 1953-1956 was 515 million yuan. Hence a cumulative total of 3 billion yuan in 1953-1957 may be regarded as a high estimate.

12. For a fuller discussion of the communes see Yuan-li Wu, "Communes in a Changing China," Current History, December, 1959, pp. 345-350.

13. China News Service dispatch, December 10, 1959, quoted in Chung-kung Shih-nien (Ten Years of Communist China), China Weekly Publishing Co., Hong Kong, 1960, pp. 233-238.

14. For a fuller discussion of the "new look" of Communist China's economic policy and an analysis of the economic crisis beginning with the unfavorable crop of 1961, see Yuan-li Wu, "Farm Crisis in Red China," in Current History, September 1962, pp. 162-167 and 182.

15. September 5, 1961.

16. See Appendix A, pp. 6-7.

17. Chang Chien-yüan, in Geographical Knowledge, no. 4, 1958, p. 154.

18. Ibid.

19. See Ten Great Years, The State Statistical Bureau, Peking, 1960, p. 84.

20. USSR Industry, A Statistical Compilation, State Statistical Publishing House, Moscow, 1957, p. 110.

21. In their study on Chinese national income, T. C. Liu and K. C. Yeh wrote: "...the Communist data on gross value of industrial production are computed on the basis of the so-called 'factory method' i.e., total gross value is the sum of the output of industrial enterprises. Consequently, interenterprise sales of industrial output are double counted, and intraenterprise sales are excluded. "

However, no adjustment is made "for the intraenterprise relationship between steel products and steel, because there is fairly clear indication that the gross values of both are included in the Communist figure on the 'values of industrial production.'" "According to the Communist instructions for compiling industrial statistics," stated the authors, "the gross value of the following products is included in the gross value of industrial production, even though they are generally consumed within an enterprise. They are: iron ore, coke, steel ingots and casting, mineral ores of nonferrous metals, wood pulp, coal, fuel oil, and natural gas produced and consumed by the same enterprise. Notably absent in this list are pig iron and cotton yarn. " Ta-chung Liu and Kung-chia Yeh, The Economy of the Chinese Mainland: National Income and Economic Development, 1933-1959, The Rand Corporation, Santa Monica, Calif., 1963. Appendix F.

22. The percent distribution of the several categories included in Soviet statistics of "ferrous rolled stock" in 1940, 1950, and 1955 were:

Category	1940	1950	1955
Total ferrous rolled stock	100	100	100
1. Pipes produced from ingots	2.8	3.0	2.6
2. Forgings produced from ingots	2.2	1.3	1.3
3. Rolled stock for reprocessing at other plants	8.2	9.9	10.1
4. Finished rolled stock	86.8	85.8	86.0
(a) Quality rolled stock	(21.3)	(19.1)	(19.2)
(b) Ordinary rolled stock	(65.5)	(66.7)	(66.8)

(Source: USSR Industry, p. 110.)

Similar divisions may also be found, for instance, in Central Statistical Department, Soviet of Ministers, R.S.F.S.R., Promyshlennost' R.S.F.S.R. Statisticheskii Sbornik (Industry of R.S.F.S.R., Statistical Compilation), Moscow, 1961, p. 59, which gives the following proportions:

Category	1957	1960
Total ferrous rolled stock	100	100
Pipes and forgings produced from ingots	3.9	3.8
Semifinished goods for reprocessing at other plants	10.1	11.7
Finished rolled stock	86.0	84.5

23. USSR Industry, op. cit., p. 124.

24. Ibid., p. 120.

25. Figure for 1945 from Appendix B.

26. See Appendix B.

27. Based on a comment from Mr. Tamotsu Takase of the Hoover Institution and correspondence with Mr. Jiro Okawa of the Cabinet Research Office, Tokyo.

28. In 1953, the ratios of designed or rated capacity to operating capacity were: pig iron, 55 to 58 percent; ingot, 79 percent; finished steel, 63.2 to 64 percent.

29. See, for instance, C.M. Li, The Statistical System of Communist China, University of California Press, Berkeley, California, 1962.

30. The 1960 capacity and production estimates are not independent of each other and should not therefore be compared. See Appendix B.

31. Geometric mean of the year-to-year rates of growth.

32. Annual rates for 1949 to 1956 and 1952 to 1956.

33. Major Aspects, op. cit., p. 20.

34. See Table B-13, Appendix B.

35. See the author's article, "China's Industry in Peace and War," in Current History, December, 1958.

36. According to Clark, op. cit., p. 254, the Soviet coefficient averaged 2.9 in 1930 to 1933, which compares with Communist China's record in 1949-1950.

37. The following data are taken from USSR Industry, op. cit., pp. 119 and 123:

Use Coefficients for Blast Furnaces and Open-Hearth Furnaces of
Various Sizes at the Most Efficient Plants of Both, 1955
(based on actual operating time)

	Blast Furnaces		Open Hearth	
	cu. m. per ton	ton per cu. m.		
All furnaces	0.80	1.25	All furnaces	6.55
-100	1.34	0.75	-10.0	3.51
101-200	0.76	1.32	10-20.9	5.24
201-500	0.79	1.27	21-30.9	5.48
501-900	0.87	1.15	31-40.9	6.14
901-1000	0.83	1.20	41-50.9	5.92
1001-1300	0.80	1.25	51-60.9	6.38
over 1300	0.76	1.32	over 61.0	7.76

	Use Coefficients of		
	Blast Furnaces		Open
Plant	cu. m. per ton	ton per cu. m.	Hearth*
USSR Average	0.80	1.25	6.55
Magnitegorsk Metallurgical			
Combine	0.65	1.54	8.60
Serov Metallurgical Plant			
Imeniserov	0.66	1.52	---
Zaporozhe Zaporozhstol'			
Metallurgical	---	---	8.26
Kuznetsk Metallurgical	0.73	1.37	8.22
Novo-Tagil' Metallurgical			
Plant	0.77	1.30	7.74
Dueprodzerzhinsk Metallurgical			
Plant imeni Dzerzhinskiy	0.77	1.30	---
Chelyabinsk Metallurgical Plant	0.77	1.30	---
Zazakh Metallurgical Plant	---	---	7.97

*Average daily steel yield per square meter.

38. People's Daily, editorial, January 19, 1957.

39. Metallurgical Bulletin, no. 30, September 27, 1957, p. 33.

40. Ibid., no. 13, October 8, 1956, pp. 6-12.

41. Issue of May 25, 1956.

42. See, for instance, the report on An-shan, in People's Daily,
January 23, 1956.

43. Computed from Clark, op. cit., p. 10.

44. Ibid.

45. See Appendix C.

46. January 7, 1958.

47. China News Analysis, no. 403, Hong Kong, January 12, 1962.

48. Peking Review, no. 41, p. 4, Peking, October 12, 1962. A virtually identical report may be found in Kung-jen Jih-pao, Peking, September 26, 1962.

49. Chin-jih Hsin-wen (Today's News), Hong Kong, reported on December 30, 1957, that 80 percent of the steel products needed in Communist China could then be produced domestically. It neglected to mention whether the figure referred to 80 percent of the varieties or 80 percent of the total quantity.

50. People's Daily, Peking, February 4, 1956.

51. For a fuller discussion of the "Great Leap Forward" and its industrial and agricultural policies see the author's articles in the December, 1958, December, 1960, and September, 1961, issues of Current History, and the August, 1961, issue of Current Scene, Hong Kong.

52. See Chapter 7.

53. See the author's article in the September, 1962, issue of Current History.

54. Jen-min Shou-ts'e (People's Handbook), pp. 89-95, Peking, 1959.

Chapter 4

1. Op. cit., pp. 210-211.

2. Sources: 1952-1956, Major Aspects, op. cit., pp. 13, 29, and 42. 1957, estimated at 8 percent of 65,020 million yuan, which is in turn obtained by subtracting from the total gross industrial output of 78,390 million yuan the output of the cottage handicraft industry or 13,370 million yuan. Wei-ta ti Shih-nien, English translation, p. 86. All figures include the output of "workshop or factory handicraft" and are therefore larger than that of the "modern sector" only.

3. The physical output statistics used in this computation are given below. See Chapter 3 for iron ore, pig iron, crude steel and "finished steel," and Liu and Yeh, op. cit., Appendices F and H. The data include the output of the "native" or "handicraft" sector.

Commodity	1952	1953	1954	1955	1956	1957
			(thousand metric tons)			
Iron Ore	4,287	5,821	7,229	9,597	15,484	19,370
Manganese Ore	190	195	172	276	524	655
Pig Iron	1,929	2,234	3,114	3,872	4,826	5,936
Crude Steel	1,349	1,774	2,225	2,853	4,465	5,350
Finished Steel	1,312	1,754	1,965	2,505	3,921	4,260
Coke	2,860	3,600	4,540	5,690	7,160	7,460

The 1952 prices of the items above, in yuan per metric ton, are: iron ore, 39; manganese ore, 53; pig iron, 200; crude steel, 690; finished steel, 1,000; coke, 44. These are the same prices as those used by Liu and Yeh, with the exception of iron ore and crude steel, for which Liu and Yeh use 20 yuan and 600 yuan, respectively. Explanation of these prices is found in the discussion on the subsector estimates later in this chapter.

4. The differences are as follows (billion 1952 yuan):

	1952	1953	1954	1955	1956	1957
Sum of six items	2.94	3.82	4.62	5.88	8.92	10.26
Total gross value output given	1.37	1.87	2.33	2.90	4.12	5.20
Difference	1.57	1.95	2.29	2.98	4.80	5.06

These differences may be explained in several ways, apart from the obvious catchall reason of "statistical discrepancy" or inaccuracy, and the possibility that the prices used in estimating the value output of the individual items are too high.

5. For instance, pig iron added to inventory and cast iron products would be included in the gross value output reported.

6. These differences may in turn be presented as follows (billion 1952 yuan):

	1952	1953	1954	1955	1956	1957
Total gross value output given	1.37	1.87	2.33	2.90	4.12	5.20
Estimated gross value output of "finished-steel products"	1.31	1.75	1.97	2.51	3.92	4.26
Difference	0.06	0.12	0.36	0.39	0.20	0.94

7. See Liu and Yeh, op. cit., Vol. II, p. 657.

8. The differences are as follows (billion 1952 yuan):

	1952	1953	1954	1955	1956	1957
Sum of five items (excluding pig iron)	2.55	3.37	4.00	5.11	7.95	9.07
Total gross value output given	1.37	1.87	2.33	2.90	4.12	5.20
Difference	1.18	1.50	1.67	2.21	3.83	3.87

These differences should be regarded either as a refutation of the preceding interpretation or as evidence of other statistical inaccuracies.

9. If the adjusted output data developed in Appendix C are adopted and substituted for those used earlier, we should find (1) the difference between the official output statistics and the sum of the five items and (2) that between the official series and the adjusted value output of finished steel as follows (billion 1952 yuan):

	1952	1953	1954	1955	1956	1957
(1) Sum of five items (adjusted)	2.05	2.74	3.32	4.25	5.77	6.69
(2) Total gross value output given	1.37	1.87	2.33	2.90	4.12	5.20
(3) Value output of finished steel (adjusted)	.81	1.12	1.29	1.65	1.74	1.88
Differences						
(1) − (2)	.68	.87	.99	1.35	1.65	1.49
(2) − (3)	.56	.75	1.04	1.25	2.38	3.32

The diminishing difference between (1) and (2) suggests that the discrepancy in their coverage may not be too great after all. The larger difference now obtained between (2) and (3), on the other hand, seems to indicate that the official output series may include end products that did not undergo finishing and intermediate products prior to the stage of steel finishing and that some of the latter, though fabricated within the same enterprise units, may nevertheless have been included in the official value output statistics.

10. T'ieh-lu Piao-chun She-chi Yü-suan Shou-ts'e (Standard Railway Design and Budget Handbook), JPRS: 10913, October 31, 1961, p. 33.

11. Survey Report, op. cit., pp. 619 and 633.

12. Liu and Yeh, op. cit., Appendix F.

13. For electricity consumed per worker in 1952 and 1956, see Major Aspects, op. cit., p. 123.

14. The data on labor productivity in 1953 are based on reports from An-shan and Ta-yeh; cf. Survey Report, op. cit., pp. 1, 64, 643, and 665.

15. For the output per man index, see Ten Great Years, op. cit., p. 110.

16. The detailed computations are tabulated below:

Item	1952	1953	1954	1955	1956	1957	1958	1959	1960
Open hearth output (thousand metric tons)	1,038	1,366	1,713	2,197	3,438	4,120	6,160	6,645	9,184
Output per man-year (metric tons)	211	211	260	309	358	407	407	407	407
Estimated number of full-time workers	4,900	6,500	6,600	7,100	9,600	10,100	15,100	16,300	22,600
Kwhr. consumed per worker	4,176	5,123	6,071	7,020	7,969	7,967	7,968	7,968	7,968
Electricity consumed per ton of steel	19.79	24.28	23.35	22.72	22.20	19.58	19.58	19.58	19.58
Total electricity consumed (thousand kwhr.)	20,500	33,200	40,000	49,900	76,500	80,500	120,-600	130,-100	179,-800
Cost per ton, 1952 yuan	1.43	1.75	1.68	1.64	1.60	1.41	1.41	1.41	1.41
1957 yuan	1.19	1.45	1.40	1.36	1.33	1.17	1.17	1.17	1.17
Total million 1952 yuan	1.48	2.39	2.88	3.60	5.51	5.81	8.69	9.37	12.95
million 1957 yuan	1.23	1.98	2.39	2.98	4.57	4.82	7.20	7.77	10.73

Notes: For explanation, see text. The 1952 and 1957 prices of electricity were 72.04 and 59.70 yuan per thousand kilowatt hours, respectively. Figures are rounded. See Yuan-li Wu, op. cit., Chapter 6.

313

17. <u>Yeh-chin Pao</u>, no. 6, February 27, 1958, p. 32.

18. Computation of miscellaneous nonlabor cost:

Item	1952	1953	1954	1955	1956	1957	1958	1959	1960
Estimated number of nonproduction workers in open hearth steel shops	192	253	257	277	375	395	590	637	880
Miscellaneous expenses per nonproduction worker in current yuan	1,103[a]	997	891	785	679	572	572	572	572
Wholesale-price index[b]	100	98.7	99.1	99.7	99.2	100.1	100.1	100.1[c]	100.1[c]
Total administrative expenses per ton									
1952 yuan	0.20	0.19	0.13	0.10	0.08	0.06	0.06	0.05	0.05
1957 yuan	0.20	0.19	0.13	0.10	0.08	0.06	0.06	0.05	0.05

(a) The 1952 figure is computed on the basis of relative labor productivity by multiplying the 1957 rate of 572 yuan by the ratio 407/211. See the section on electricity consumption and number of workers.

(b) <u>Wei-tati Shih-nien</u>, English translation, p. 149.

(c) Assumed to be the same as in 1958.

19. <u>Yeh-chin Pao</u>, no. 1, January 2, 1958, p. 35.

20. See Appendix B.

21. See the author's article, "An Interpretation of the Industrial Cutback in Communist China," <u>Current Scene</u>, Vol. 1, no. 9, Hong Kong, August 1961.

22. In the July 15, 1960, issue of <u>Jen-min Jih-pao</u>, for instance, it was stated that quality should be improved through drastic testing measures in inspecting raw materials, slags and products, proper storage of pig iron by grades, and feedback of information from the users of iron. Many other similar reports can also be found in the official press and journals.

23. K. P. Wang, "A Review of Mining and Metallurgy in Communist China," Department of the Interior, December 26, 1960, p. 28.

24. Kung-jen Jih-pao (Workers' Daily), Peking, July 2, 1960.

25. Union Research Service, Hong Kong, August 9, 1960.

26. No. 195, May 10, 1960, p. 2.

27. No. 4, January 25, 1960, pp. 38-39.

28. Metallurgical Bulletin, April 11, 1960, pp. 14-15.

29. Chi-hua yü T'ung-chi, no. 2, February 1959, p. 23.

30. Metallurgical Bulletin, October 9, 1959, quoted in Ronald Hsia, "China's Steel Industry since 1958," China Quarterly, no. 7, July-September 1961, p. 119.

31. No. 12, March 25, 1960, p. 27.

32. Chi-hua yü T'ung-chi, no. 2, February 1959, p. 23.

33. No. 21, 1958, p. 25.

34. Planned Economy, no. 11, November 1958, p. 19.

35. Metallurgical Bulletin, no. 9, March 1960, p. 43.

36. Red Flag, no. 3-4, February 1, 1961.

37. For the modern furnaces the coefficients have been estimated at 1,299 kg. in 1959 and 1,359 kg. in 1960. See Table 4.9.

38. Planned Economy, no. 6, June 1958, p. 9.

39. Ibid., no. 10, October, 1958, p. 5.

40. Planned Economy, no. 10, October 1958, p. 5.

41. Ibid., p. 12.

42. Actually, this does not mean that the aggregate estimates embodying the adjusted output of finished steel as suggested in Appendix B should be discarded. Inasmuch as the six principal items do not really correspond exactly to the entire industry, inclusion of the now omitted commodities would raise the "adjusted totals."

43. The ratios of gross value-added to value output in Communist China, based on the "unadjusted" series given above and the value output of the six items given at the beginning of Chapter 4, are (in percent):

1952	1953	1954	1955	1956	1957
44	44	45	46	47	48

44. G. Warren Nutter, The Growth of Industrial Production in the Soviet Union, Princeton University Press, Princeton, N.J., 1962, pp. 510-511.

45. American Iron and Steel Institute, Charting Steel's Progress in 1961, New York, p. 57. The estimates are based on sales revenue of 182.3 billion dollars and materials and other purchases of 81.9 billion dollars. Differences are, of course, observed in the case of individual companies. For 1961 and 1962, some illustrations may be cited:

Year	Bethlehem	Republic	Armco
1961	63.8	51.6	49.4
1962	60.8	49.4	47.7

Differences in the degree of integration would of course also play a role in these cases. (Data derived from the annual reports of the above companies.)

46. Nutter, op. cit., p. 366.

47. Ibid., op. cit., pp. 510-511.

48. Gardner Clark, op. cit., pp. 99-100.

49. The ratio is S/V, where S = net value-added less the wage bill and V = the wage bill.

50. Yuan-li Wu et. al., op. cit.

51. See Chapter 3.

52. Major Aspects, op. cit., p. 46.

53. See Yuan-li Wu et. al., op. cit. Two of the statistical peculiarities producing an exaggerated rate of economic growth were the overpricing of new industrial products at high pilot costs and the underreporting of grain production in the early 1950's.

54. See Table 3.3.

55. No effort has been made here to establish the changes in the capital-output ratio in the metallurgical industry, partly because of deficiencies in the investment data and partly because of the practical difficulty of relating increases in output in any year to specific investments in the industry in prior years.

56. This is the mean of 1952-1955 and 1957. The year 1956 has been omitted as the value output given is slightly below the estimated value-added, indicating therefore a possible error in either or both of the estimates. We have used the "unadjusted" series containing the unadjusted estimates of finished-steel output under the assumption that any overestimate would be compensated for by other omissions. If the adjusted series of iron and steel industry output were used, the corresponding estimates of modern industry output would be slightly lower. They are: 1958, 62.93 billion 1952 yuan; 1959, 67.88 billion; 1960, 78.77-83.07 billion.

57. The basic data are for 1952-1957 and can be found in Table 4.18 for modern industry and on page 93 for the iron and steel industry. The coefficient of correlation is +.994.

58. See Yuan-li Wu, Economic Development, op. cit., Appendix C.

Chapter 5

1. The output of electric furnace steel is obtained as a residual from the total output and estimates of converter and open-hearth steels. For simplicity the pig iron input coefficient is an average of the coefficients for converters and open hearths.

2. The iron input is assumed to be 1,744 kg. in 1958 and 1,569 kg. in 1959-1960. See Chapter 4, pages 124 and 125.

3. No. 9, September, 1957, pp. 11-15.

4. The percent distribution was: 1952, 17.41 percent; 1953, 23.27 percent; 1954, 26.07 percent; 1955, 33.24 percent.

5. Planned Economy, no. 9, September, 1957, p. 13.

6. Jen-min Shou-ts'e (People's Handbook), Vol. II, 1959, p. 465.

7. Bureau of Information, Executive Yuan, Chan-hou Ti-i-ch'i T'ieh-tao Chi-hua (The First Phase of Postwar Railway Reconstruction), Nanking, 1947, p. 64; and Chao Tseng-chüeh, Chan-hou Chiao-t'ung Chien-she Kai-k'uang (Transport Reconstruction after the War), Shanghai, 1947, p. 68.

8. According to the People's Daily, October 17, 1959, 50 tons less of finished steel are required when light instead of heavy rails are used in building spur lines; hence the estimate of 80 tons (i.e., 130 less 50).

9. Planned Economy, no. 3, March, 1957, p. 8, and Chung-kuo Kung-jen (The Chinese Worker), no. 23, 1958, p. 6.

10. U.S. Consulate-General, Current Background, no. 407, 1950, p. 4.

11. January 24, 1960, quoted in the Iron and Steel Overseas Market Study Committee (Japan), Interim Report on the Chinese Iron and Steel Industry, Vol. 7, p. 9.

12. China News Service, Peking, September 17, 1958, and October 29, 1960; NCNA, Peking, January 27, 1960.

13. Tzu-kuo (China Weekly), no. 561, October, 1963, p. 39. See also Cabinet Research Office, Gunji josei shiryo (Information on Military Affairs), no. 66, p. 5, Tokyo, October, 1963.

14. July 14, 1957, p. 31.

15. Ibid.

16. See Table 5.8.

17. Pauley, op. cit., p. 120.

18. Computed on the basis of a population of 43.23 million reported in the 1940 census. Japan-Manchoukuo Yearbook, 1941, Tokyo, p. 610.

19. Thus not all the steel absorbed by "personal consumption" was actually consumed at home. The export figures include, however, only exports in the original forms.

20. Op. cit., no. 13, July 14, 1957.

21. No. 9, September, 1957, p. 16. The index numbers are:

Year	Index
1953	100
1954	98.3
1955	101.8
1956	74.6
1957	74.1

22. From 1957 on, the inventory changes do not include unplanned additions; hence, much larger residuals are left. Furthermore, as pointed out in Appendix C, as well as in the earlier chapters, if double counting is present in the production data and if this exaggeration is magnified in the years after 1956, a series of substantially higher residuals beginning in 1957 would also be the result.

23. Ryszard Wraga, "Soviet Militarism (II)," The Eastern Quarterly, London, vol. II, no. 2, September, 1949, pp. 58-59.

24. Cf. also the following sections.

25. T'ung-chi Kung-tso, no. 13, July 14, 1957.

26. It will be noted that the "other" category among the allotments includes addition to stock and allocation to central government agencies not otherwise listed.

27. See Table 5.3.

28. See Appendix C and Chapter 3.

29. See the article in <u>Chi-hua Ching-chi</u>, September, 1957, cited earlier.

30. The capital construction and machine building estimates in Table 5.10 in 1958-1960 were also not wholly independent of the output estimates.

31. <u>Major Aspects</u>, <u>op. cit.</u>, p. 46.

32. As a further illustration of the nature of finished-steel imports, the following data on listed imports from the U.S.S.R. in 1950-1957 may also be used as a reference (thousand metric tons):

Year	Railway Track Material	Heavy and Light Sections	Wire Rods	Strip	Plates
1950	70.6	137.8	7.2	---	111.2
1951	105.3	180.5	10.1	---	131.2
1952	95.1	162.6	7.2	---	98.2
1953	120.2	178.3	10.1	4.2	155.2
1954	50.2	132.7	7.8	3.2	103.4
1955	130.8	145.8	16.5	2.9	110.2
1956	39.3	88.0	17.5	2.8	95.5
1957	10.0	20.0	10.0	2.3	39.1

Year	Sheets	Steel Tubes and Fittings	Wire	Tin-plate	Wheels, Tires and Axles
1950	5.3	19.5	---	---	4.7
1951	12.3	18.9	---	---	---
1952	---	13.6	---	---	---
1953	11.1	9.4	---	---	---
1954	10.6	21.8	---	---	---
1955	27.5	51.0	0.7	7.0	12.3
1956	14.5	54.4	0.6	7.7	7.5
1957	25.0	26.0	0.4	---	5.0

From United Nations, E.C.E., <u>Statistics of World Trade in Steel, 1913-1959</u>, Geneva, 1961, quoted by M. Gardner Clark in <u>Bulletin of the Association for the Study of Soviet-Type Economies</u>, June, 1961, pp. 19-20.

33. Yuan-li Wu et al., <u>op. cit.</u>, chapter on investment.

34. See Chapter 2. China proper was, of course, dependent on pig iron imports during the 1930's.

35. Ore exports to Japan were 29,000 tons in 1956 and only 3,000 tons in 1957.

Chapter 6

1. No estimate was available for Shansi at the time.

2. For the approximate annual capacity of pig iron output see Table 6.5.

3. M. Gardner Clark, The Economics of Soviet Steel, Harvard University Press, Cambridge, 1956, p. 113.

4. H.D. Fong, op. cit., p. 635.

5. Ibid., p. 365.

6. Tan Hsi-hung, op. cit., p. G-2.

7. General Statement, 5th issue, op. cit., p. 184.

8. Oldest daily newspaper in China, published in Shanghai.

9. See Table 6.7.

10. General Statement, 7th issue, op. cit., pp. 10, 89, and 93.

11. National Resources Commission Quarterly, vol. VI, nos. 1-4, June-December, 1946, pp. 102-103, and Kang-t'ieh, 1947, pp. 20-21. For details, see Appendix B.

12. Kang-t'ieh, p. 20.

13. See Tables B-5 and B-13, Appendix B.

14. Inclusion of Hupeh in this list is, of course, a result of the wartime relocation noted earlier and lack of complete information in 1945.

15. A quick survey on this basis would provide us with a starting point for an examination of changes under the Communists.
It seems at first glance that more steelmaking plants should be established in all the provinces in group (1). Upon closer examination, however, we shall find that the annual pig iron capacities of Kiangsi and Kwangsi (1,500 and 3,500 metric tons, respectively) were negligible in comparison with those of Hopeh, Shantung, Hunan, and Szechwan. By ignoring those provinces which had only a small pig-iron production or a negligible excess capacity in pig iron, the candidates for additional steelmaking facilities would be reduced to the following:
(a) Hopeh. Here the annual pig iron capacity was 498,000 metric tons as compared to 25,800 metric tons of steel ingot, leaving no doubt at all about the nature of the imbalance.
(b) Hunan. In this province, both steel ingot and finished-steel capacities were lacking while pig iron capacity was as high as 154,200 metric tons per year.

(c) Shantung. With 150,000 metric tons of annual pig iron capacity and no steel-ingot and finished-steelmaking facilities at all, there was a potential need to establish steelmaking plants.

(d) Szechwan. As of 1945 the degree to which new plants were needed depended on the material input coefficients per metric ton of steel ingot. With 123,300 metric tons of pig iron capacity but only 45,000 metric tons of steel ingot capacity per year, there was indubitably such a need. Roughly speaking, one-quarter of the total steel ingot capacity of Szechwan was from open hearth furnaces; one quarter came from Bessemer converters; the remaining 50 percent was from electric furnaces. By using the material input coefficients per metric ton of crude steel for the year 1953 in the same proportion as the output by types of furnace (see Chapter 4), we find that the amount of pig iron required to produce an annual production of 45,000 metric tons of steel ingot would be only 45,000 tons. Therefore the excess in pig iron capacity would approximate 78,000 tons.

(e) Liaoning.

Before Soviet removals. The annual capacities of pig iron, steel ingot, and finished steel in 1945 were 2,510,000, 1,600,000 and 962,400 metric tons, respectively. According to Chapter 4, the material input coefficients per metric ton of crude steel in 1952 for open hearths and Bessemer converters were 0.769 and 1.230, respectively. For simplicity, we may assume that it was equal to 1.2. Thus only 1,920,000 metric tons of the 2,510,000 metric tons of pig iron capacity would be utilized for the annual steel ingot production. The excess in pig iron per year would thus approximate 59,000 metric tons.

After Soviet removals. The story was entirely different after Soviet removals, however. There was no longer an excess in pig iron capacity. In fact, what was needed was more capacity in pig iron as well as finished-steel output. Steel ingot capacity, on the other hand, was not deficient.

(f) Shansi. With 89,500 metric tons of pig iron as compared to 50,000 of steel ingot per year, there would be no need for a new mill if the material input coefficient remained above 1.5. A need for new mills would arise if the coefficient fell below 1.3.

In the case of provinces in group (2), more plants for finished steel were needed. The more favorable candidates were:

(a) Liaoning. Here the need for plants for finished-steel products was not affected by Soviet removals.

(b) Yunnan. With a production capacity of only 18,000 metric tons per year in steel ingot, there was nevertheless a potential for steel finishing as compared with almost all of the other provinces.

(c) Hupeh. With only 15,000 metric tons of steel ingot per year, whether a plant should be established would depend on the degree of rehabilitation of the local iron- and steelmaking facilities.

Chapter 7

1. See Chapter 3.

2. See Table 3.12 for the distribution by size.

3. There is some uncertainty about the regional divisions. Seven regions are listed in Table 7.5. More recently, according to one source (Ta-kung Pao, Peking, June 27, 1962), the Central and South regions have been shown as one, which would correspond to the regional administrative divisions introduced under the Communist regime in the early 1950's. Furthermore, it appears that Fukien may have been moved to the South China region from East China. However, in so far as the major steel centers are concerned, these changes would make little material difference.

4. Ti-li Chih-shih (Geographical Knowledge), Peking, No. 4, April, 1958, p. 155.

5. In other words, a province with very little iron ore may nevertheless have enough to warrant the establishment of a modest-sized mill or two. On the other hand, from a dynamic point of view, it may be wiser to concentrate the developmental effort on the more promising locations where much greater expansion is desirable in the long run. This may lead to the acceleration of development.

6. Chung-kung Shih-nien (Ten Years of Chinese Communism), issued by the China Weekly, Hong Kong, 1960, pp. 233-234.

7. 370,600 out of 2 million is about 18.5 percent. But since the "semi-modern" furnaces are not included in the total, the actual proportion of the sample is smaller. The many press sources on which the above data are based include the following:

(a) People's Daily, July 5, 6, 7, 8, 9, 19, and 26, 1958; August 3, 8, 22, 23, 25, 26, and 30, 1958; September 2, 3, 4, 5, 6, 8, 9, 12, 13, 14, 19, 21, 23, 25, 28, and 29, 1958; October 1, 2, 3, 5, 13, 14, 15, 17, 18, 19, 23, 24, 25, and 29, 1958; November 3, 9, 10, 15, 20, and 24, 1958; December 3, 4, 8, 15, 18, 29, and 30, 1958; January 1, 3, 5, 13, 16, 18, 22, and 29, 1959; February 1, 3, 12, 20, 21, 23, 25, and 27, 1959.

(b) Liaoning Daily, July 7, 9, and 27, 1958; October 1, 1958, and November 18, 1958.

(c) Kansu Daily, November 1, 1958.

(d) Tientsin Daily, August 30 and September 2, 1958.

(e) Hopeh Daily, August 23, 1958.

(f) Shansi Daily, October 1, 18, and 24, 1958, and February 22, 1959.

(g) Inner Mongolia Daily, September 1, 12, 17, 1958.

(h) Shantung Daily, November 11, 1958.

(i) Honan Daily, August 19 and 21, 1958.

(j) Anhwei Daily, November 2 and December 12, 1958.

(k) <u>Shanghai Liberation Daily</u>, August 5 and September 27, 1958, and February 26, 1959.

(l) <u>Nanking New China Daily</u>, October 24, 1958, and February 1, 1959.

(m) <u>Shanghai Daily</u>, August 4 and 14, and October 26, 1958.

(n) <u>Hupeh Daily</u>, August 4 and 14, and October 24 and 26, 1958.

(o) <u>New Hunan Daily</u>, October 1 and 24, 1958, and February 22, 1959.

(p) <u>Fukien Daily</u>, October 3 and 25, 1958, and January 27, 1959.

(q) <u>Canton Daily</u>, October 17, 1958.

(r) <u>Kwangsi Daily</u>, October 18 and 20, 1958.

(s) <u>Yunnan Daily</u>, October 23 and 24, 1958.

(t) <u>Szechwan Daily</u>, February 2, 1959.

(u) <u>New Kweichow Daily</u>, October 23, 1958, and January 27, 1959.

(v) <u>New China Semi-monthly</u>, no. 10, 1958, p. 71.

(w) <u>Red Flag</u>, no. 11, 1958, p. 24, and no. 1, 1959, pp. 6 and 8.

(x) <u>Kiangsi Daily</u>, October 12, 14, and 24, 1958.

8. By Yuan-li Wu, currently under preparation.

9. <u>Chinese Year Book</u>, vol. II, 1948, pp. 1507-1514.

10. Pao-t'ou and T'ung-hua, though new steel centers now supplying established machine industry centers (T'ai-yüan and Ch'ang-ch'un, respectively), may be designed to supply new machine industry concentrations not yet developed. Accordingly, they have not been included in the above list and have not been classified as "market-oriented."

Appendix A

1. Yuan-li Wu, <u>An Economic Survey of Communist China</u>, New York, 1956, p. 26.

2. <u>Op. cit.</u>, p. 12.

3. K. P. Wang, <u>op. cit.</u>, 1960, suggested that 5 billion tons might be a more likely figure.

Appendix B

1. Tokyo, March 1941, pp. 712-714.

2. <u>Op. cit.</u>, 7th issue, p. 110, Chungking, 1945.

3. <u>Major Aspects</u>, <u>op. cit.</u>, Peking, 1958, p. 5.

4. Geological Survey of China, <u>op. cit.</u>, 1945, p. 106; and Bureau of Information, <u>Kang-t'ieh</u> (Iron and Steel), Nanking, 1947, pp. 20-21.

5. Op. cit., p. 115, and Appendix 5.

6. Op. cit., pp. 4 and 10.

7. Op. cit., pp. 712-714.

8. Op. cit., pp. 5, 10, and 14.

9. Op. cit., p. 103, Peking, 1960.

10. The Economic Development of Communist China, 1949-1958, Oxford University Press, 1959, p. 211.

11. Mineral Trade Notes, Special Supplement No. 59, March 1960, p. 10.

12. Op. cit., p. 92.

13. Op. cit., pp. 105 and 109; figure represents the sum of An-shan and Pen-ch'i-hu outputs.

14. General Statement, op. cit.

15. Op. cit., pp. 21 and 35.

16. National Resources Commission, Quarterly Journal, vol. VI, nos. 3-4, 1946, p. 104.

17. Yuan-li Wu, The Economy of Communist China, Council for Economic and Industry Research, Inc., 1954, p. 23.

18. Pauley Report, op. cit., p. 115 and Appendix 5.

19. General Statement, op. cit., 7th issue, pp. 4 and 110.

20. Op. cit., pp. 92, 95, and 115.

21. Op. cit., pp. 127-128.

22. Op. cit., vol. 2, p. 1569.

23. Cabinet Research Office, Survey Report on the Steel Industry of Communist China, Tokyo, 1955.

24. This gives rise to ratios between rated and operating capacities different from those obtained when both have been adjusted to the same coverage.

25. Op. cit., p. 22.

Appendix D

1. Kang-t'ieh (Iron and Steel), No. 18, Peking, 1959, p. 799.

2. Yeh-chin Pao (Metallurgical Bulletin), op. cit., No. 4, 1960, p. 7.

3. Kang-t'ieh, op. cit., pp. 799-800.

4. Ibid., p. 800.

5. Ibid.

6. Major Aspects, op. cit., p. 24.

7. K'o-hsüeh T'ung-pao (Science Bulletin), No. 5, Peking, 1959, p. 137. [Semi-monthly.]

8. Kang-t'ieh, op. cit., p. 802.

9. According to official reports, Mainland China produced a total of 20.5 million tons of pig iron; output of blast furnaces with a volume of 100 cubic meters or less amounted to 11 million tons.

10. The average coefficient for January-June, 1959, was 1.56 for furnaces over 100 cubic meters and 0.70 for furnaces of 100 cubic meters or less.

11. Yeh-chin Pao, No. 4, 1960, p. 20.

12. Ibid.

13. Kang-t'ieh, No. 6, 1959, pp. 190-197.

14. Ibid., No. 14, 1958, pp. 22-28.

15. Ministry of Metallurgical Industry, Kuan-yü T'ai-yüan Kang-t'ieh-ch'ang San-ts'ao-ch'u-kang ti Pao-kao (Report on the three-ladle steel-tapping experiment of the T'ai-yüan Iron and Steel Works), March, 1958; Kang-t'ieh, No. 23, 1959, p. 1126.

16. NCNA, Peking, August 7, 1958.

17. Kang-t'ieh, No. 18, 1959, p. 809.

18. Ibid., pp. 787, 809. See also Chapter 3. In 1958, the national average was about 8 tons.

19. Report by the An-shan Chapter of the Metallurgical Society in April, 1958.

20. Kang-t'ieh, No. 6, 1957, p. 13.

21. Ibid., No. 9, 1958, p. 19; Jen-min jih-pao, September 23, 1959.

22. Kang-t'ieh, No. 18, 1959, p. 823.

23. Ibid.

24. Ibid.

25. Jen-min jih-pao, March 3, 1960.

26. K'o-hsüeh T'ung-pao (Science Bulletin), No. 5, 1959, p. 138.

27. Yeh-chin Pao, No. 12, 1956, p. 30.

28. Kang-t'ieh, No. 18, 1959, p. 815.

29. Jen-min Jih-pao, December 12, 1958.

30. The temperature of the molten iron reaches $1,350-1,410^{\circ}$ C, and as much as 80 percent of the sulphur content of the "native iron" can be removed in the hot-air basic melting furnace.

31. NCNA, Wu-han, November 27, 1958; Jen-min Jih-pao, August 1, 1959.
Prospects for further improving the quality and for increasing the variety of converter steel are encouraging in view of the successful experiments undertaken by the Ta-yeh Steel Plant with the assistance of the Iron and Steel Research Institute. These were experiments conducted on the mixing of converter steel with the ferro-alloy melt in the electric furnace and with the electric-furnace slag. Thus mixed in the ladle, while the slag promotes further desulphurization and oxidation of the converter steel, alloys from the electric furnace react with it to form alloy steels. As a result, the quality of converter steel is improved and its variety increased.

INDEX

China: Central, 16, 17, 37, 43,
194, 205, 208, 210, 214, 217,
218, 220, 223, 228, 239
_____: East, 16, 43, 201, 208,
210, 214, 218, 220, 223, 224,
228, 238
_____: North, 16, 18, 33, 35, 37,
43, 201, 208, 210, 218, 220-
221, 223, 224, 238-239
_____: Northeast, 36, 43, 50,
208, 210, 214, 217, 218, 223
_____: Northwest, 16, 50, 208,
209, 210, 214, 218, 220, 221,
222, 223, 228, 239
_____: South, 43, 208, 210, 214,
220, 223, 239
_____: Southwest, 29, 35, 37, 43,
50, 201, 105, 208-210,
214, 218, 220, 223-224,
239
Chin-ling-chen: 18, 192
Ching Lin: 42
Ching-t'ieh-shan iron ore de-
posits: 222
Chiu-ch'üan district (Kansu
province): 222
Chou En-lai: 90
Chou-k'ou-tien furnace: 127
Chungking iron and steel complex:
29, 34, 38, 64, 201, 205, 218,
220
Civil war (1945-48): 37, 61
Clark, Gardener: 171, 176, 192
Clay, deposit of: 221
Coal: material input in open hearth
crude steel production, 99
Coal deposits: 14, 29, 142, 192
Coal industry: 42, 97, 158
Coal mines: 17
Coal production: cost of inputs,
192
Coke: 33, 97, 98, 192
"Cold down repairs": 74
Communes, agricultural: 144; contri-
bution to "backyard furnace"
drive, 1, 47
Communist bloc exports to China:
188

Communist Chinese armed forces:
172
Communist Chinese economic
policy: 1-12, 36, 39, 40-45,
47-49, 134-144, 172-176, 213-
220, 223, 228. See also Five-
Year Plans, "Great Leap
Forward."
Communist party of China, 37
Communist period: growth of the
iron and steel industry, 37-90,
45
_____: Official Development Plan
for 1949-1957, 40-45, 50, 55-
61
_____: First Five-Year Plan (1953-
1957), 42-45, 49-50
_____: Second Five-Year Plan (1958-
1962), 45-50
_____: "Great Leap Forward" (1958-
1959), 47-50, 53-56, 62-65
_____: Economic Crisis (1960-1963),
48-59
Communist regime, installation
of: 39
Cost of production: 94-108, 120-
129
Converter steel: 80, 180
Converters: 17, 48, 108
Crude steel: 37, 72, 99-
108
Demand, domestic: 27, 29
Depreciation: 99, 122-123, 127
Disinvestment: 33
"Double" counting: 51-52, 83-84,
236
Economic development: 2, 3, 11,
17, 38, 64, 189
Economic policy: Communist, 1-12,
39-45, 47-49, 144, 172-176,
213-220, 223, 228
_____: pre-Communist, 20, 33-34,
175, 195-196
Electric power: 99
Electric power industry: 97
Employment: 64
Emulation campaigns: 78-79
"End products": 52, 92
End use: 152-153

Exports: 18-19, 22-27, 34, 169-171, 188, 236-238

"Factory method" of accounting: 52, 53, 93-94

Fan-ch'ang: 18, 192

Feng-t'ien province: 18

Ferrous metals industry: 1, 2, 12, 141

Ferrous rolled stock: 35

Finished steel: 31-34, 37, 40, 55-62, 65-79, 152-178, 178-188

First Five-Year Plan (1953-57): 1-2, 55, 65-79, 91-148 passim, 155, 178, 214, 220-223, 236-238

Fixed assets: 42

Foreign influence: 18-20, 35, 195, 205

Foreign policy: 40

Fuel input cost: 98, 122, 220-223

Fukien province: 121, 208-209

Fu-la-erh-chi special steel works: 64

Fu-shun steel mills: 33, 64

Geological Survey of China: 14, 16

Geological surveys: 16, 32, 38, 48, 96, 222

Geographical distribution of iron and steel industry: 21-22, 36, 189-211, 213-232, 239-240

Germany, coke consumption by: 92

"Great Leap Forward" (1958-59): 1, 13, 47, 88, 150-152, 163, 178, 236-237, 240-241

Gross national product, prices, and cost of structure: 91-148, 237

Gross value-added in iron and steel industry: 94-127; and wage ratio in China, Soviet Union, United States, 238

"Gross value output": 92

Growth of iron and steel industry: 53-65; Communist annual rates of, 63

Government ownership of iron and steel industry: 2-3, 36, 40

Hainan Island: 34, 205, 207

Hankow: 18, 194

Han-yang: iron and steel complex at, 17, 29-30, 195; first Chinese steel mill at, 34; Iron and Steel Co.'s history, 17; replacement of, 17; relocation of, 201. See also Wu-han, tri-city of.

Han-yeh-p'ing Coal and Iron Co.: 192

Heilungkiang province: 121, 208

Ho-hsi corridor: 222

Ho-hsin Co.: 194

Honan province: 121, 195, 198, 205, 208, 210, 211

Hopeh province: 121, 190, 205, 208, 210, 211, 223

Hsiang-pi-shan iron ore deposits: 18, 190

Hsiang-t'an coal mines: 221

Hsin-hsiang mill: 195

Hsüan-hua: 18, 190

Huai-nan Coal Mining Co.: 194

Huang-tai iron ore deposits: 190

Hunan province: 118, 121, 205, 208, 210, 211

Hungary, exports to Communist China: 49

Hung-yü Iron Works: 195

Hupeh province: 17, 18, 34, 36, 38, 50, 121, 189, 190, 192, 194, 198, 205, 209-211, 221

Hydroelectricity: 98, 105, 221

Imports: 27, 29, 49, 65, 84, 141, 186, 188, 241, 237

Incentives, monetary and honorary to workers and plants: 78

Indochina: 29

Inflation: 33

Industry, modern: characteristics of, 79-88; and interindustry balance, 64; and intraindustry balance, 79-94; Nationalist development plans for, 20

329

Marxist concepts: 136
Mass furnaces: 47
Metallurgical Bulletin: 119, 122
Metallurgical industry, divisions of: iron and steel, and machinery industry, 91-92; investments allocated and shares for iron and steel and machinery, 41; priority for machinery production, First Five-Year Plan, 41-45; ferrous sector, 39; metal processing, 42, 92
Miao-erh-kou iron ore deposits: 18
Mica deposits: 221
Mining Bureau, Hupeh provincial government (1920): 18
Ministry of Agricultural Machinery: 167
Ministry of Commerce: 168
Ministry of Electrical Equipment Manufacturing: 165
Ministry of Foreign Trade: 169
Ministry of Geology: 167
Ministry of Heavy Industry: 78, 165
Ministry of Industry and Commerce (Nationalist): 20
Ministries of Machine Building: 165-168, 171
Mukden incident: 20
Mukden iron and steel center: 64
Multiple iron and steel centers: 218-220
Multiplier effect: 65
"Mutual assistance" regions: 218-219, 239
Nanking: 20
National income: 52
National People's Congress: 90
Nationalist government: 20, 33, 195, 201, 239
Native sector furnaces: 47, 88-90, 108-127, 167, 236
Ningsia area: 121
Ningsia Hui Autonomous Region: 208

"Nominal time": 74
Nonferrous metals: 91
North China Iron and Steel Co.: 33
Northeast Industrial Engineering Institute: 124
Oceania: 14
O-ch'eng iron ore deposits: 50, 221
Official Development Plan (1949-1957): 40-45
Open hearth furnaces: 33, 58, 99-108, 198
Open hearth steel: 99. See also crude steel.
Output-per-unit capacity index: 65-74; comparison of Chinese and Soviet coefficients of use for blast and open hearth furnaces, 67-68
Oversupply: definition of, 149
Pai-yün-o-po mine: 50
Pai-yün-o-po Mountain: iron ore deposits at, 221
P'an-chang-chuang iron ore deposits: 50
Pao-chi seamless tube mill: 49
Pao-t'on complex: 43, 45, 47, 50, 64, 78-79, 218, 220, 221, 234
Pa-tung iron ore deposits: 50
Pauley mission: 31, 33, 169, 229
Peking – Wu-han railway: 221
Pen-ch'i: 33, 119, 194, 221
Pen-ch'i-hu Iron Manufacturing Co.: 18-19, 30, 198, 205
Pig iron: 17-19, 55-62, 92, 150-152, 188
Ping-hsiang: iron ore deposits at, 49, 221; coal and iron works at, 17, 194, 221
P'ing-liang basin iron ore deposits: 50
P'ing-lo basin coal deposits: 222

Pipe mills: 33

Planning, Communist: role in industrial development, 2; design of central plan, 39-41; Soviet model for, 229-232; and investment, 41-43, 144; and errors, 1, 11, 90, 144, 150-152, 177-186; poor locational design in "backyard furnace" drive, 223; abuse of labor-intensive method and drive for quantity, 240; effects on regional distribution and intra-industry balance, 228, 241; validity of statistics, 240-241. See also "Factory method"; Communist Chinese economic policy; Five-Year Plans; Statistics.

Postwar devastation (1945-49): 31-34, 37-40

Power installations: 97, 158

Pre-Communist period growth of iron and steel industry: 14-26, 189-211, 234

Production: costs and prices, 93, 105, 108, 118-125, 127; incentives, 78; processes, 50-53; norms, 78-79; relation to plant location, 61-62; to number and size of plants, 74-77; coefficents of use of, 68-74

Products of iron and steel industry: 51-53, 92

Provinces. See under name.

Quality control and labor productivity: 78

Quality of products: 49, 84-89, 108, 118-123, 235, 237, 238-241

Quantitative production records: 78, 84-88, 235, 238-239, 241

Railways: 17, 158, 221

"Rate of exploitation": 136

Ratio of "surplus value" to "variable capital": 136

Raw material availability: 43, 220-223

Refractory materials: 192, 221

Regional distribution of iron and steel industry: pre-Communist, 33-35, 189-211; Communist, 48, 213-233, 237; underlying locational pattern of, 189

"Rehabilitation Period" (1949-52): 41, 55, 58-61

Relocation of iron and steel plants, World War II: 29, 33, 201-207, 210, 239

Removals of iron and steel plants by Soviet Union: 29, 31, 33, 35, 201-207, 235, 242

"Replacement" of capital equipment: 61

Rivers and plant locations: 194

Rolling mill: 64

Rolled products: 92

Rolled steel: 51, 52

Safety standards: 78

Savings, domestic: relation to growth of the industry, 38-39; and capital-output ratio, 54

Scrap iron: 97, 99

Second Five-Year Plan (1958-62): 45-49, 62-65, 79-84, 87-88, 105-108, 118-123, 144, 223-242

Sectors of iron and steel industry: 92, 98-127

Semimodern furnace: 47, 88, 108-127

Shanghai: 38, 43, 64, 189, 194, 198, 201, 205

Shansi province: 14, 18, 121, 189, 192, 205, 208, 210, 211

Shantung province: 18, 121, 189, 192, 195, 205, 208, 210, 211

Shensi: 121, 208

Shih-ching-shan mill: 30, 33

Silicon: 221

Sinkiang province: 29, 121

Sino-Japanese agreement (1915): 19

Sino-Japanese War: 195, 198, 201, 207

Small Industry Drive, "backyard furnaces" and side-blown converters: 47-48, 88-90